Feeding Your Horse for Life

Published in the United States of America by

Half Halt Press, Inc.
P.O. Box 67
Boonsboro, MD 21713
www.halfhaltpress.com

Book and jacket design by Design Point Studio
Cover photos and interior photos as noted by Helen Peppe
Illustrations by Pam Tanzey

The publishers also wish to thank for photos as noted
Dan's Saddlery: www.dans-saddlery.com
Purina Mills: www.purinamills.com

Library of Congress Cataloging-in-Publication Data

Morgan, Diane, 1947-
  Feeding your horse for life / Diane Morgan.
      p. cm.
  Includes bibliographical references and index.
  ISBN 0-939481-68-5
    1. Horses--Feeding and feeds. 2. Horses--Nutrition. I. Title.

SF285.5.M67 2004
636.1'085--dc22

2004054078

To my good friends,

Rheeanna Benner and Jane Jones,

for their dedication

and love for all animals.

And special thanks to my partner

and collaborator John Warner.

Contents

Contents

Introduction

YOUR HORSE DEPENDS ON YOU TO CARE FOR HIM AND provide for his dietary needs. You buy his grain, buy or grow his hay, and supply his water. If your horse is pastured all day long—you are the one responsible for the quality of the pasture. Your horse is what he eats, and so what he becomes is largely in your hands.

Nowadays, we know about more nutrition than ever before. It can make the difference between a good a horse and great one, between a stressed out, emaciated or obese animal, and a sleek, finely tuned partner for fun and adventure.

It can seem a daunting responsibility, and indeed it is, but this book can help you make the right choices. You'll learn how the digestive system functions, so you'll understand exactly how hay turns into horses. You'll learn about the basics of nutrition: protein, fats and carbohydrates. You'll learn how water, vitamins and minerals make the crucial difference.

You'll discover how to choose good hay and maintain a good pasture, what kind of grain (and how much) to feed. You'll pick up hints on nutrition for breeding mares, foals and performance horses. You'll learn how poor feeding can cause disease, and good nutrition cure it. You'll find out what poisonous plants and toxins may be lurking in your fields. You'll get to check out supplements and nutraceuticals—and find out which ones make a difference and why. We'll even provide you with a resource list, so you can discover more on your own—and a conversion table for changing those pesky metric units into familiar English ones.

Most of all, you'll be learning the basic principles of good horsekeeping —and nothing can be more fun and important than that. Your horse will thank you!

Hay into Horses: The Equine Digestive System

IT'S NOT EASY TO LIVE ON GRASS, and the fact that so many animals manage to do it anyway is a tribute to their anatomical ingenuity. (Horses belong to an elite subclass of plant-eaters called "contrarian digesters." They are joined by rabbits, elephants and rhinoceroses. Contrarian digesters run their food through a special enzyme/chemical process before they set about fermenting it.) Grass is tough, low in nutrients, and often difficult to locate. It tends to mingle freely with toxic plants, and in a drought it's the first thing to wither up. When grass is dried artificially it's called hay, which has most of the disadvantages associated with grass, but, since it's dried up already, is little affected by drought. (Mold is a different story.)

OFFICIALLY THE horse is classified as a non-ruminant herbivore. Herbivore means that the horse lives mainly on grass (not herbs) and non-ruminant means that the horse has a single-chambered stomach, as opposed to the multi-chambered stomach of ruminants, like cows, goats, and deer, who chew their cud (which is where the word "ruminate," meaning to chew over something and consider it thoughtfully, comes from.)

Anyway, the best way to understand the process of turning hay into horses is to take a magical mystery tour down the horse's digestive tract. (Don't worry, I won't let anything bad happen to you while we're down there.) The process is studded with exciting features like peristaltic contractions, enzymatic action, and bacteria fermentation. We certainly don't want to miss any of that!

So, please join me for a leisurely stroll down along the gastrointestinal (GI) tract to see the sights. (The GI tract is sometimes called the Alimentary Canal, not to be confused with the Suez or Panama Canals.)

Oh, Those Sweet Lips

Once the horse finds his food source, a process that includes memory, desire, vision, and the olfactory system, he begins to munch down, using those amazing lips. Horses have about the best lips in the business (with the possible exception of some collagen-clotted female film stars). Horse lips are really big and just chock full of muscles, which makes them mobile. This is why horses are better kissers than dogs, cats, and most people. The fancy name for this important lip muscle is the orbicularis oris. The technical word for this kind of muscle ability is "prehensile," a word usually applied to the tails of New World monkeys. Horses have a chin muscle as well—the mentalis muscle, which despite its name has nothing to do the mind, except possibly for the fact that horses have their minds on eating pretty much all the time. They are programmed to be that way.

The reason horses' lips are so mobile and strong (almost like fingers) is that it helps them select the best grasses and tidbits from their pasture. It helps them avoid noxious and poisonous plants, an especially handy trick since their digestive systems aren't able to deal with these materials as effectively as ruminants like cows. Partly because of their choosiness, and partly because of their more finicky digestive system, horses don't take in as much material per mouthful as other grazers. They also chew their food very, very carefully, and grind it into small particles. In fact,

Horses' lips help them select the best grasses and tidbits from their pasture.
Helen Peppe photo.

one stalwart researcher estimated that the average horse uses about 60,000 jaw movements per day. (How that compares with the average talk show host, I can't imagine.) Ponies chew even more. Horses make up to 1,000 "jaw sweeps" to devour two pounds of grain, and more than 3,000 to deal with a similar amount of hay.

Let's Talk Teeth

Once the grass gets scooped up by the lips, the teeth take over. Horses' teeth are designed to nip grass into manageable pieces, and then grind it up (or down, depending how you look at it) into edible particle size. This is important for more than just mechanical reasons, too. Smaller particles have more surface area, and that's critical when it comes to the digestive enzymes. The more area they have to work on, the easier their job becomes. Consequently, a horse with bad teeth is jeopardizing his entire digestive system. In fact, teeth are so critical to the process, it might be a good idea to grind to a halt (pun intended) and take a closer look at them.

Like people and dogs, horses get two sets of teeth during their lifetime. First come the baby, milk, or deciduous teeth. (Call them what you like, they will fall out when the 40 adult teeth come in, a process that is usually completed by the time the horse is four years old.) In the tooth count statistics, this puts horses somewhere between people (32 adult teeth, counting the wisdoms) and dogs (42 adult teeth).

The 40 teeth of the horse include 24 (wow!) molars to grind, 12 incisors to pluck, pull, and nip, and four small canine teeth. Since it doesn't seem right to call horse teeth canine teeth, they are also known as "tushes." I can't say that's much of an improvement. Wait. I need to back up. I was talking about male horses. Female horses may be a bit different, since most of them do not have tushes. You know what I mean.

Both male and female horses sometimes develop non-functional "wolf teeth," which are small sharp teeth that erupt in the upper jaw. (Wolf teeth are not considered in the tooth-count.) I am tempted to make a remark about how wolf teeth were left over from the time when horses used to battle wolves on the open plain, but this may not be true. Wolf teeth are often removed in domestic horses, since they can get in the way of the bit.

The grinding of the molars is often uneven, however, since the lower jaw is slightly wider than the upper one. Horses chew in a circular pattern in order to bring the molars in opposition for grinding. Eventually, if the wear on the teeth is not even, sharp points form on the edge of the molars. These sharp points tend to form on the outside border of the top cheek teeth, and on the

---

ENZYMES ACT as facilitators for chemical reactions. Your horse (and you too) contains thousands of different kinds. Each one is a specialist, often facilitating just one chemical reaction. Without enzymes, you will die -- fast.

ALL THE HORSE'S adult teeth continue to "grow" throughout its life. They don't actually grow, of course, but it seems that way because they are being continually pushed up from the bony bed of the jaw. The grinding motion of the molars keeps them the same length, but the more forward teeth, which aren't opposed, get longer and longer—which is where the expression "long in the tooth," meaning "old age" comes from. Extremely old horses, however, can grind their teeth down to the root. Everything has an end.

HORSES CAN BE born with abnormalities like parrot mouth, where the lower jaw is shorter than the upper; sow, bulldog, or monkey mouth, in which the lower jaw is longer than the upper, and shear mouth, where the upper jaw is too wide. All these conditions interfere with proper mastication. No horse with any of these abnormalities should be bred.

WITH ALL THIS saliva-making going on, it's a wonder that horses don't drool, but there's a reason. Oddly enough, unlike Pavlov's dogs, horses can't start salivating until they start chewing or at least moving their jaws around. Then, too, unlike dogs, horses don't need to salivate to cool themselves off. Like humans (and like no other mammal) horses are well equipped with sweat glands. The expression "sweating like a pig" is thus a poor one. Pigs couldn't sweat even if they wanted to.

inside edge of the lower cheek teeth. The sharp edges interfere with proper eating, and can cut the horse's mouth, causing still more trouble.

Horses who develop this problem tend to eat less and lose weight. Equally seriously, they may try to swallow their food in unwieldy chunks rather than chew it properly. The food can then become trapped in the esophagus and the horse may choke or come down with colic. This is why older horses need to have their teeth "floated" or filed regularly, generally once a year. Even young horses, especially those on a concentrated grain diet, should have their teeth checked regularly.

In general, the more grinding a horse has to do, the more likely he will be to need his teeth filed. Even horses fed on "soft" feeds might be in need of dental work, because soft foods may not encourage sufficient "sweeping" action of the jaw for even grinding. Horses who slobber a lot, take longer to eat, or drop partially chewed food back in the manger are often suffering from dental pain. The horse's manure might also reveal sign of incomplete chewing by the retention of long pieces of hay and whole pieces of grain.

The Tongue and Salivary Glands

Shakespeare advised us to keep a good tongue in our heads, and I suppose this applies as well to horses as to anybody else. A horse's tongue is pretty much like our own. It's a powerful muscle, with a full complement of taste buds, nerves, blood vessels, salivary glands and mucus. Its purpose is to push food around in the mouth and eventually to deliver it to the pharynx, a muscular tube that connects the mouth to the esophagus. The horse can also use his tongue like a straw for drinking. Dogs can't do this at all, which is why dogs are messier drinkers than horses.

Horses have three pairs of salivary glands: the great big parotid gland at the back, the smaller submaxillary gland, also in the back and under the jaw, and the sublingual gland, which, as the name suggests, lies under the tongue. These glands produce a prodigious amount of saliva—up to 85 pounds of the stuff a day—about 10 gallons. Saliva adds a lot of weight to horse feed. A well-chewed mouthful of oats doubles in weight, while hay absorbs about four times its own weight in saliva.

The saliva (good old horse slobber) serves to soften the food to make its passage down the gullet easier. The saliva helps glue the food together in a ball called the bolus, which goes down more easily than a dry, formless chunk. Horse saliva also contains the digestive enzyme amylase (as does human saliva), which starts digesting carbohydrates. After all the chewing and softening and grinding are over with, the horse swallows—and the fun begins!

Once the food is well chewed and softened, the tongue pushes the food past the soft palate, into the pharynx, which opens into the esophagus.

The Esophagus

The flexible esophagus is the next stop on our downward spiral (figuratively speaking.) It connects the pharynx to the stomach. The esophagus moves food by muscular contractions called peristaltic waves down to the tummy. The horse esophagus is a strange creation, with a major drawback. It is about five feet long and constructed in such a way that it is almost impossible for the animal to vomit—or even burp. And although you may have felt at certain times in your life that neither burping nor vomiting were all that much fun, they do serve a purpose not available to horses. They enable us to rid our bodies of toxins, gases, and other nasty things we'd rather not have to deal with. Deal with them he must, however, and while the rest of the horse's system is admirably developed to handle problems, once in a while the lack of vomiting capability can land a horse in really deep—perhaps fatal—trouble. If a lump of food meets an obstruction in the esophagus, it returns to the outside world through the nose, not the mouth.

This evolutionary oversight is made much worse by modern feeding methods, in which a large amount of food is crammed into the horse at one meal, rather than the natural plan of leisurely munching and strolling.

As the horse swallows you can see his dinner (the so-called ingesta, in vet language) passing along down the left side of the neck, just below the windpipe.

The horse's digestive system. Pam Tanzey.

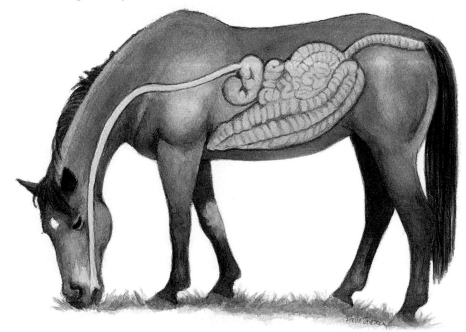

HORSES NATURALLY eat all the time, up to ten hours a day. Wild horses eat for even longer periods. They have to, since grass is relatively low in real nutrients. They can do this partly because their stomachs have little storage capacity (holding only about 2 to 3 gallons of liquid), passing everything along rather quickly along the digestive tract.

The Tummy

The esophagus empties into the J-shaped stomach (or tummy, as I prefer to call it). The entrance to the stomach is protected by the cardiac sphincter (a band of muscle). This is yet another barrier to vomiting. A horse's stomach will actually rupture first. The stomach lining (gastric mucosa, to be technical) excretes digestive juices like pepsinogen and hydrochloric acid. The hydrochloric acid changes the pepsinogen into pepsin, a digestive enzyme designed to handle protein. The hydrochloric acid isn't finished either. It then turns its attention to the mineral content of the food, dissolving it so that the nutrients are more absorbable.

The horse tummy can hold "only" about two gallons of material, either food or water, at a time. (Horse historians attribute this restriction to a horse's natural, nomadic past.) This is only about 10 percent of the horse's digestive system, and its main job is to mix the food up, although it also does some actual digesting. (Cows, on the other hand, have stomachs that handle about 70 percent of the digestive work.) They say that a horse's stomach was designed to be small so that the horse could flee from danger quickly. I suppose that's possible. But didn't wild cows need to flee from danger also?

Horses manage to eat so much anyway because they are very efficient about not letting food just lie around in the stomach doing nothing. On average, a full horse tummy starts to empty in about 12 to 15 minutes, while if the horse has been fasted first, it may take a whole day. To digest a small meal may take only half an hour—a large one may take up to three hours. A lot of water passes quickly along the folds of stomach wall straight into the small intestine. This comes in very handy, so that the horse can rehydrate the small intestine even if he has a full stomach.

Horse tummies begin the work of handling concentrated high-protein foods like grain or supplements, which it breaks down into component parts by bacterial or enzymatic action. But it hands over most of this work to its partner in digestion, the small intestine.

The Small Intestine

The passage between the stomach and small intestine is called the pyloric sphincter. The small intestine is small only in a manner of speaking. To my mind, anything inside a horse that is 70 feet long isn't really that small. But there you have it. If I had been given the job of naming horse innards, I would have called it "the really, really, really *long* intestine." But no one asked me. Well, never mind. Of course the whole thing is intricately looped and coiled up, held in place by the fanlike mysentery membrane. It would have to be, otherwise we'd have a 70-foot-long horse.

The first part of the small intestine is the U-shaped duodenum. The U is probably designed to keep food from going back up into the stomach in case a problem arises (which inevitably seems to happen). The small intestine is more distendable than the stomach, so presumably it is in better shape to handle crises.

The small intestine contains mostly fluid. (It can hold about 17 gallons, about 30 percent of the GI's total capacity) The small intestine continues to break down nutrients to be absorbed by the blood stream, which carries them to all the organs of the body.

It breaks down about half the soluble carbohydrates (largely found in cereal grains) into sugars, and most fats into fatty acids, and proteins into amino acids. (It does a better job with grains than forage.) The small intestine turns the starch that hasn't been digested by the saliva into maltose, and this and the other complex sugars and carbohydrates into simple sugars (mainly glucose) to be absorbed from the intestinal wall. It also absorbs calcium, iron, zinc, copper, manganese, and magnesium, as well as the B and most other vitamins. The small intestine shares the job of absorbing phosphorus and the electrolytes sodium, potassium and chloride with the large intestine.

The intestinal lining or wall is covered with small projections called villi. The villi, which in turn are loaded with even tinier microvilli, greatly increase the surface area of the small intestine to further aid digestion. They absorb the nutrients to be carried off by the capillaries into blood stream and liver.

The small intestine is suspended in loops from the roof of the abdominal cavity, a very curious arrangement. It is supported by fanlike mesentery, which is a double fold of the peritoneum. The small intestine is divided into three sections: the duodenum (about 3 or 4 feet), the jejunum (55 feet) and the ileum (6 to 8 feet). When it's empty, the diameter of the small intestine is only about 2 inches (hence the real derivation of the term "small.")

The small intestine moves food along its path at the rate of about 1 foot per minute, depending somewhat on the kind of food the horse is eating. Loose hay moves more slowly than pelleted feed or wafered hay. On average, the ingesta spends between 30 to 60 minutes in the small intestine, but can take up to eight hours.

The ileum is the last part of the intestine. (The ileum has nothing to do with Ilium or Troy, although I wish it did. There's an iliam, too—but that's a bone in the pelvis. No wonder anatomy is confusing.) The ileum leads straight up into the hindgut, which follows after the small intestine.

THE ACTUAL percentage of carbohydrate digestion that is handled in the small intestine depends upon the type of carbohydrate involved. For example, while the small intestine can handle about 55 percent of the oats it receives, that percentage drops to 29 percent for corn and only 21 percent for barley. The cecum handles most of this work.

SOME DIGESTIVE help is received from the liver and pancreas, both of which have other jobs, but don't mind lending a hand (so speak) when the subject is such an important one as food. The liver, which is the largest internal organ, produces a continuous flow of bile, to help digest fats by breaking fat into smaller particles and suspends it in water. (Horses don't have gall bladders like people, dogs, and cattle in which to store the bile. This tragic omission doesn't stop them from handling fat in their diet, any more than it does people who have had their own gall bladders removed.) The pancreas produces individual digestive enzymes, each of which is designed to work on fat, protein, or carbohydrates. The bile and enzymes from the liver and pancreas work in the small intestine.

The Large Intestine: Cecum, Large Colon, Small Colon and Rectum

The large intestine handles most of the digestion of tough carbohydrates like fiber and cellulose. The hindgut, instead of using enzymes for its dirty work, relies upon bacteria, which also synthesize certain vitamins and bacterial protein, which ultimately revert to the horse when the bacteria die and are themselves digested. This is why horses are sometime referred to as hindgut fermenters. (If you yourself have never called your horse a hindgut fermenter, don't worry. You will some day.) The job of these bacteria (and there are billions of the things) is to turn fiber into volatile fatty acids (VFAs), which are absorbed through the hindgut wall into the system.

Food moves slowly through the various parts of the large intestine, taking as long as several days; during this period the microbial digestion continues. The slow rate of passage allows for extensive fermentation to take place.

The Cecum (Hindgut)

The cecum is a truly amazing structure, about four feet long, that can hold about 10 gallons of food and water. (The closest thing we have to a cecum is our appendix, which we have apparently forgotten how to use. All it does is cause trouble.) The horse's cecum is right behind the right flank, if you want to know. The cecum of the horse (and donkey and mule and zebra) performs a similar function to the rumen in a cow or sheep. The cecum is a blind pouch or gut, folded into itself. Its entrance and exit (separated by only about two inches) are both near the top; the food enters the top, gets mixed and digested some more, and then is expelled through another opening near the top.

It's the cecum's job to handle tough carbohydrates like grass and hay, stuff that managed largely to elude the stomach and small intestine. In fact, all the "real" digestion work takes place here, and the cecum contains lots and lots of microbes to help it do its job. These good microbes produce vitamin K and the B vitamins, more bacterial proteins, and fatty acids. The cecum handles about 55 percent of protein digestion, and practically all the soluble carbohydrate digestion (not counting fiber.) All true horse digestion is accomplished by enzymatic action, which happens both in the cecum and the colon. Food remains in the cecum between seven and 30 hours.

As the food ferments in the cecum, the byproducts include gas, heat, ammonia and acid.

The Colon—Large and Small!

The material then moves along to the large intestine (colon) that finishes the digestion process, and equally important, removes most of the remaining water from the food to redistribute to the system. The large intestine has no digestive juices—only fermentation bacteria and mucus to help move the fibrous food along. Horses who spend more time foraging develop longer colons than those who eat less forage and more grain.

Curiously, the large intestine is considerably shorter than the small intestine, being only about 12 to 24 feet long (quite long enough, in my view). Its diameter is a different matter, varying between 2 and 18 inches for the large colon, and 3 to 4 inches for the small colon. (The horse's large intestine is bigger than that of any other animal of its size. The large (ascending) colon is 10 to 12 feet long and can hold 15 to 19 gallons, about 38 percent of the entire GI tract; the small (descending) colon is about 10 feet long, but can hold only about four gallons, due to its narrower diameter (about four inches). The job of the small or descending colon is to collect the indigestible parts of the food, and form horse manure. Most of the digestion has already been done. The small colon makes manure with the help of little sac like structures that make the fecal balls. The whole thing lies coiled against the floor and wall of the abdomen, unlike the small intestine. This "sacculated" design, meaning done up in pouches, is great for breaking down lots of food, but isn't great when gas can't escape.

The Rectum

Finally we arrive at the rectum, a foot-long tube, which holds the waste until it can be excreted out through the anus. The whole trip can take 72 hours.

So What's the Point of All This Digestion?

Shortly put, digestion is the process that turns a horse's food into a horse's body and energy. And that's what the rest of this book is about. ▬

BACTERIA ARE so good at synthesizing B complex vitamins that they produce more of them than the horse can ever use. In fact, studies have shown that horse manure contains more B vitamins than were present in the original feed. When a horse has been on a long course of antibiotics, however, the good microbes can be killed off and need to be reestablished, preferably with a commercial supplement.

THE DIAMETER of the colon can change rather dramatically and without advance warning, so to speak. The resulting "funnel" can cause a lot of digestive problems for the horse.

THE ENTIRE digestive process, from first bite to manure pile can take two to three days. Pellets and fresh grass move through about twice as fast as hay.

CHAPTER

Water:
The Vital Elixir

OF THE SIX CLASSES OF SUBSTANCES WE call nutrients (water, carbohydrates, protein, fat, vitamins and minerals), water is the most immediately important. In fact, about 70 percent of your horse is water! The percentage is even higher for foals and colts. It's a good thing water is cheap.

Water is so critical to your horse's health that if he loses only 12 to 15 percent of it from his body, he will die. (Yet he can survive the loss of nearly all his fat and half the protein in his body and still live on—although poorly.) A loss of about 6 percent will result in dry mucous membranes, a tucked-up abdomen, and sunken eyes. A 3-percent loss can substantially inhibit performance.

WATER HELPS
regulate body tem-
perature because it
has a high specific
heat, meaning that
it can absorb the
heat generated by
metabolic reac-
tions with only a
slight increase in
temperature. It also
transports heat away
from hard working,
heat-generating
organs. And water,
of course, is an
essential compo-
nent of sweat, the
major temperature
regulator of the
horse.

WATER IS STORED
in the body in four
different "compart-
ments." About 64
percent of it resides
within the cells; 22
percent lies in the
intercellular (also
called interstitial)
spaces; 7 percent is
in the blood plasma;
and the remaining
7 percent is pres-
ent as transcellular
fluid; in the eyes
(vitreous and aque-
ous humor), cerebral
spinal fluid, joint
(synovial) fluid, and
digestive secretions
in the stomach and
intestines.

One of the terrific things about water is that it is so easy for your horse (and you and your dog) to use. It doesn't have to be digested or broken down, since it comes ready made in usable form. It only has to be absorbed.

Growing horses will take in a little more water than they excrete ("growing" water) while adults maintain a pretty even balance. (Otherwise, they'd get waterlogged or dried out.) Total body water balance is maintained by dietary water intake and metabolic water production. This means that your horse can make some water from his feed. Horses absorb water mostly through the cecum, although some is also absorbed in the large intestine proper. It is excreted in urine, sweat, feces, and as water vapor from the lungs.

Water, of course, is necessary for the life of every cell. In addition, it performs several critical functions in the system:

- Carries nutrients
- Major component of saliva, blood, mucus, milk, cerebrospinal fluid and sweat
- Flushes waste out of the body
- Aids certain chemical reactions
- Helps regulate body temperature
- Transports sound in the ear
- Lubricates joints
- Provides shape and resilience to the body

The following factors can influence your horse's need for water:

- Temperature and humidity
- Feed type
- Feed amount
- Exercise level
- Health
- Lactation and breeding status

Amount

A non-working stall- or pasture-potato might get by with as little as four gallons of water a day in temperate weather; a hard working horse of the same size might need 15 gallons. One commonly used equation figures that a resting horse drinks about half a gallon per 100 pounds in cool weather, up to four times that amount when the weather is hot. An increase of ambient temperature from 55 degrees to 70 degrees increases a horse's need for water by up to 20 percent! In fact, a high-performance horse can lose 60 pounds in just a few hours, especially if the temperature and humidity are high. (Most of this is sweat, of course. Along with the water, sodium and chloride are also lost.)

Horses prefer water served cool—below about 75 degrees Fahrenheit. Obviously, it helps to keep your horse's drinking water in a shady place if at all possible. Optimum water consumption seems to occur when the water temperature is between 45 and 75 degrees.

Horses also need more water if they are fed a grain supplement laced with molasses (sugar increases thirst, as we all know), or a diet high in protein and minerals, since more water is needed to process these nutrients in the digestive system. Excess salt in the diet also leads to increased thirst. Horses can get some water through the digestive process itself as they break down fats, proteins and carbohydrates (this is called metabolic water). But most of a horse's water has to be supplied by a nearby pond, or stream, or most likely, you with a hose or bucket.

Water Quality

Having sufficient water is only part of the picture, however. For water to be useful to your horse, it must be clean. Filthy water introduces nasty organisms into your horse's digestive tract. Keeping water clean means keeping the water container clean, although I must tell you I had a horse once who enjoyed putting her hoof into the watering tub the instant I had gotten it clean and filled with fresh water. She wasn't happy until the water was restored to its original dirty state. However, this horse was an aberration.

In a similar vein, the water needs to be palatable. If it isn't, your horse won't drink as much as he needs, and will suffer as a result. Stale water is much less palatable to a horse than fresh water, and a horse will consequently drink less of it.

Palatability can also be affected by the amount of minerals present in it, which in turn depends upon the soil type. (Minerals are not usually toxic, but some like sulfur can affect water palatability. Sulfur, of course, makes water smell like rotten eggs.) Water can also affect the mineral balance in your horse's body, especially if the water is high is calcium, magnesium, manganese, iron, copper, zinc, sodium, chloride, lead, or various sulfates and nitrates. On the positive side, the minerals in some water may provide all the iodide your horse needs, and between 4 and 20 percent of the daily requirements for salt, calcium, magnesium and cobalt. It is a negligible source for other minerals.

So-called "hard" water contains more dissolved minerals than "soft" water. Such minerals commonly include sodium, potassium, calcium, magnesium, iron, chloride and sulfate. Most horses prefer the taste of soft water, and some horses may refuse (at first) to drink hard water when they are moved to a hard water location. Most horses won't drink water with dissolved solids over 1,000 ppm (1 gram/liter). One solution is to mask the taste of the water

WATER HELPS move food through the large intestines. If these are not sufficiently lubricated, the dry matter can get stuck in any one of the hairpin turns and twists.

IT HAS BEEN shown that if horses have to travel to get their water, they tend to drink less often. If water is readily available, they drink more than they need.

MOST HARD water does not provide enough mineral content to make up for mineral deficiencies in feed, with the exception of areas where calcium-rich limestone is plentiful.

LEAD CAN BE TOXIC to horses as well as to people, although its effects are not well studied. Water itself usually has little lead, but some old plumbing systems contain lead pipe or fixtures. These should be replaced, or else a calcite filter should be installed.

with a little molasses or some other flavoring the horse enjoys. Just a couple of tablespoons per bucket will do the job. It is especially important to get your horse to drink enough water when he is working—and that is often the case with a traveling horse!

If your horse is not used to drinking chlorinated city water, let the bucket "settle" for a night—the chlorine will evaporate. Gradually, the horse will get used to the taste. You might also consider adding a couple of tablespoons of an iron supplement to the water. This will speed the release of the chlorine, and seems to make the water taste more like "home."

And of course, the presence of pollutants like pesticides are dangerous as well as unpalatable. These contaminants are more common than we might like to believe. Discouragingly, toxic substances, that do not taste bad, are more dangerous than those that do, since the horse is more likely to ingest them.

Water is the universal solvent. Nearly everything that falls in it, flows through it, wades or swims through it, or lies beneath it, eventually imparts some if its "flavor" (or other features) to this unique substance. Certain dissolved minerals can be dangerous if present in high enough concentrations (in mg/liter). These include arsenic (over 0.20); cadmium (0.05); chromium (1.0); cobalt (1.0); copper (0.5); fluoride (2.0); lead (0.1); mercury (0.01); nickel (1.0); nitrate nitrogen (100); nitrite nitrogen (10); vanadium (0.10); and zinc (25). You should have your water tested once every three years or so for total dissolved solids (TDS). This is the single most important test for water quality. High levels are usually considered to be over 1,000 parts per million (ppm). A level of 6,500 ppm is the upper safe limit for horses.

Water with a high salt content is of course undrinkable, a problem that is most likely to occur in western states, or in locations close to a salt storage site, or to a street that is heavily salted in winter. Saline water changes the electrolyte balance and intracellular pressure in your horse's body and can actually produce dehydration, which is one reason why you feel even thirstier if you drink salt water. Your water source can be tested for salinity: levels of total salts under 7,000 mg/liter are relatively safe for nearly all horses, but the lower the better. Higher levels may cause performance problems. Levels over 2,500 mg/liter might cause diarrhea in animals not used to drinking it. Levels over 10,000 are dangerous. Young horses, and pregnant or lactating mares, are in the most danger from high salinity water.

The alkalinity or acidity of water may also be a factor for palatability. It measures the amount of alkali metals in the water. These metals are mostly sodium and potassium, but can include lithium, rubidium and cesium. The total alkalinity of the water will be lower than the TDS, which also includes other metals.

Another dangerous water source can be shallow ponds heavy in blue-green algae. (This condition is more commonly observed in the summer in quiet, sunlit parts of the water.) The algae may be enriched by excess nitrogen or phosphates from fertilizer runoff. When the algae bloom dies off, toxins are released into the pond. These nasty little creatures can cause bloody diarrhea, convulsions, and sudden death. Although blue-green algae are usually visible (sometimes clustered at one end of the pond because of prevailing winds), they are equally likely to be mixed with the water so not readily seen. Copper sulfate will kill these algae—but will also kill any other living thing in the pond. See Chapter 14 for more information.

City water is usually quite safe, since it is checked at the source, but of course this means little if there is a break or contamination in the system at your end. Of course, if this is the case—you might be getting sick as well....

Another problem horse owners face is the threat from bacteria in the water source. Water high in nitrates and phosphates (something easily checked) tends to be high in bacteria as well. This is because nitrates often come from manure contamination. However, other sources of nitrates like crop fertilizers, may also be to blame. Nitrates can even leach into well water from the soil. This is yet another reason to get your well water checked regularly. Nitrates dissolve in water, and can't be filtered out. However, it is possible to buy anion exchange units, which remove nitrates and sulfates. Luckily, nitrate poisoning is pretty rare in horses, and when it does occur, it is more likely to come from forage, not water. Horses can tolerate sulfate levels of 1,000 PPM and even higher (given time) without associated diarrhea; however, the real danger of nitrates in the water is that they suggest a high level of bacteria.

Salmonella is the biggest danger to farm animals. Believe it or not, flowing surface water is most likely to have bacterial contamination, but well water can also be infected.

If your barn water comes from a well, it's best to have a Total Cloriform test done by your agricultural extension agent. This test should be performed annually if you have an old or shallow well, but only every two or three years if you have a new, deep well which has tested negatively for two years. You should also have this test done on any new water source, or if any human or animal in your home becomes ill from a water-borne disease. (Potomac Horse Fever, which may be spread by fresh water snails, is an example of such a suspicious disease.) This test will analyze the water sample for bacteria that might be found in the surface water, surrounding soil and human

HARD WATER refers to how easily water precipitates soap or forms scales on heated surfaces. High levels of calcium and magnesium are usually responsible for hard water, although iron, strontium, zinc and manganese can also contribute.

and animal waste. Coliform levels typically rise during a drought, sudden downpours or flooding, or when the well has a damaged cap or other defect. A well located too close to manure piles or a septic tank is also suspect. You can often, but not always, notice a severe coliform infection by a change in color, odor, or taste of the water.

Some well water contains high levels of iron. This stuff imparts a rusty red color to waters, stains clothes, and tastes bad. More seriously, iron can sometimes be accompanied by "iron bacteria," which need iron to grow, but in the process exude a nasty, rust-colored slime to whatever it touches, including the insides of water pipes.

Water in Food

While some foods like growing grass may be 60 to 80 percent moisture, dry food like hay may contain only about 15 percent water. Horses living on rich growing grass may actually not need to drink water at all, although they generally will if it is available. Horses also require less water with more digestible food, regardless of the actual water content. This is because more digestible food means fewer feces—and a horse uses up a lot of water just to make feces. So feeding your horse a higher quality diet will not only make fewer bucket-carrying trips for you—but also less manure to pick up. And that has to be a good thing, unless you have a really big garden.

Dehydration

Without sufficient water, a horse's entire digestive system goes awry. A horse needs water to properly absorb nutrients from the gut. Water loss can also result in colic, since the food can become impacted in the digestive system.

If a horse is not provided sufficient water, he will need to draw it from his tissues and organs, first from the gut, then from the interstitial spaces (between the cells), and finally from the blood plasma. If a horse becomes dehydrated, his whole appearance and bodily functions will suffer.

Technically, a horse is supposed to be able to live for six days without water, but I really wouldn't recommend testing this theory. Horses deprived of water stop eating after a couple of days.

Too Much Water

Although it is extremely unlikely that a horse left to his own devices will drink too much water, overhydration can sometimes occur as a result of medical intervention in an emergency like choke. Certain diseases can also cause a horse to retain water unnaturally. Overhydrated horses usually exhibit swelling (edema) in the legs or general swelling. The latter is quite serious and often indicates kidney or heart disease. Even a localized swelling in the legs can be a sign of kidney problems.

Water Sources and Methods

Usually the horse owner has only limited control over his horse's water source. Either one has a natural source such as spring, pond, or creek, or one does not. Sometimes, however, access to such sources can be blocked or opened. Although a natural source certainly is easiest for horse owners, and often, especially if the source is a cool flowing stream, preferred by horses, it may not be the watering method of choice. You generally have little control over the quality of a natural source, and have less opportunity to monitoring your horse's water intake. This is especially important since the first signs of illness often manifest themselves by a horse's refusal to drink.

Timing

If possible, horses should have access to cool water at all times, except after heavy work. Horses fed large amounts of cold water after work are in danger of colic or even a type of laminitis. Wait at least fifteen minutes before allowing your horse anything more than a swallow or two of water after work. Common wisdom says that on a trail ride, water consumption is permissible if the horse resumes moving right after drinking. This lessens the likelihood of problems. However, it should be added that competitive endurance riders often water and rest their horses at the same time, without ill effects.

When free water access is not possible, the water should be provided at a set time daily. Most hard working horses also seem to benefit if they are watered before they are fed.

Water Troughs and their Kin

Horses kept in a stall are usually provided water in buckets. This presents no problems, so long as the bucket is regularly filled and cleaned. (This means cleaned daily and disinfected at least twice a week, more frequently if your horse is ill.) Water buckets that have had electrolytes or sweeteners added are especially in need of thorough cleaning—they can draw flies.

If you will not be able to visit your horse during the day, it may be necessary to leave an extra bucket for him. The flat-sided kinds that hang right against the wall are most preferable.

Flat back water buckets are preferable in stalls because they're a little more stable.
Courtesy Dan's Saddlery.

IF YOU ADD electrolytes to your horse's water, it's best not to add them to an automatic waterer which contains metal fittings—the salt could corrode them.

The bucket should be at an easy to reach height, to encourage the horse to drink all he needs. (This means in most cases that the bucket should be no higher than the point of the horse's shoulder. The most natural drinking position, of course, is head down.)

If possible, get an automatic waterer for your horse. It saves time and trouble, and insures that your horse will always have a fresh supply. The only drawback is that you can't monitor consumption. And of course, automatic waterers must be periodically cleaned and checked.

If possible, locate the water bucket at some distance form hay and feed troughs. Too near a proximity encourages the horse to drop wisps of hay and food particles into the water bucket which only hastens the inevitable dirtying up process.

If your pastured horse uses a trough, it's important to keep it clean; this is a whole lot easier if the trough has a drain. Trough or tubs with round corners are less likely to cause injury. Position the trough so that it's in a shady place during the summer, preferably so that it isn't right against the fence line, where a fence-running horse could run into it. ■

Troughs with rounded corners are less likely to cause injuries. Courtesy Dan's Saddlery.

3

Carbohydrates: The Staff of Life

CARBOHYDRATES, SUCH AS SUGAR and starches, are produced by plants. Using photosynthesis, plants combine carbon dioxide from the air with hydrogen from water to make carbohydrates. Plants are commonly considered to be really rather stupid, but you try it sometime.

Carbohydrates supply about 85 percent of your horse's energy requirement. About 75 percent of all plant material is carbohydrate. And most of a plant's dry matter (about 93 percent) comes straight from the air. And when you think that most of your horse comes from plants—well—I guess that means that your horse materialized from thin air, so to speak.

Carbohydrates perform the following functions:

- Provide energy
- Supply a heat source for the body when they are metabolized for energy
- Can be stored as glycogen or converted to fat
- Help regulate protein and fat metabolism
- Serve as building blocks for other biological components, such as glycoproteins, vitamin C, nonessential amino acids, glycolipids, and lactose (milk sugar)

Carbohydrates turn into glucose, the sugar found in blood. (Glucose can also be derived from proteins, or the glycerol found in fats.)

The body is desperate for glucose, getting it from wherever it can, even if this means metabolizing amino acids needed for muscle development. In fact, your horse needs a steady supply of glucose to keep every system in his body in good working order. Not just horses, but all animals, have a requirement for glucose. After glucose is absorbed into the body, the liver has two enzymes, glucokinase and hexokinase, that change glucose into its usable glucose-6-phosphate form.

Monosaccharides

Monosaccharides are simple sugars; they are highly palatable and easily digested. In fact, the general rule is that the more simple carbohydrates present in a feed, the more digestible the feed is. Simple sugars are the only form of carbohydrate that can be directly absorbed from the intestinal tract; all others must be broken down first. Most simple carbohydrates are found in grain. They consist of a single 3 to 7 (usually 6) carbon atom unit.

Most soluble forms of carbohydrate are broken down by amylase, a digestive enzyme made by the pancreas and secreted into the small intestine. (There's some in saliva, too.) More complex forms of carbohydrates are broken down into simple carbohydrates by the enzymes in the small intestine before they are absorbed and go into the bloodstream to be delivered to the cells for energy use. If the complex carbohydrates are not completely digested (usually because the horse is given too much grain at one meal), they pass on to the large intestine where the gut bacteria have a chance to work on them, producing energy-supplying volatile fatty acids in the process. In large amounts these may cause gastric disturbance, so it's better to feed horses several smaller meals than one large one.

Some of the most important monosacchride sugars include:

- **GLUCOSE** (found in fruits like berries as well as in corn syrup and similar products) is the end product of starch digestion. Glucose is a simple, moderately sweet sugar which supplies energy to vital organs, especially the central nervous system, brain, red blood cells, and muscles. It also provides the starting material for the synthesis of other compounds. Glucose is sometimes called dextrose, but it's really all the same thing.

- **FRUCTOSE** (honey, many ripe fruits, and some vegetables) is a very sweet sugar formed from the digestion of sucrose (a disaccharide).

- **GALACTOSE**, (not found "free-form" in food, although it makes up about 50 percent of the disaccharide lactose, which is found in milk) is released during digestion and converted to glucose by the liver.

Disaccharides

Monosaccharides and disaccharides are often grouped together as "simple sugars." Disaccharides are formed from two linked monosaccharides like fructose and glucose. Disaccharides include:

- Sucrose (sugar cane, sugar beets, molasses, maple syrup) is basically table sugar; it's composed of a molecule of glucose and a molecule of fructose.

- Lactose (milk sugar) is made up of a molecule of glucose and a molecule of galactose. This is the only carbohydrate of animal origin with dietary significance.

- Maltose (not commonly found in food) is composed of two linked glucose molecules. It is formed as an intermediate product during starch digestion.

Molasses, consisting largely of sucrose, is often added to horse feed—for two reasons. First, it increases the palatability of the food. Second, it helps keep down "dust" from rolled or ground feed. It is often added at a level of 2 to 4 percent—anything above this "cakes" the feed, especially in the cold.

Polysaccharides

Polysaccharides, often called complex carbohydrates, have three or more sugar units. They are found in hay and forage. Complex carbohydrates include starches, hemicellulose, cellulose, pectin and gums. Most of these are made largely of glucose molecules strung together. Starch is digested first

**LACTASE AND
sucrase are diges-
tive enzymes which
are secreted from
the interior intesti-
nal wall. They go to
work if milk sugar
(lactose) or table
sugar (sucrose) are
present in the gut.
Lactase activity is
high at a foal's birth,
but decline as a
horse ages.**

**SOME KINDS OF
starches, including
corn, rice, barley
and wheat are more
digestible than
other starches, like
potatoes or tapioca.**

**GLUCOSE STORED
by animals is called
glycogen. It is found
in the liver and mus-
cle. Glycogen serves
as a ready, easily
utilized reserve of
glucose. Only so
much glucose can
be stored as glyco-
gen; the rest is con-
verted to fat, where
it is used by the
body during times
of stress or famine.**

by amylase, which breaks down the polysaccharide molecule into the disaccharide maltose. Then the enzyme maltase breaks maltose down into its constituent monosaccharides (glucose). The other polysacchrides have similar patterns of digestion, often facilitated by bacteria in the gut.

Most polysaccharides convert to glucose, but some, called insoluble fiber or roughage provide little or no nutrition, although they may have other benefits. The way the sugar units are linked differs from grain to grain, and that affects the way the horse can digest the food. Oats, for example, are much easier for a horse to digest than barley.

Complex carbohydrates come in two forms: *starch* and *dietary fiber*. Carbohydrates that are digested easily are called *starches*, while those more resistant to digestion are termed *fiber*.

Starches

Starches are complex, long chains of simple sugar molecules, usually glucose. Starches are the nonstructural parts of plants; they make up a large portion of the grain you feed your horse. Cereal grains are a main source of carbohydrates; these foods also provide some minerals and vitamins.

Starches are highly palatable, but require more digestion than simple sugars before they are absorbed into the bloodstream. However, between 87 and 100 percent of the starch a horse eats is eventually absorbed.

The complexity of the starch molecule makes it take longer to be digested; often the small intestine can't finish the job, and passes it along to the large intestine, and that's when trouble can occur. The arrival of the unexpected starch induces a kind of feeding frenzy among the bacteria designed to digest it, and they multiply far beyond their usual numbers. They do get the starch digested, but also produce lactic acid, which acidifies the gut lining. The normal bacteria that live there just can't stand their new acidic environment and begin to die off, thus making it harder for the horse to digest forage, his natural food.

Fiber

Although it sounds boring, fiber is a critical element in a horse's diet. Fiber does a lot of things: it allows for more efficient "mixing" of the digestive juices, enzymes and bacteria. It also helps the horse retain water and electrolytes in the digesta in the large bowel. It is fermented by special cellulose-chomping bacteria, which, as a by-product, produce a lot of heat. (Everybody knows how warm a snug barn can be—in the dead of winter. This is one reason why it's a good idea to feed your horse some extra hay when it's cold outside.)

Remember that fiber plays two main functions: digestible fiber is a source of dietary energy, while indigestible fiber is necessary to maintain normal movement through the GI tract, and to maintain normal pH. It keeps the digestive system moving at the correct rate; without it, the stuff would move through too fast, and put the horse at grave risk of colic or founder. All fibers increase fecal volume, since horses can digest only about 50 percent of structural fibers, even with the help of the friendly bacteria. The more insoluble fiber a feed contains, the less energy even a horse can extract from it.

Horses were designed live largely on fiber; they like the stuff, and it provides the average horse with everything he needs to live on. Without sufficient fiber in the diet, a horse will die; it's that simple. Only high-performance animals actually need anything more. And even the highest performance horses need a diet composed of at least 50 percent fiber.

Fiber is composed of a number of complex carbohydrates, primarily cellulose and hemicellulose; it makes up the structural component in plant cell walls. No animal in and of itself possess the digestive enzymes necessary to break up cellulose—all animals rely on intestinal (in the cecum and colon) bacteria to do the job. For animals without the requisite bacteria (like us) the stuff simply passes largely unchanged through the digestive tract. And if something bad happens to the fiber-chomping bacteria, something bad happens to the horse. Of course, the bacteria aren't doing all this fiber digesting from the goodness of their hearts—they need the stuff for their own purposes,

IN CASE YOU'RE wondering, the volatile fatty acids include acetic, proprionic, lactic, isobutyric, isovaleric, and valeric acids. If you are not wondering, you can skip reading this box, but I suppose it's too late for that.

Horses were designed to live on fiber—and they like the stuff! Helen Peppe photo.

Pectin is found both in plant cell walls and intercellular regions. It is found primarily in fruits and vegetables like apples, raspberries, potatoes, sugar beet pulp, citrus fruit skins, and broccoli. It's what makes jellies gel.

Donkeys are much better at getting energy from high-fiber diets than are horses or ponies. Considering the dry areas they come from, this doesn't surprise me. But the champion fiber buster is the llama. And look where they come from. No, not Tibet, that's the one-l lama. The 2-ll lama is from the desert regions of South America— Peru and such places.

whatever those may be. Their unintended good works convert fiber to volatile (short-chain) fatty acids (SCFAs) which can provide 30 to 70 percent (depending on how much grain your horse receives) of your horse's total energy needs.

Nutritionists classify fibers by both solubility and fermentability. Solubility refers to the ability of fiber to disperse in water. Insoluble fibers just lie there; soluble fibers disperse into a slurry. Fermentability refers to the time it takes for a fiber to be broken down into short-chain fatty acids, primarily by bacteria in the large intestine. Highly fermentable fibers break down more quickly.

Soluble fibers (pectins, gums, mucilages) are found in pysllium seeds, fruits, oats, legumes, guar, and barley—the stuff coming from the secretions and inside parts of a plant. These fibers have high water-holding capacities; they delay gastric emptying and probably slow down the rate of nutrient absorption across the intestinal surface. Most soluble fibers are also highly fermentable. They are highly digestible, but usually comprise only a minor portion of a horse's diet.

Tough, rigid, insoluble fibers like cellulose, lignin, and most of the hemicellulose, are found in the structural parts of plants. In fact, cellulose has been compared to the hollow reinforcing rods that hold buildings together; like those rods, cellulose holds together the plant's cell walls.

Famous insoluble fibers (which come from the non-seed, non-fruit portions of a plant) include:

- **CELLULOSE:** the most abundant fiber found in plants, forming the material of the plant cell wall. Cellulose is found in whole-wheat flour, bran and vegetables.

- **HEMICELLULOSE**: closely associated with cellulose in plant cell walls. As the plant ages, hemicellulose converts to the less digestible cellulose. Some forms of hemicellulose, like psyllium, are soluble, while others like wheat bran and some other grains, are insoluble. *Cellulose and hemicellulose provide most of the energy required in a horse's natural diet.*

- **LIGNIN:** not strictly a carbohydrate, but close enough. (Technically lignin is a phenylpropane polymer, if that's any comfort.) This totally insoluble fiber helps make up the structural part of plant cells, a kind of cement that holds plant cell walls together. Lignin is found in woody plants, wheat and vegetables. It is not digestible, and has no nutritional value.

Your horse, with the help of his intestinal bacteria, can digest cellulose and hemicellulose in his cecum and large intestine. Lignin, which is present in woody plants, is something else again. Not even a horse can digest lignin—he just doesn't have the right microbes. Only termites do. One source I consulted referred to lignin as "completely resistant." This is really too bad. Think of how much fun a walk in the woods would be if we could eat trees.

Fiber performs a balancing act. First, it speeds the passage of food through the stomach, often before it is fully broken down. It then slows it down through the lower part of small intestine and colon.

Fiber serves as a natural laxative and stool softener. (By distending the large intestine, it stimulates defecation.) On the other hand, it also helps manage diarrhea. Thus fiber plays a role in "normalizing" the digestive process. Some kinds of fiber appear to lower cholesterol and to regulate blood sugar and insulin levels. The exact way fiber is handled by the digestive system, however, depends on the specific type and amount of fiber given.

It's generally understood that both moderately and highly fermentable fibers increase colon weight and mucosal surface area, which in turn increases the absorptive capacity of the colon.

A few minerals may be adversely affected by rapidly fermenting fibers, including calcium (beet pulp and pea fiber), copper, iron (beet pulp, apple pectin, citrus pulp), phosphorus (beet pulp, soy hulls, soy cotyledon fiber, guar gum), and zinc (beet pulp and peanut hulls).

Horses get fiber mostly in the form of grass and hay. If they don't receive enough fiber in the diet, they may develop poorly formed feces that resemble cow patties more than normal horse manure. But precisely how much fiber your horse gets from any particular batch of hay depends on the season, soil conditions, type of plant, and time of cutting. Usually early cut hay has less fiber than hay from older, more mature fields. It has more of other kinds of nutrients, however. Luckily horses are pretty forgiving, within limits. Grains, are more consistent in their fiber content than hay.

Since fiber is present in all plants, it's present in the contents of your horse's feedbag. The label on the bag will give the crude fiber of the feed, but this number is usually wrong, over-rating the non-fiber part of the food and underestimating the cellulose content. It's only a best guess. Another way of estimating fiber content is the NDE test, which measures the amount of "neutral detergent fiber." This test manages to get all the cellulose and about half of the hemicellulose, but it tends to overestimate the amount of digest-

Starch and fibers are chemically different: in starches, the glucose units are linked together with ∂-glycosidic (between sugar) bonds; sugars in fibers are linked by ß-glycosidic bonds. In simple terms, ∂-bonds are "up" while ß-bonds are "down." This doesn't sound like a big deal, but it is. Animal enzymes can break up ∂-bonds, but only the enzyme in microbes can break up ß-bonds. These microbial enzymes are found in the colon.

THERE'S ACTUALLY an enzymatic test available to show how much soluble versus non soluble material is contained within a feed. No one bothers with it, though.

VITAMIN B12 can also be bound by various fibers.

THE INFAMOUS *hay belly is caused not by too much food, but too much poor-quality fiber that distends the digestive tract.*

ible starches. The best test is the ADE, which measures acid detergent fiber. Even this test tends to underestimate the insoluble fiber content. In this world, it seems that nothing is perfect.

Still and all, many feed companies can conduct a test (it costs about 40 dollars) using all three tests to give a you a pretty accurate idea of what your feed or pasture contains. In order to get an accurate analysis of forage, however, make sure you bring in samples of the stuff your horse actually eats. This may take a bit of observation on your part. You should get samples from at least 20 different bales (or sections of the pasture) and try to get as representative a sample as possible. Obviously, if you buy hay from different people, it becomes prohibitively expensive to conduct an analysis on every hay sample so you may have to rely on common sense and your horse's sturdy digestive system. ▬

4

Protein and Fat: The Body Builders

Protein

Proteins are long, complex molecules made from amino acids linked together like beads on a chain by peptide bonds. (Amino acids, in turn, are made mostly of carbon, hydrogen, nitrogen, and oxygen with a little sulfur thrown in for good measure.) Proteins and their constituent amino acids are the "building blocks" of the body. They are the basic substance of protoplasm, comprising about 50 percent of every cell.

All animals need protein for body maintenance and healing, and young animals also need it for growth. (If a foal doesn't get enough protein, his tissues, hoofs, and organs won't develop properly.) Proteins are critical in building enzymes, hormones, hemoglobin and antibodies. They maintain and repair muscle tissue, connective tissue, blood cells and cartilage. (Horses with cancer, trauma and burns need additional protein to help heal.) Horses can also use protein for energy, although it's a fairly inefficient and expensive way to produce it. Energy production from protein produces a lot more body heat than the energy produced from fats or carbohydrates; this can lead to more sweating and even heat exhaustion.

When your horse munches down, his digestive system separates the protein into its original constituent amino acids using clever combinations of enzymes and acids. Following absorption, the amino acids are then dispersed to all the body cells where the amino acids are re-combined into new proteins more suitable for horses. (During their travels, some of amino acids change their structure in the liver.)

The Essential Amino Acids

Although your horse needs all 22 amino acids, he can manufacture half of them in his own body tissues. These "made-at-home" amino acids are called "nonessential"—they don't need to be supplied in the diet. Amino acids that must be supplied in the diet (or synthesized by microorganisms in the intestinal tract) are called *essential amino acids (EFA)*. This designation is somewhat different from dogs and people in whom we consider amino acids synthesized by the intestinal bacteria "nonessential." The reason for the difference is that intestinal bacteria in horses tend to be variable, depending upon what the horse's diet is at the moment. Some essential amino acids can be synthesized by the horse, but not in sufficient quantities to meet his needs.

Different foods have different "amino acid profiles," which is a fancy way of talking about the number and position of amino acids in a single protein. For example, most cereal grains lack certain essential amino acids (like lysine), while many grass forages are low in protein generally. Among plant proteins, only soybean and canola meal contain sufficient amounts of lysine and methionine; they are two very tricky amino acids to find in most plant proteins. Cereal grains like oats, corn and barley tend to have less complete or more unbalanced proteins than soybean meal.

Linseed and cottonseed meal have much poorer amino acid profiles, so feeds based on these meals must be supplemented by the manufacturer. Amino acids must conform to a perfect pattern; if just one essential amino acid is missing from the diet, then the quality of the entire protein is lowered. All this being said, it should be pointed out that amino acid deficiencies have never been identified as a specific problem in horses. Nearly all commonly used horse feeds contain the right number of amino acids to meet a horse's needs. What matters is how much total protein a horse gets, and how digestible that protein is. In general, horses can digest between 45 and 85 percent of protein found in most horse feeds.

About 10 amino acids are essential; we'll look at these more closely below. In addition, some amino acids are "conditionally essential"; this means that although they are not ordinarily required in the diet, certain physiologic conditions may occur in which the animal cannot properly synthesize them from other amino acids. Young horses are much more sensitive to getting the right kind and amount of amino acids, especially lysine and methionine, than are older ones.

High-quality proteins have a high proportion of essential amino acids; those with a higher percentage of nonessential amino acids are considered low-quality protein.

The following amino acids are considered to be essential for all phases of equine life:

- **LYSINE:** Enhances growth and nitrogen balance. Promotes bone growth in foals, and stimulates gastric juices. This particular amino acid is often called the "first limiting" amino acid—meaning that if your horse doesn't get enough of it, he won't be able to use any of the others either. Horse feeds should contain a minimum of 0.65 percent lysine (dry matter).

- **METHIONINE:** Important for hair coat and growth. Helps prevent deposits and adhesions of fat in the liver, is essential for selenium bioavailability, and is an antioxidant and anti-arthritic. Methionine is second only in importance to lysine as a "limiting" amino acid.

- **ARGININE:** Stimulates the release of insulin and growth hormone. It has been shown to be helpful as a nutritional aid in cancer therapy, as it fights tumor growth. It stimulates the immune system by boosting T-cell production.

- **HISTIDINE:** Maintains plasma, hematocrit (the portion of the blood occupied by the red blood cells), and serum albumin. It releases histamine from body stores, and helps control pain. Helps treat arthritis. It stimulates stomach acid secretion and so improves appetite.

- **PHENYLALANINE:** Produces adrenaline and noradrenaline and is an antidepressant.

- **THREONINE:** Enhances growth and food efficiency. Produces adrenaline and is a precursor to the thyroid hormones.

What's really important for gauging your horse's nutrition, however, is the amount of digestible protein (DP) a food contains. Unfortunately, this number is extremely hard to determine, unlike the crude protein (CP) figure. It requires studies of live animals, which are long, complicated, and expensive. Mostly, we have to make do with the crude protein number. We do know, however, that cereal grains are higher in digestible protein, while mature grass forage is lower.

CONTRACTILE proteins, like myosin and actin, regulate muscle action. Other proteins control glucose levels in the blood, digest nutrients, transport oxygen and iron, and regulate the acid/base balance. Although there are only 22 amino acids, there are thousands of proteins. This is because the amino acids can combine in different ways, just as the 26 letters of the alphabet can make a nearly infinite variety of words.

- **TRYPTOPHAN:** Produces serotonin, and so is a mood stabilizer. Precursor to niacin and may aid in blood clotting.

- **VALINE:** With fellow amino acids isoleucine and leucine, valine regulates protein turnover and energy metabolism. Vital for muscle co-ordination.

- **LEUCINE:** Keeps muscle protein from degrading.

- **ISOLEUCINE:** Helps form hemoglobin and fights nervous system degeneration.

Protein Digestion

Protein digestion begins in the stomach, where the enzyme pepsin goes to work in the presence of hydrochloric acid. How and where protein is digested depends largely upon its source. Most of the protein derived from grain and other concentrates is digested in the small intestine, while that derived from high-fiber feeds must be digested in the large intestine, the organ equipped to handle fiber.

Like fats and carbohydrates, amino acids can be "stored"; however, they are stored only as protein in muscle. If the body needs extra energy or amino acids, it must draw them from the muscle, which over time can lead to muscle wasting. So extra amino acids are not stored in the sense that fats are; instead the liver removes the nitrogen (deaminates it), and the kidneys excrete the by-products as urea and creatinine. The leftover parts (keto acid analogs) are stored as body fat or used as energy.

Protein Requirements

An 1,100-pound mature working horse does very well on a diet of 9 to 12 percent crude protein, provided by good hay and adequate grain. (This means about 600 to 800 grams per day.) The harder work the horse does, the more protein he needs (up to a point.) A layabout horse can get along well on as little as 8 or 9 percent protein. Pregnant mares need 11 or 12 percent, and lactating mares, which need it for their milk, need 13 or 14 percent. During lactation, mares need a total of 1,400 grams a day for a mare with a newborn foal and 1,000 gram a day when the foal is three months old. By far the highest levels of protein are required by weanlings, who are growing at an incredible rate; weanlings need 14.5 to 16 percent protein. Once they reach a year old, that requirement goes down to about 13.5 percent. These levels are somewhat higher than those recommended by the National Research Council, which many experts regard as too conservative.

Protein Deficiency

Normally we see protein deficiency in horses kept for long periods on a protein-poor pasture. Protein deficient horses lose weight, perform poorly, and develop poor, unkempt-looking coats which fail to shed out well. In serious cases you may even notice muscle deterioration in the hindquarters, where the muscles mass is most evident. The horse has been taking his necessary energy from the protein intended to build muscle.

Young horses fail to grow properly, and lactating mares give less milk. Hooves grow more slowly than normal; they can also crack and splinter. Protein-deficient horses may lose their appetites—or even resort to copraphagy (feces eating). (A horse restored to the correct amount of protein will resume normal eating patterns in a week or so.) A horse that loses his appetite due to protein deficiency, of course, is on a downward spiral, since by failing to eat he loses even more protein. He may "stock up" due to a decrease in plasma protein concentration.

Many grass forages are very deficient in protein, but protein deficiency can be cause by more than just not enough protein in the diet. The protein may be of poor digestibility as well, as sometimes happens with heat-damaged feed. And of course, a horse that is not getting enough food in general is almost certain to have a protein deficiency as well. For example, if a horse is getting enough protein, but not many fats or carbohydrates, the horse will use the protein for energy not for muscle building as nature intended, and he will lose condition as a result. Remember: carbohydrates and fats for energy—protein to build a strong body.

Protein Excess

Protein excess occurs more frequently than protein deficiency. If a horse gets extra protein in the diet, he will convert it into energy just as he does with carbohydrates; however, proteins, in the nature of things, are a much more expensive source of energy than plain old carbohydrates. Protein not used right away is metabolized so that the nitrogen within is released. (The rest of the molecule is stored.) These nitrogen atoms are converted to urea and ammonia, which are excreted in the urine.

Excreting the extra protein does require some extra work on the part of the kidneys, but no studies exist to suggest that this is a problem for a healthy animal. Only horses with kidney or liver disease are in danger from extra protein. If a horse can't excrete enough urea, the amount of urea or ammonia in the body increases, which can lead, in the worst case scenarios, to coma or even death. One study showed that growing horses fed 25 percent extra protein (that's a whole lot more) did suffer slower growth rates and developmental bone disease.

NONESSENTIAL amino acids are alanine, cistine, proline, aspartic acid, glutamine, serine, carnitine, glycine, taurine, citrulline, hydroxyproline and tyrosine.

CURIOUSLY, researchers have determined that aged horses, those 20 years old and over, require greatly increased levels of protein—in fact, they return to the protein needs they had as young, growing horses.

RUMINANTS, LIKE cows, can synthesize protein from nitrogen-rich non-protein sources like urea. Horses, however, are much less capable of doing this, since most of the non-protein nitrogen is absorbed from the small intestine and excreted in the urine before it reaches the cecum and colon, which contain most of the bacteria able to perform the synthesis.

Even worse, excessive non-protein nitrogen is toxic, since the process that turns urea nitrogen into protein involves a middle step: the products become ammonia, which is obviously poisonous. Curiously, horses are more resistant to ammonia poisoning than cows or sheep (because they excrete the extra nitrogen rather than digest it), so the amount of urea present in cattle or sheep feed is harmless to horses—although it doesn't do them any particular good, either. However, colts are considerably more sensitive than grown horses, so they should definitely

Tradition says that a horse getting excess protein in his diet will produce a foamy sweat and a strong ammonia smell in the urine. In addition, extra protein will be excreted in the urine; the more protein a horse gets the more he urinates. The more he urinates, the more water he needs to drink—this becomes especially important if *you* are the one carrying the water. And of course, if your horse is stalled, the more he urinates, the wetter the stall. This seems to be the main problem with high-protein forage like alfalfa, especially if the stable is not well ventilated.

Your Horse's Protein Needs

The amount of protein your particular horse needs in his diet largely depends upon how of much of that diet he eats. For example, a horse eating a high-energy diet will tend to eat less than one on a lower-energy diet. Therefore it's very important that such high-energy diets contain enough protein, or the horse may eat his "fill" without receiving enough amino acids. The same is true of all nutrients, of course. You know yourself that you can consume a candy bar or two or three, which may make you not hungry for dinner, yet which doesn't give you the nutrients you need to survive indefinitely, should you make M & M's your permanent sole fare.

The amount of protein needed also depends on how digestible the protein is, and your horse's own particular need for protein. Most adult horses do well on 0.60 grams of *digestible protein* per kilogram of body weight per day. I talk more about this subject in Chapter 11. For growing horses, the amino acid content of the protein is also important.

The most serious problem with large amount of protein can occur in young horses. If colts are fed rapidly increasing amounts of protein *without sufficient quantities of minerals like copper and zinc to support increased growth* they may be liable to a host of bone problems including osteochondrosis.

In general, we can say that the higher quality of protein your horse consumes, the less of it he needs in his diet. The quality depends mostly on the proteins' availability and digestibility in the food. High-fiber foods usually mean lower protein digestibility, while poor curing or storing procedures can also lower the digestibility of protein. As the concentration of protein in the diet decreases, so does its digestibility. Some forages, like fresh-cut alfalfa, are very high in protein, while others, like brome grass, can vary from a low of 5 percent to a high of 14 percent, depending on when it is cut and baled.

Since protein utilization produces three to six times more heat than carbohydrates, extra protein may be useful on a cold winter day—and less so in the hot summer, where the extra heat production encourages sweating.

Fats

Technically, fats are one of the substances we call lipids. The other major class of lipids is called oils. (This distinction between fats and oils is somewhat arbitrary and both are more accurately called triglycerides.) Oils and fats are pretty much the same except that at room temperature, fats are solid, while oils are liquid. Both fats and oils are made up of fatty acids and glycerol. Fats are digested through both physical and enzymatic processes before they are absorbed from the small intestine. The fatty acids that result go to the horse's liver, from which some are used for energy needs, while the rest are stored by the body as—well—fat, to be used later or not, as the occasion arises.

Fats have about two and a quarter times the number of calories per gram as protein or carbohydrates. They are packed with energy that keeps cells in good working order.

Fatty Acids

Fatty acids are the principal energy-providing components of fat. Some fatty acids are derived from the diet, while others, the volatile fatty acids, are produced by bacterial digestion in the hindgut. These acids are essential for all sorts of biological functions. They circulate all through the body and are stored mostly between muscle cells.

Horses not only use fat, of course; they also store it. Horses store fat under their skin, around their vital organs, and in the membranes surrounding the intestines. Fat storage serves not only as an energy reserve, but also as an insulator against both cold and injury.

Lipids have the following functions:

- Supply energy
- Make up, in the form of phospholipids and sphingolipids, the main part of membranes surrounding cells
- Carry the fat-soluble vitamins A, D, E and K, and aid in their absorption in the body
- Help make calcium more available

Fats in Feed

The precise requirements of fat in the horse's diet are not established. Certainly wild horses don't get much. The current recommendation is for 0.5 percent in the diet dry matter. Most horse feeds contain several times that amount, and horses that do lot a work can benefit from higher levels of

not be fed feeds containing urea or biuret.

Federal law states that feed labels must state the amount of non-protein nitrogen contained in the feed. To figure out how much usable protein your horse is getting, subtract this amount from the total protein provided. For example, if the total protein is 22 percent, with a 10 percent "protein equivalent" from urea, that food contains only 12 percent usable protein, so far as your horse is concerned.

DIETARY LIPIDS consist of triglycerides, a group of three fatty acids linked to glycerol. There are other kinds of lipids besides fats and oils, including cholesterol. Most of these diverse substances bear little resemblance to fats, but chemists classify them as lipids for lack of a better category. Cholesterol forms the bile salts necessary for fat digestion and absorption, is present in cell membranes, acts as a precursor for steroid hormones, and forms a protective layer in the skin. Horses can synthesize their own cholesterol and do not need it in their diet.

OILS DERIVED from plants provide large amounts of essential fatty acids (EFAs). EFAs are polyunsaturated. They stimulate growth, condition skin and coat, and aid the development of the nervous system. The essential fatty acids include linoleic acid (an omega-6) and linolenic acid, also called alpha-linolenic acid,

fat. Among the grains, oats have the most fat, with 5.1 percent; corn has 3.6 percent. Hays run lower, as you might expect. When fat must be added to a horse's diet to help supply energy, it is usually added as vegetable oil or even hydrolized animal fats. (Horses need encouragement in eating both, especially the latter.)

"Good" Fat versus "Bad" Fat?

The easiest way to think about this is to drag out the old chemistry book. Oh. You threw yours away after college. That's okay—here's all you really need to know. Sadly, fat has a bad name in the popular imagination. For people, bad fat is saturated fat, the kind present in meat and butter. Most saturated fats are solid at room temperature while unsaturated fats, or oils, are liquid.

In most cases, the more unsaturated the fat, the lower its melting point. This all has to do with so-called double bonds, a carbon linked twice to another carbon. A saturated fat has no double bonds. Unsaturated fats have at least one. Let's take olive oil. Olive oil is largely comprised of oleic acid. Oleic acid is a monounsaturated fat: it has one double bond.

Linoleic Acid (Omega 6)

Linoleic acid is the most common omega-6 fatty acid, and can be used by the body to synthesize others, and is probably the only truly essential fatty acid for horses. In other words, linoleic acid can provide the horse's total physiological requirement for omega-6 fatty acids. Linoleic acid has two double bonds. That makes it a polyunsaturated fat. The two richest sources of linoleic acid are corn oil and safflower oil, containing 55 and 73 percent respectively.

Omega-3 fatty acids, such as linolenic acid, usually have three double bonds. (That's not why they're called omega-3s, though, unfortunately.) Their requirement by horses has not been established, but some benefit may follow from including them in the diet, and small amounts certainly won't do any harm. Gamma-linolenic acid and arachidonic acid (both omega-6 fatty acids) are synthesized from linolenic acid. Linolenic acid is the most common omega-3 fatty acid and is found abundantly in flaxseed (*Linum usitatissimum*) and a few other vegetable oils. Most other vegetable oils commonly are much higher in the omega-6 family. Other omega-3 fatty acids are found mostly in fish oils.

> **Tidbit:** *As we all know, fats tend to break down and become rancid. Not only do rancid fats fail to supply the body's linoleic acid needs, they also deplete the body of vitamin C, E and beta-carotene. In addition, they form free radicals,*

and break down into evil smelling ketones and aldehydes. A few of these prod-
ucts are positively dangerous. Omega-3 fatty acids are more susceptible to ran-
cidity than omega-6s. This is one reason why foods containing omega-3s must
include a preservative, and should be refrigerated after opening.

Essential fatty acid deficiency, as a condition separate from fat deficiency, is
not known in horses.

Essential fatty acids:

- Are required for growth and reproduction
- Are precursors of eicosanoid and prostaglandin synthesis
- Contribute to cell membrane structure and fluidity
- Keep skin and coat healthy
- Promote proper development of the nervous system
- Increase food efficiency during growth, keep skin in good condition
- Are essential for the normal development of retina and nervous system

Fat Deficiency

Although very rare, horses can develop a fat deficiency, especially if they
consume low-quality fats containing insufficient EFAs in the diet. Fat deficiency is signaled by:

- Slower wound healing
- Harsh coat
- Dry skin and dandruff
- Dermatitis
- Lesions
- Emaciation

Some horses have to be encouraged to consume a higher fat diet, but
most take to it fairly readily. A higher fat diet will improve your horse's
appearance and performance. (One reason for the performance improvement may be that fats produce more water as they are metabolized than
do protein or carbohydrates. This may help keep horses from dehydrating
so quickly.)

NOT ALL HORSE feeds reveal the amount of fat by listing it as "crude fat." The label may use the term "ether extract," which amounts to the same thing. Fat is soluble in ether, and so its amount in feed is measured that way.

Minerals:
The Bone Builders

MINERALS ARE INORGANIC SUBSTANCES, which cannot be synthesized in the laboratory—or in your horse's body. They are elements, and thus neither die nor are reborn. They are simply there or not there—although some that are there may be present in a form that makes it almost as if they were not there. But perhaps this is a quibble.

Many minerals are essential to your horse's health, and must be supplied in the diet. Only about 3 to 4 percent of your horse's total body weight is mineral—this is pretty amazing when you think of the skeleton! Your horse's bones are about 35-percent calcium combined with about half that much phosphorous.

AN EXCESS OF minerals in the diet can cause as many problems as too few. Any mineral supplementation should be done very carefully, and with your veterinarian's approval.

AS A GENERAL rule, legume hays like alfalfa are richer in minerals than grass hays. Horses living on poor pastures, or pastures containing only one kind of forage, are more likely to need mineral supplementation than others.

THROUGHOUT this book, I'll be using the abbreviation mg, which stands for milligram. A milligram is a thousandth of a gram. A gram is about the size of a raisin. (There are about 454,000 milligrams in a pound. So if you ate a pound of raisins— never mind.)

Minerals participate in nearly every function of the body. They build teeth and bone, serve as enzyme cofactors, and are a vital part of the blood and other body fluids. Some minerals also play a role in muscle contraction, the transmission of nerve impulses, and in cell membrane permeability.

One of the notable things about minerals is the way they interact with each other; the action of one often enhances, is necessary for, or impedes the action of another. These interactions can occur during digestion, at the tissue storage sites, during transport out of the digestive system, or even within pathways of excretion. Although I am considering each mineral pretty much separately in his book, it's important to recall that as dietary elements, they work as group.

Not every mineral in the world has importance in the diet. Some, like uranium, cadmium, lead and mercury are harmful in any amounts, and gold and silver, while not harmful, don't do your horse any good either. (This is a good thing, since gold or uranium supplements would be fairly pricey.)

Although minerals themselves are inorganic in that they do not contain carbon, they are presented to the body in organic and inorganic forms. "Inorganic" minerals are supplied as sulfates, oxides, phosphates, chlorides and carbonates. Organic minerals come in polysaccharide or amino acid complexes, chelates and proteinates.

But how does your horse get his minerals? Well, through the plants he eats, plants which have extracted the minerals from the soil. Since this amount can be extremely variable, some owners supplement their horse's mineral needs by supplying a mineralized salt block (which may be helpful, but doesn't provide enough minerals to counteract a seriously mineral-deficient diet) or through the purchase of specially fortified pre-mixed feeds. However, it's important to remember not to add minerals to your horse's diet unless you know for a fact that he needs them.

Of the minerals needed by the body, seven are termed *macrominerals*, meaning that your horse (and you) needs them in fairly large amounts. These minerals include calcium (Ca), phosphorus (P), magnesium (Mg), potassium (K), sodium (Na) and chloride (Cl), which together make salt, and sulfur (S). Usually they are measured as parts per hundred (percent) in the diet. As a group, macrominerals are used for body structure and maintaining acid/base and fluid balance. They also help cellular function, nerve conduction, and muscle contraction.

The other minerals are called *microminerals*, or trace minerals. They include selenium, iodine, copper, zinc, manganese, iron and cobalt. They are often expressed as parts per million (ppm or mg/kg which are the same thing).

Most trace minerals are used by the body as components of metalloenzymes, which control many biological reactions. With the exception of selenium, most trace minerals are more easily absorbed by the horse in their organic, as opposed to their inorganic, forms.

One of the great myths in nutrition is that horses will automatically seek the minerals they need. Tests have shown that a calcium-deficient horse does not select calcium rich foods over others. It is your job as the owner to give your horse what he needs.

Calcium (Ca)

Calcium is the major inorganic component of bone, comprising about 35 percent of the skeleton. (It also makes up from 30 to 50 percent of the mineral content of milk.) In fact, about 99 percent of the body's calcium is found in the skeleton and teeth, and it is generally considered the most important mineral in the body, even though it makes up only about 2 percent of the entire body weight. Blood moves calcium around in the body, and researchers estimate that about 20 percent of the calcium in the bones is replaced every year.

The average maintenance horse needs about 20 grams of calcium, plentiful in some hays and legumes, per day. Foods high in calcium include alfalfa and leafy green vegetables. Although horses don't eat a lot of spinach, they do consume leafy legume hay when given the opportunity. In fact, alfalfa is so richly supplied with calcium (up to 2 percent) that it is wise to mix alfalfa with other hays or a phosphorus supplement, like monosodium phosphate, when feeding young horses, whose skeletal development can be adversely affected by too much of the stuff. The next most calcium-rich hay is timothy (0.43 percent) followed by bromegrass (0.25 percent), then grains such as oats (0.08 percent), and corn and barley (0.05 percent each). Most grains and grass forages are poor sources of calcium.

Function

- Forms and strengthens bones and teeth
- Helps in blood clotting
- Aids metabolism
- Helps regulate temperature
- Aids fluid transport through cell walls
- Participates in muscle contraction
- Activates certain enzyme systems
- Regulates nerve function and excitability

MINERALS ARE A sociable lot, and enjoy teaming up and working together. Some famous pairs include calcium and phosphorus, and sodium and chloride. Copper and zinc often pair off, and even sometimes footsie around with iron or other minerals. Selenium is the most renegade mineral of all, since its partner is a vitamin—vitamin E.

HORSES WITH impaired kidney function should not be given food too high in calcium. The phosphorus/calcium balance, however, should still be maintained.

**FOR BOTH CALCIUM
and phosphorus
the main effects of
too much or little
is skeletal disease.
Horses are more
likely to get too
little calcium than
too much.**

Calcium is more easily absorbed by the body than most other minerals; its absorption rate varies between 50 and 70 percent, depending upon a number of factors, including the horse's age. Older horses are less efficient at absorbing calcium than young ones.

Calcium from inorganic sources like limestone (calcium carbonate) or dicalcium phosphate is more readily absorbed than calcium from most organic sources. One reason for this is that many plants contain large amounts of phosphorus, phytates, and/or oxalates, all of which can bind to calcium and inhibit absorption. Horses eating diets containing low but adequate levels of calcium while eating substantial amounts of oxalate-rich plants, such as sorrel (or other members of the *Oxalis* genus), halogeton, or greasewood, may develop a calcium deficiency. The greatest danger of such diets is to growing horses and lactating mares. Excess oxalates may also lead to kidney stones and subsequent renal damage.

Alfalfa is high in oxalates, although it doesn't seriously reduce calcium absorption. The ever popular bran mash is high enough in phosphates that horses consuming a lot of it may need a calcium supplement. Oats are also high in phytates. Horses getting lots of these kinds of feed should receive a calcium supplement.

Too much iron, magnesium, or zinc likewise inhibits calcium absorption. (However, some magnesium must be included in the diet—otherwise the calcium cannot be used.)

Increasing the amount of vitamin D increases the body's ability to absorb calcium. Other things can make a difference, too, like fat in the diet. Horses need some fat to help absorb calcium, but if they get too much, it inhibits calcium absorption.

Deficiency

A calcium deficiency is most likely to occur in a high grain/low legume diet, resulting in:

- Slower, incomplete growth
- Hyperparathyroidism
- Anorexia and weight loss
- Loss of muscle tone, tendinitis
- Extensive bone demineralization
- Shifting leg lameness that worsens with exercise
- Bone fractures and loose teeth

- Epiphysitis (swollen knees and fetlocks causes by the bony plates pressing against each other)
- Miller's disease (big head or bran disease)

Excess

Calcium excess usually comes about when too much of a calcium supplement is added to the diet, or when the Ca:P ratio is greater than 6:1 in adults or 3:1 in weanlings. This is probably the most common (and one of the most dangerous) mineral imbalances to occur in horses. Excess calcium results in:

- Decreased feed efficiency
- Nephrosis (kidney tubule degeneration)
- Lameness and bone/joint problems
- Swollen knees and fetlocks (epiphysitis)
- Lower absorption of magnesium
- Decrease in thyroid function
- Possibly fractures

The Calcium/Phosphorus Ratio

Calcium levels in the horse's body must be coordinated with phosphorus levels. Horses not only need both calcium and phosphorus, but they need them in the correct ratio. Fortunately, this ratio is pretty forgiving in the horse. Anything from 1:1.1 to 6:1 calcium/phosphorus seems acceptable, with the ideal ratio about 1.1 to 1.5:1. This is a good thing, because lots of grain and little forage can result in too little calcium (cereal grains like oats, corn and barley have twice as much phosphorus as calcium), while the reverse situation may result in too little phosphorus. In addition, alfalfa has eight times as much calcium as phosphorus, which can be dangerous, especially for a young horse. If a horse gets too much calcium, there is will be a phosphorus deficiency, and vice versa. Calcium and phosphorus balance affect bone density, growth rate, and the thickness of cartilage.

So long as your horse is getting enough calcium and phosphorus, the ratio between them pretty much takes care of itself. The only problem that may arise is if you supplement calcium in large amounts without compensating for the phosphorus. In addition, too much calcium causes a corresponding deficiency in phosphorus, zinc, iron and copper. That's because the excess calcium forms an insoluble complex with phosphorus. This can cause a rare condition called nutritional secondary hyperparathyroidism, a skeletal disease.

Calcium can be "bound" by excess phosphorus (in a largely bran diet, say) or

HORSES WHO HAVE suffered calcium deficiency (or phosphorus excess) should receive twice the amount of recommended calcium for the first two or three months of treatment. The Ca:P ratio should be from 1:1 to 3:1 during this period. If the condition is due to excess oxalate intake, decrease the oxalates by keeping the horse away from dangerous plants. If for some reason, this is not possible, then calcium and phosphorus intakes must be increased.

ONE EASY RULE (at least to remember) is that the diet should contain a little more calcium than phosphorous.

PHYTATES, THE primary phosphorus storage reservoir in plants, consist of inositol (a kind of sugar) molecule linked to six phosphorous units.

by certain oxalates contained in some plants. These plants include halogeton (halogeton glomeratus), greasewood (sarcobatus vermiculatus), and sorrel or shamrock (Oxalis spp). There are a lot more, but I thought these would do for starters. These plants can also cause acute oxalate poisoning, so they're just plain no good. The problems caused by these plants are worse in lactating mares and weanlings, mainly because they need so much calcium.

Adult idle horses should get about 0.25 percent calcium in the diet, an amount that can be increased to 0.3 in working horses. Pregnant mares in mid and late pregnancy, and first-stage lactating mares, need 0.5 percent calcium. From the third month of lactation on, the amount can drop to 0.35. The main users of calcium, however, are growing horses.

Calcium and Vitamin D

Calcium needs to work with vitamin D to get its job done properly; luckily horses seem to know this, and the average well-fed horse has no problems in regulating his calcium intake.

Phosphorus (P)

After calcium, phosphorus is the most plentiful component of bones and teeth. Over 80 percent of the body's phosphorus combines with calcium to form the compound hydroxyapatite in teeth and bone. About 15 or 16 percent of the skeleton actually is phosphorus. It is absorbed from the large intestine, unlike calcium, which is absorbed in the small intestine. However, phosphorus is not so easily absorbed as calcium—only 30 to 55 percent of it gets to its target. Like calcium, it is better absorbed by young horses, and the best absorption rates come from inorganic sources like monosodium phosphate.

> **Tidbit:** *Phosphorus in the body is nearly always in the form of phosphate, a phosphorus atom linked to four oxygen atoms. Three of the oxygen atoms are linked to something else as well, such as a fat molecule to make phospholipids. Simple phosphates, with the oxygen linked to things like hydrogen, sodium, or ammonia are used as plant fertilizers. Plant fertilizers should NOT be fed to horses or any other animal.*

Plant-based phosphorus is mainly in the form of phytates; the bioavailability of plant-based phosphorus depends upon on the particular plant.

For example, most phosphorus in cereal grains, oilseed meals, and bran is in the phytate form, which is only 45 to 50 percent available. Phytate must be broken down in order for the attached minerals to be absorbed. What your horse needs for this is the good old phytase enzyme, which is plentiful in wheat and rye, but low in corn. This is why some folks like to add some rye or wheat to their horse feed. You can also buy phytase commercially. Still, barring any unusual antagonistic mineral or other weird circumstances, phosphorus is well supplied in the normal feeds that make up a horse's diet.

Function

- Aids growth and repair of cells
- An essential part of bones and teeth
- Helps regulate the acid/base balance
- Aids kidney function
- Help muscle activity
- Metabolizes nutrients
- Part of the phospholipids needed to make cell membranes
- Necessary for energy production
- Aids reproduction

Protein-rich foods also contain phosphorus in abundance. Oilseeds and protein supplements contain large amounts of phosphorus; however, many low-calcium plants like cereal grains and grass hays are also low in phosphorus.

The recommended requirement for phosphorus is 28.6 mg per kilogram of body weight. That means the average horse needs about 14 grams (about half an ounce) of phosphorus a day, an amount normally supplied in the horse's diet.

Deficiency

Phosphorus deficiency can be caused by excess calcium supplementation. It can also occur when no extra phosphorus is available for growth. Although a calcium/phosphorus deficiency is rare in a well-balanced diet, when it does occur, it can be serious. It has many of the same results as a calcium deficiency. Consequences include:

- Pica and other strange eating habits
- Dehydration
- Loose teeth and bone demineralization
- Decreased feed efficiency
- Constipation
- Decreased growth
- Poor coat
- Lameness and reluctance to move
- Spontaneous fractures
- Infertility

CERTAIN FORAGES, like orchard grass and brome grass, may contain enough phosphorus early in the season, but lose it as the plants mature. Since phosphorus aids growth, it is theorized that one reason wild horses seldom reach the size of domesticated ones is that they eat a low-phosphorus diet for a prolonged period

PICA IS A condition in which an animal (or human) compulsively devoirs inappropriate non-food material.

THE MOST
detrimental
effect of too
much phosphorous
is that it binds
calcium, making it
unavailable for use.
When this happens,
severe skeletal
deformities result.
The less calcium the
horse gets in his
diet, the more seri-
ous a phosphorous
excess becomes.

Horses with a phosphorus deficiency may benefit from the short-term addition of a yeast culture in their feed, or the straight out supplementation of *lactobacillus acidophilus*. This will help the horse absorb phosphorus better.

Phosphorus Excess

Excess phosphorus can be extremely harmful to horses. However, it occurs only if bran is the major part of the diet, or if the horse owner supplies an excess amount of phosphorus containing mineral supplements.

- Binds calcium and so inhibits its absorption, causing a calcium deficiency that produces bone loss
- Causes kidney damage
- Causes loss of muscle tone
- Leads to calcification of soft tissues
- Decreased weight gain
- Convulsions
- Decreases absorption of magnesium

Magnesium (Mg)

About 60 to 70 percent of the body's magnesium is in the bones and teeth, usually in the form of phosphates and carbonates. The rest is found within cells or in the extracellular fluid. The average horse is walking around with about half a pound of magnesium in his body, which may sound like a lot until you figure that that makes only about 0.05 percent of his body weight. Of course, without that little bit, your horse would not be able to survive.

Magnesium is interdependent with calcium and phosphorus for bone development, working with calcium and phosphorus to build bone and teeth. Just as calcium stimulates muscles, magnesium helps them relax.

Dietary absorption of magnesium is between 40 and 60 percent. At the lower absorption rate horses need 15 mg per kg of body weight (about 7 mg per pound). So an 1,100 horse needs about 7.5 grams a day. Magnesium is absorbed mostly from the small intestine. Interestingly, horses can get magnesium not only from their diets, but also from their bones. Young horses are especially adept at this, so it's critical for youngsters to get enough magnesium in the diet, so that they won't have to draw any form the bone. Magnesium is important for:

- Many of the enzyme functions that produce energy
- Synthesis of protein
- Digestion of starch

The magnesium requirement for maintenance adult horses is 6.8 mg/pound (15 mg/kg) body weight. That's about 7.5 grams. Hard working horses need about twice that, a little over 15 grams a day. Total magnesium requirement for growing foals is 4 to 6 grams a day depending on their age.

A horse needs about 0.1 percent magnesium in his diet; this is easily met by most horse feeds and forages which contain between 0.1 and 0.3 percent. Luckily, since magnesium is contained within the chlorophyll of green plants, it is plentiful in the normal horse's diet. Only high-performance horses on grass hay rather than alfalfa might be a little low. The richest source for magnesium is alfalfa (0.30-0.35 percent). Other hays, like timothy, bromegrass and orchard grass contain only about 0.10 to 0.11 percent, as does corn. Oats (0.16) and barley (0.14) are in the middle.

A horse generally absorbs about half the magnesium he receives in his feed. However, he can absorb about 70 percent of magnesium obtained in inorganic forms such as magnesium sulfate and magnesium oxide. Magnesium absorption can be limited by excess phosphorus.

Deficiency

Magnesium deficiency is very rare in horses. When it happens, it is usually due to the stress of traveling, or in lactating mares. This particular condition has the rather daunting name of hypomagnesemic tetany. If it does occur, it causes:

- Muscle tremors and nervousness
- Ataxia
- Convulsions and collapse
- Poor coat
- Sweating
- Mineralization in the arteries
- Heart damage

Horses who don't get enough magnesium require more calories to do the same work as horse correctly supplied with magnesium. Toxicity from excess magnesium does not occur.

Potassium (K) and Salt (NaCl): The Electrolytes

These minerals are often grouped together because they work together to keep all the body fluids in balance. Sodium, chloride and potassium (and sometimes small amounts of calcium and magnesium) added together are called electrolytes. That's because they are capable of conducting electricity, although in chemical language, it refers to the way a substance behaves in solution. Potassium and salt work together to regulate both osmotic pressure and the acid/base balance. Potassium also aids in the transmission of nerve impulses. Chloride is an important constituent of bile and hydrochloric acid.

Horses crave salt, and some crave it more than others do. They don't crave potassium or iodide or magnesium, although they need them all—but salt they like. All horses will select a diet with a salt concentration of 0.5 to 1 percent in preference to a salt deficient diet. A horse which is heavily exercising also consumes more salt than one who rests.

A horse on a maintenance diet requires at least 0.1 percent sodium in the diet (which means about 0.25 percent salt, which is 39 percent sodium and 61 percent chloride). An active horse, however, who can lose a lot of salt through sweat, needs at least 0.3 percent sodium (0.75 percent salt). Between 75 and 95 percent of sodium and chloride ingested are absorbed; any excess is excreted in the urine.

Many commercial feeds are low in sodium and chloride, so experts often recommend that the horse owner add 0.5 to 1 percent salt to the feed mix. And, of course, there is always the salt block, which is often fortified with trace minerals like zinc, manganese, iron, copper, cobalt and iodine. You can even get specialized blocks with contain higher than usual levels of copper, zinc, or selenium if you live in an area where this is necessary. The only problem with these things is that horses seem to prefer plain salt. So some

Two ways to make salt available to your horse all the time. Courtesy Dan's Saddlery.

horses using a trace-mineral block may not be getting either enough salt or enough trace minerals.

Besides its role in maintaining the acid/base balance and osmotic pressure, potassium is especially important for heart function. In a natural diet, mature horses require about 0.4 percent potassium (27 mg/pound or 60 mg/kg of body weight). That's about 30 grams a day for an 1,100 pound horse. Horses in heavy training or lactating mares may need twice that amount.

Most forages contain between 1 and 4 percent potassium, with 1.5 percent about average. That's plenty to satisfy the horse's requirement of 0.4 percent, so long as the horse receives a diet of 40 or 50 percent forage.

Of the forages, orchard grass has the most potassium (2.9 percent). Cereal grains, in contrast to forages, are usually low in potassium (0.30 to 0.45 percent). Only horses in heavy training who are not eating much grass or hay need supplementation. (Protein supplements also contain lots of potassium, as do molasses and oilseed meals like soybean or cottonseed meal.) It is very rare for a horse to overdose on potassium, although it has happened. In some cases horses have developed hyperkalemia (which just means too much potassium in the blood), resulting in cardiac arrest. In cases when the horse does need more potassium, you can buy commercial electrolytes or add about 75 grams of "low sodium" salt to the diet. Low sodium salt is half sodium chloride and half potassium chloride

As a supplement, most electrolyte products contain equal amounts of sodium and chloride. Potassium is added in the ratio of a third to a half that of sodium and chloride—that's the amount usually lost in sweat. These supplements are beneficial when it's hot and humid, and any time when your horse is sweating heavily. Nervous and fearful horses, which tend to sweat more, may also benefit from electrolytes. Extra electrolytes must be accompanied by plenty of extra water.

Sodium Deficiency

Sodium deficiency can occur when a salt block or salt supplements are not available in the feed. If the salt is present, the horse will consume enough for his needs. Sodium deficiency results in:

- Lowered performance
- Reduced food and water intake
- Weight loss
- Decreased milk production
- Weakness

- Dehydration
- Pica
- Constipation

Basically, there are two kinds of sodium deficiency. Acute deficiency results from exhaustive exercise. An affected horse will walk with an unsteady gait and have muscle contractions. Horses with chronic salt deficiency may lick plastic, wood, or metal (in an apparent attempt to find salt) and have a rough coat and "puffy" appearance.

Sodium Excess

As long as your horse has access to fresh water, he really can't overdose on salt. Sodium toxicosis can, however, occur when not enough fresh water is available to flush out the excess. It can cause:

- Colic
- Diarrhea
- Excessive thirst
- Weakness and staggering
- Hindleg lameness

Potassium Deficiency

Potassium deficiency can be cause by a high-grain diet or by diuretics. Sweating can also increase potassium loss; this is more common in high-performance, especially three-day event horses. Its effects include:

- Weakness
- Lethargy
- Reduced feed and water intake
- Weight loss

Potassium excess is not known clinically, except in potassium-induced periodic paralysis, a disease limited to Quarter Horses, Paints and Appaloosas. Under normal conditions, your horse cannot overdose on potassium.

Sulfur (S)

Sulfur is a critical component of several amino acids including methionine, cystine and cysteine, and is obtained primarily through the sulfur-containing amino acids methionine and cysteine. Your horse can make cysteine on his own if he is getting sufficient methionine. It is also a part of biotin, thiamin, insulin, the anti-coagulants heparin, glutathione, taurine, and chondroitin sulfate, which is part of the joints and connective tissue. Although your horse carries around about a pound and a half of sulfur, most of it is in his hair and hoofs (each of which is about 3 percent sulfur, contained in the protein keratin).

The necessary dietary requirement for sulfur is not currently known, but most feed contains at least 0.14 percent non-mineral (organic) sulfur. Horses don't seem to be able to make much use of mineral sulfur, which curiously make up about 12 percent of the sulfur found in plants. (Cows can use this mineral sulfur, but that's a different story.) Horses have better luck with organic (amino-acid based sulfur). However, there is so much sulfur in plants that horses can extract what they need. In addition, food which has sufficient protein always has enough sulfur.

Excess sulfur is excreted through the urine and feces. Sulfur toxicity and deficiencies do not normally occur in horses. However, in a reported case of horses accidentally ingesting a whole lot of mineral sulfur, the animals suffered serious problems, including convulsions. Two of the 12 affected horses died.

Microminerals

Some minerals are required in such small quantities that they are called trace minerals, or microminerals. Researchers are still learning about their precise functions in the body, and about the complex interactions between them.

Iron (Fe)

Iron is present in every cell of the body, but its greatest concentration is in the proteins hemoglobin and myoglobin. Hemoglobin molecules are found in the red blood cells and transport oxygen from the lungs to all other tissues. Myoglobin holds oxygen in the muscles and releases it as needed. About 60 percent of the iron is found in the red blood cells; the rest is found in myoglobin, enzymes, and in storage throughout the body. Iron absorption increases with increasing need, and decreases with excessive intake of cadmium, copper, zinc or cobalt. It is absorbed mainly from the small intestine and stored in the liver, spleen and bone marrow.

Function:

- Combines with protein to make hemoglobin, which carries the oxygen in red blood cells
- It's a cofactor of enzymes in heme synthesis
- Helps produce myoglobin, which binds oxygen for immediate use by the muscle cells

UNFORTUNATELY, due to adverse environmental factors, our soil seems to be losing some of its most important trace minerals—copper, iron, and zinc. This is one reason why supplementation is become more and more necessary for our horses.

DESPITE THE importance of iron, it is truly a trace mineral. The average horse has about 33 grams of iron in his body.

"DRY MATTER" (DM) is the residue of plant or animal tissue after the the moisture has been removed. So if we refer to 1 milligram of iron or poison or whatever per 50 pounds feed DM, we mean the amount that exists in the feed after the moisture is removed. Obviously, the concentration of such a substance will be somewhat higher using DM than it would be if the water was still there. Why do we use DM? Because the amount of moisture in a particular hay or grain can be extremely variable. Using DM as a basis guarantees uniformity, so we know how much of a substance is present for nutrients, or how much would be toxic.

- Helps the immune system
- Is a cofactor in some of the enzymes that turn sugar into energy

The dietary maintenance requirement for maintenance horses is 40 ppm (about 18 milligrams in each pound of feed). Most forages and grains contain 200 to 400 mg/kg DM. Growing horses, pregnant, and lactating mares need about 50 ppm (22.6 milligrams per pound of feed.)

Rich iron sources include alfalfa, soybeans, wheat bran, beet pulp and pumpkin. Although iron absorption rates are pretty low (10 to 15 percent), most foodstuff contains enough of it (between 50 and 250 ppm) to supply the average horse. Alfalfa has 200 ppm of iron—an extremely high amount. (Iron from some sources like wheat bran is not so available as iron from soybeans.) Some commonly fed horse feeds, however, like corn and timothy are on the low end, containing only the minimum amount for maintenance (even if the horse absorbed all of it) and not enough for growing horses.

Deficiency

Iron deficiencies in adult horses are seldom reported and those that do occur are on account of chronic or severe blood loss, not to a deficiency in the diet. Such blood loss can occur from parasites just as surely as from bleeding. A horse with high levels of cadmium, copper, manganese, cobalt, or zinc may have trouble absorbing iron. Iron deficiency results in two different types of anemia, microcytic and hypochromic.

Excess

Iron excess is much more common than iron deficiency, but it rarely occurs in nature. The body has no way to excrete excess iron—the only thing it can do is decrease the amount it absorbs. Extra iron is stored in the liver. Large amounts of iron in the diet can interfere with the absorption or metabolism of other minerals, especially zinc, copper and calcium. This leads to other mineral imbalances, including a problem with phosphorus metabolism.

Excess usually occurs only when too much iron is given as a supplement, (especially as an injection) in which case it can be a real problem. Toxicity is most likely to occur in horses with a vitamin E or selenium deficiency, or in foals. Newborn foals have reduced ability to control iron absorption and too much iron supplementation can be fatal to them.

Copper (Cu)

Copper is important for the synthesis of collagen and elastin necessary for bone development, and for skin pigmentation. It is a component of many

metabolic enzymes. Large excesses of zinc may decrease copper utilization, and copper and iron each affect the absorption of the other. In fact, copper is necessary for the absorption and transport of iron and is essential for all cells. Copper is found everywhere in the body, but is most highly concentrated in the liver, brain, heart and kidneys. In many animals, copper is a necessary part of hemoglobin and red blood cell development, but this is less true of horses than of other species, including human beings.

Function:

- Helps absorb and transport iron
- Maintains mitochondria in the cell nucleus
- Affects skin and possibly hair color
- Aids cellular energy production
- Mineralizes bone and helps prevent osteoporosis
- Helps cartilage and connective tissue formation
- Helps cardiac function
- Promotes healing

The optimum amount of copper necessary for horses hasn't been established; the NRC recommends about 10 ppm, which is probably low for young, rapidly growing horses, but higher than needed for other animals. Most feeds are well supplemented with copper, containing between 3 and 20 mg/kg. Copper supplements include cupric sulfate, cupric carbonate and cupric chloride.

Copper is absorbed mainly from the small intestine. Like iron, the body can control the amount absorbed depending on need. Copper is metabolized in the liver, which incorporates it into the protein ceruloplasmin to be transported in the blood to the rest of the body. Excess copper is excreted through the bile.

Deficiency

In adults less than 5 ppm in the diet (which is virtually unheard of) is considered a deficiency. The average horse needs 80 mg per day, although young horses in training can use twice that amount. Very young foals need as much as 50 ppm, while weanlings need at least 25 ppm. Research suggests that young horses may benefit from additional dietary copper to prevent osteochondrosis and other developmental orthopedic diseases. Copper deficiency can also be caused by dietary levels higher than 700 ppm zinc; a copper: molybdenum ratio of 1:8 or higher affects copper absorption by cows but this has not been established in horses. Certain other minerals, including lead, silver and cadmium decrease copper absorption.

MANY SPECIES of animals seem to lose their color when deprived of sufficient copper; that doesn't seem to happen with horses. Still, some people swear that copper-deprived horses will experience a fading of the coat.

Deficiency

- Slow growth
- Bone lesions and thinning
- Neuromuscular disorders
- Osteochondrosis
- Uterine artery rupture in aged mares

Excess

Excess amounts of copper are practically unknown in horses—at least under natural conditions. Grain contains 4-11 mg/kg of copper with corn the lowest and barley the highest. Grass hay (0.5 to 30 mg/kg) and alfalfa (2 to 30 mg/kg) copper content is quite variable. Supplementation is beneficial for growing horses.

Copper excess is rare but may occur when very high levels of copper supplement are added to the diet. Toxicity has been observed at total copper dietary levels exceeding 800 mg/kg. It produces:

- Acute hemolytic anemia
- Lethargy
- Liver and kidney damage

Zinc (Zn)

Zinc is a component of more than 200 enzymes. It is found in many body tissues, and is a cofactor in the synthesis of DNA, RNA and protein, and is critical for the normal metabolism of carbohydrates, lipids, and protein. It is found in high concentrations in the eye and prostate gland.

Zinc is necessary for the enzyme function relating to the skeleton and the horse's immune system. Horses living solely on forage may be deficient in zinc, which is especially critical in young horses, which need it for skeletal development. The National Research Council has recommended a level 40 mg/kg DM, although studies have shown that horses can get by on much less than this amount—as little as 15 mg/kg. Other studies, however, suggest that foals need about 60 mg/kg zinc in the diet. It's the same old story—even the people who should know aren't really sure.

Function:

- Essential for skeletal development
- Aids fetal development and growth rate
- Necessary for the synthesis of protein and collagen

- Helps hoof growth and maintenance
- Necessary for digestion
- Keep cell membranes healthy
- Aids the immune system
- Helps the pancreas produce insulin
- Important for skin and hair growth and wound healing
- Helps reproductive system and prostate function
- Promotes taste and appetite

Source

Most common horse feeds contain between 15 and 40 mg/kg DM. Of grains, oats have the highest amount, 35 ppm, corn and barley about half that. Of the hays, timothy is the highest (38 ppm), followed by orchard grass (36 ppm). Plant-based protein supplements are very high in zinc, between 30 to 70 mg/kg.

The dietary requirement for zinc is complicated by several factors, but is reckoned to be at least 20 ppm for adults and 50 ppm for weanlings. Zinc absorption occurs mostly in the small intestine, but may be reduced by excess dietary iron, calcium, copper, fiber and phytates, although the extent of interference by these substances is not definitely known for horses. The absorption rate of zinc is usually low, ranging from 10 to 15 percent, but can vary with the animal's needs.

Deficiency

Inadequate amounts of copper and zinc in the diet may produce osteochondrosis, osteodysgenesis and other developmental orthopedic diseases. Luckily zinc deficiency has not been observed in horses, even though many feeds appear low in it. Zinc deficiency also causes:

- Reduced feed intake
- Reduced growth
- Hair loss, scaly skin (especially in foals)

Most horse feeds are well supplemented with zinc, so zinc deficiency is not a problem with most horses.

Excess

Toxicity occurs when dietary zinc is over 700 ppm, where interference with the utilization of copper is observed, and is thus a contributor to orthopedic diseases. Zinc toxicity is not common, and horses are fairly tolerant of high amounts in the diet, but it can occur where pastures have been contaminat-

SELENIUM HAD a bad reputation until the mid-1970s—so bad that it could not be legally added to horse feeds! This made things tough on owners of horses in selenium-deficient areas.

IT HAS ALSO been shown that, to a lesser extent, the addition of some other anti-oxidants like vitamin C or the amino acid cystine decrease the need for both vitamin E and selenium.

ed from residue from smelting, and even from air pollution from industries using zinc.

- Developmental orthopedic disease
- Lameness and stiffness
- Induced copper deficiency

Very high levels of zinc, equivalent to 3,600 ppm in the diet, have caused anemia and reduced growth in foals.

Selenium (Se)

As an integral part of the enzyme glutathione peroxidase, selenium protects cell membranes from oxidative damage, much like its partner vitamin E. It scavenges free radicals and destroys lipid peroxides which are released into the cell by normal metabolic processes. If there is inadequate vitamin E in the diet, more selenium is needed; if there isn't enough selenium, more vitamin E is necessary. The best plan, of course, is to have optimum amounts of both.

Unfortunately, selenium can be toxic especially when it accumulates in certain "selenium-accumulating" plants. I call them selenium-soakers. The functions of selenium include:

- Interacts with vitamin E to maintain the required level of coenzyme Q_{10} (ubi-quinone)
- Antioxidant which helps protect against pollutants in the environment
- Helps the immune system
- Protects cell membranes
- Has been reported to help cardiac function
- Aids reproduction

Selenium is found largely in cereal grains. Some areas of the country including the Atlantic seaboard, Great Lakes region, and northwest, may be selenium-deficient, while places in the Dakotas may have enough excess to produce the toxicity. In general, selenium deficiency is a more common problem than selenium excess. However, it should be noted that the amount of selenium can vary wildly from pasture to pasture. In horses, the absorption rate for selenium is high—about 75 percent. This is one reason why selenium toxicity is a greater problem in horses than in many other livestock species—they absorb it better.

The proper dietary amount of selenium for a maintenance horse is calculated to be 0.1 to 0.3 mg/kg DM. This may be a little low, and horses in training and pregnant or lactating mares may benefit from twice this amount. The maximum amount is said to be 2 ppm, only 20 times the minimum dose. This is a very narrow margin, and it makes some people nervous. Most feed stuffs contain 0.05 to 0.3 mg/kg DM, depending upon the soil from which the feed was obtained.

Deficiency

Scientists have discovered six general types of problems that can arise from a deficiency of selenium/vitamin E. These include vascular disorders, nutritional myopathies, encephalopathies, organ damage, reproductive disorders, and adipose tissue inflammation.

With today's supplemented food selenium deficiencies are not common in adult horses. However, it appears fairly often in foals, especially those under one month old. When a mare does not get enough selenium in her diet (less than 0.05 ppm), the foal may have:

- Reduced immunity
- Decreased growth
- Stiffness
- White muscle disease

Excess

Selenium has the lowest toxicity level of any mineral critical in equine nutrition, and selenium toxicity is much more common than a deficiency. Selenium toxicity stems from interference with the action and metabolism of the very important sulfur-containing amino acids methionine and cystine. The minimum lethal dose of selenium is about 150 to 200 mg/kg (70 to 90 mg/lb) in the diet. This may sound like a lot, but selenium is actually quite a bit more toxic to horses than to cattle or pigs. In fact, selenium toxicity to equines has occurred with dietary selenium levels of only 5 to 40 mg/kg (2 to 18 mg/lb).

States which contain areas with toxic levels of selenium include Wyoming, Colorado, California, Idaho, Montana, Utah, Oregon and South Dakota. Alkaline soils in areas of low rainfall yield the highest selenium concentrations in plants. That doesn't mean every place in these states has toxic levels. In places, the selenium might actually be deficient. You must get your soil tested if your horse is pastured; if you buy all your hay, you should check the source for selenium levels. Never supplement selenium (it appears in many trace minerals blocks) without first finding out if it is needed in your area.

CHEMICALLY
selenium is related to sulfur, which may help to explain the apparent bad taste and smell, making horses reluctant to eat most plants containing high levels of selenium.

Most plants contain 0.05 to 0.3 mg/kg selenium, but "selenium-soakers" can contain as much as 10,000 mg/kg. Some of these plants include milk vetch (*Astragalus*), asters (*Machaeranthera*), wheat grass (*Agropyron*), broomweed (*Gutierrezia saraothral*), and others. Many of these have an unpleasant smell or taste, but horses may eat them if the pasture is overgrazed. Even horses getting as little as 2 to 5 ppm from high-selenium plants can suffer toxic effects. These, or inappropriate supplementation, which is even more common, produce selenium toxicosis, the effects of which are:

- Stiffness
- Patchy sweating
- Head pressing
- Anemia
- Enlargement of liver, heart and kidney
- Abnormal hoof growth or hoof sloughing
- Dark liquid stools
- Blind staggers (alkali disease)
- Decreased appetite and listlessness
- Dyspnea
- Rough coat and hair loss from mane and tail

Molybdenum (Mo)

Most horse feeds contain between 0.3 to 8 mg/kg molybdenum, although plants growing in areas contaminated by industrial waste may be considerably higher—up to 231 mg/kg DM. In addition, shale soils, poorly drained soils, and alkaline soils may be high in this mineral.

Function

A component of xanthine oxidase enzymes, it is involved in purine metabolism and production of uric acid.

Excess

Excess of this mineral occurs when horses graze on alkaline or contaminated soil. It can also occur when the dietary copper/molybdenum ratio is 1:8 or more. This essentially causes a copper deficiency. Molybdenum deficiency has never been reported.

Cobalt (Co)

Cobalt is an important component of vitamin B_{12}. In fact, except as a component of vitamin B_{12}, no real function has been found for cobalt in the body—yet. The microorganisms in the horse's cecum and colon apparently perform the feat of incorporating cobalt into B12. The recommended dietary requirement ranges from 0.1 to 10 mg/kg.

Forages usually contain 0.1 to 0.6 mg/kg cobalt, and grains between 0.05 to 0.25 mg/kg. These are only ballpark figures, however. Cobalt deficiency or excess has never been reported in horses, although they have in cattle and other species.

Iodine (I)

The iodine your horse eats ends up mostly in his thyroid gland, which uses it to make various hormones, especially thyroxine (T4) and triiodothyronine (T3), which regulate the metabolic rates of the body. The minimum iodine requirement is estimated at 0.1 ppm, with feeds ranging from 0 to 2 ppm. Most feeds range from about 0.05-0.2 ppm DM. It all depends upon the soil where they were grown. Toxicity is noted at iodine levels of 5 ppm or higher. The soil around the Great Lakes is iodine deficient.

Function:

- Regulates energy
- Control metabolism

Deficiency

Iodine deficiency is not uncommon with horses fed unsupplemented foods. Most iodized salts satisfy your horse's iodine requirements. The only problem might occur if an animal does not consume enough of the iodized salt, which sometimes happens because horses just don't like the stuff as well as plain salt.

Horses getting insufficient iodine can actually develop goiter (an enlarged thyroid gland), a condition that used to be fairly common. It can still occur in foals. Other symptoms include:

- Rough coat
- Brittle hooves
- Decreased growth
- Interrupted estrus cycles in mares
- Cold intolerance
- Timidity or drowsiness

Excess

The maximum safe level of iodine has been estimated to be 5 mg/kg DM—or 40 milligrams per day. Horses, especially pregnant and lactating mares, have

A SKIN DISEASE called derma- tophilosis is often treated with iodine, and iodine toxico- sis has been known to result from this treatment.

a low tolerance for excess iodine. Toxic amounts of iodine do not occur in horses that are getting anywhere near the right diet. However, certain poor feeding practices are producing a hitherto unseen rise in iodine toxicosis. These poor habits include adding more than 4-8 percent iodized or trace- mineralized salt to the foal's or late-stage pregnant mare's diet, over supple- menting, or feeding an excess of kelp, a popular supplement in some quar- ters. Kelp can contain as much as 1850 ppm of iodine, so it wouldn't take much to give your horse a toxic dose of the stuff.

The symptoms of iodine excess are the same as the symptoms of a deficiency, which doesn't make things any easier.

Manganese (Mn)

Manganese is a component of many enzymes, particularly those involved with the production of energy. Recently people have begun a new apprecia- tion for manganese, since it is one of the main requirements for chondroitin sulfate synthesis, the natural "wonder drug" that is so helpful to arthritic ani- mals and people.

Function:

- Helps synthesize the chondroitin sulfate necessary for cartilage devel- opment
- Maintains cell integrity
- Helps utilize calcium and phosphorus for bone development
- Needed for the metabolism of fats and carbohydrates
- Helps immune system function
- Helps the reproductive system

The NRC says horses need between 40 to 140 mg/kg manganese in their diet, but this may be a high estimate. Most horse feeds contain between 3 and 170 mg/kg DM with 20 mg/kg being about average. Areas with low man- ganese in the soil are common in the Northwest, but no problems in horses have thus far been reported. Manganese is found in fiber sources like cereal products, timothy and orchard grasses. It is stored mostly in the liver, but it is also present in the pancreas, bones, and kidney. Manganese is excreted in the bile

Forage contains 40 to 140 mg/kg manganese, while grains except corn con- tain between 15 to 45 mg/kg; corn has a lower manganese content of about 3 to 9 mg/kg. The differences are largely due to the differences in soil.

NOTE: Manganese is low in grains (especially corn) and also low in alfalfa. Consequently, performance horses, which subsist largely on alfalfa and corn, may need a manganese supplement.

Deficiency

A deficiency in manganese can adversely affect growth and reproduction. Manganese deficiency is rare but can occur on heavily limed soils:

- Bone problems in newborns
- Decreased growth
- Enlarged joints and crooked legs
- Stiffness (especially in performance horses)

Excess

Manganese is a relatively nontoxic mineral, even in large amounts. No problems have ever been reported, although too much could interfere with the absorption of other nutrients.

Fluoride (F)

Fluoride is part of the teeth and bone; it makes them harder. City water generally contains 1 or 2 mg per liter (L). This is enough to reduce cavities in kids by over 60%, so it seems to be a good deal. No one knows for sure if fluoride is needed in the diet, but most forages contain between 2 and 16 mg/kg DM, while grains have between 1 and 3 mg/kg. It is possible for horses to get too much fluoride in the diet—it's a condition called fluorosis, and is usually caused by phosphorus supplements like rock phosphates, phosphatic limestone, or inadequately defluorinated fertilizer-grade phosphates. Pastures or feeds contaminated by runoff from facilities like aluminum or steel processing plants are another possibility. The upper safe level of fluorine is 50 mg/kg DM. Bones and teeth are the first organs to be affected by excess fluoride, with mottled teeth in foals being an early sign of fluoride poisoning. Bone abnormalities occur in severe cases, together with rough coat, arched back, and lameness.

6

Vitamins: The Invisible Magicians

VITAMINS ARE ORGANIC (CARBON-containing) dietary components different from proteins, fats, or carbohydrates. They are utterly essential for your horse's health, although they are needed in only small amounts. They are critical for normal body functioning and their absence produces a deficiency syndrome. Vitamins don't have calories in themselves, but your horse needs them to convert calories to energy.

NOTE: Vitamins are often measured in IU/lb—international units per pound. An IU is an amount of the substance that produces a standard, internationally agreed upon effect. Since each vitamin is defined individually in terms of what it does, an IU of vitamin A would not have the same weight as an IU of vitamin E. Moreover, any inactive material present in the vitamin that adds to the weight but not the effect, does not influence the number of IU present. Mostly, fat-soluble vitamins like A, D, and E are measured in IU's.

Each vitamin play one or more of these roles in the body:

- Act as potentiators or cofactors in enzymatic reactions; these are called "co-enzymes"
- Scavenge free radicals
- Release energy from nutrients
- Help metabolize amino acids and proteins
- Maintain cell membrane integrity
- Support bone development
- Help maintain calcium balance
- Support normal eye function
- Act as key components of body fluids
- Aid nerve impulse transduction
- Help blood clot

Vitamins come in two general catagories: fat-soluble (vitamins A, D, E and K) and water-soluble (vitamin C and the eight B vitamins). Fat-soluble vitamins need dietary fat in order to be absorbed from the gut and taken up into the body, while water-soluble vitamins need only water. Fat-soluble vitamins are handled by the body in the same way as dietary fat; the metabolites of these vitamins are excreted in the feces. Excess fat-soluble vitamins are stored in the liver. The good side of vitamin storage means that fat-soluble vitamins don't need to be made or supplied every day—the bad side is that it is possible for an animal to get too much of a fat-soluble vitamin, although this is less likely in horses than in many others animals.

Most water-soluble vitamins are not stored in the body and need to be replaced regularly. However, horses can make water-soluble vitamins on their own, and don't generally need them added to their diets as long as they have the right number and kind of healthy intestinal bacteria working in their intestines. Water-soluble vitamins can't be stored in the body, so in general, you never have to worry about your horse getting too much of them.

Believe or not, horses are very, very smart—they can make nearly all their own vitamins – although in most cases they hire out their intestinal bacteria to do it for them. Vitamins D, C and niacin (a B vitamin) are produced directly by the horse; the rest of the B vitamins and vitamin K are made by microbes in the cecum and large intestine. The liver also plays a part here. The two exceptions are vitamins A and E, which need to be provided in the diet. We can term these "essential" vitamins, since they need to be supplied in the diet. (Of course, if a horse isn't getting anything to eat, he won't be able to get the proteins, carbohydrates and fats he needs to synthesize his vitamins.) Since a horse can manufacture so many vitamins on his owns, it has been difficult to determine what the exact requirement is for many of them.

Although all the essential vitamins your horse needs are met in his fresh green diet, it's important to note that when hay is cut, dried, and stored, its vitamin content (except vitamin D) begins to drop, subject to a process called oxidation. The warmer and hotter it is, the faster this process occurs. After a period of three months in adverse conditions, it's possible for hay to lose almost all its vitamin content. The same can be true for grain, and even for vitamin supplements that are not sealed and stored properly.

Vitamin A

Vitamin A may be the most important "nutritional" vitamin of all and it was the first vitamin to be officially recognized—back in 1913. However, we now understand that the term vitamin A actually refers to a family of related compounds: retinol (the most biologically active form), retinal and retinoic acid.

The precursor to Vitamin A, beta-carotene, a plant pigment, is found in almost everything fresh (especially in the leaves) your horse naturally eats. The younger the plant, the more beta-carotene it will have. High-quality, leafy green hay cut early, has some beta-carotene, but it will deteriorate over time. Hot, humid weather is death to beta-carotene. In fact, beta-carotene is so easily oxidized that 80 percent can be lost in the hot sun in 24 hours after cutting. In six months storage under good conditions, another 50 percent can be lost. This is one reason why fresh pasture is essential to your horse's health. If he doesn't get it, his food should be supplemented.

Vitamin A itself comes only from animal sources, such as liver, and especially from fish liver oils; egg yolks and milk also contain vitamin A. However, animal sources don't contain beta-carotene.

Horses can turn beta-carotene into vitamin A on their own (so can you.) Horses can convert one milligram of beta-carotene into about 400 IU of Vitamin A. There is an enzyme in the lining of the small intestine that does the conversion, and then sends the vitamin A to the liver for storage. Some beta-carotene remains unconverted and goes straight to the fat and skin tissue and, in mares, to the ovaries, where it plays an important part in the reproduction process.

CAROTENE IN alfalfa and other legume hay is more available to the horse than that in grass hay.

FAT-SOLUBLE vitamins are hard to analyze chemically. Consequently, amounts are often given as "international units" (IU) rather than in weight units. An IU is an amount of the substance that produces a standard, internationally agreed upon effect. Since each vitamin is defined in terms of what it itself does, an IU of vitamin A would not have the same weight as an IU of vitamin E. Moreover, any inactive material present in the vitamin that adds to the weight but not the effect, does not influence the number of IU present. Sometimes vitamins are measured in U.S.P.—United States Pharmacopeia measurements. Same deal applies.

Beta-carotene is found in yellow vegetables like carrots and sweet potatoes. (You always knew there was a good reason to give your horse carrots.) It is also present in dark green plants. Most grains have no beta-carotene at all, although corn has a trace amount. Although beta-carotene is really yellow, its color can be masked by the chlorophyll. Stored (as opposed to new) hay contains about 40 mg/kg of beta carotene. This supplies an adequate, but not abundant amount of vitamin A; it's usually added to grain to make up the difference. For ultimate safety, it's probably better to add non-toxic beta-carotene rather than vitamin A proper, but this is an expensive alternative.

Other vitamin A precursors exist also, but beta-carotene is the most plentiful of them. Unlike vitamin A itself, high doses of beta-carotene have not been shown to be significantly toxic.

It has been estimated that horses need 2,000 IU vitamin A per kg of diet DM daily for maintenance, and 3,000 IU per kg of diet DM for growth, pregnancy, lactation, and performance.

Vitamin A:

- Helps maintain epithelial lining of the liver cells, gastrointestinal tract, respiratory tract, reproductive tract and kidneys
- Aids the respiratory system
- Conditions the skin and hoofs

- Maintains eye health and aids vision, especially night vision (it's the major component of the light sensitive pigments in the eye)
- Helps the immune system resist infection
- Is necessary for spermatogenesis and normal heat cycle
- Supports bone development and muscle growth
- Protects against air pollution
- May prevent cancer, since it acts as a strong antioxidant

Horse who are provided fresh green pasture for 4 to 6 months of the year can retain sufficient vitamin A to meet their needs for a whole year. Helen Peppe photo.

Deficiency

Because beta-carotene is found in anything green, vitamin A deficiency is fairly rare. Horses who are provided fresh green pasture for 4 to 6 months of the year can retain sufficient vitamin A to meet their needs for a whole year. And even with lesser opportunities to graze, the horse's liver can store a three to six month's supply. Consequently, unless your horse is stabled year round, he should get plenty. The only way we can measure the level of vitamin A is by blood testing, but even this method is not accurate, because the liver is always trying to help out by releasing its stored vitamin A into the blood stream. So a test might reveal normal levels of vitamin A, while it may all be coming from the liver. When the liver runs out (assuming the horse isn't getting enough dietary beta-carotene), the vitamin A blood level will take an instant dive. Deficiency leads to

- Poor, dry, rough coat and prolonged shedding
- Night blindness, photophobia, and tearing
- Hardening of the skin and cornea
- Anorexia
- Diarrhea
- Retarded growth
- Impaired intestinal function
- Problems with gums (gingivitis) and teeth; abscess of the salivary glands
- Reproductive difficulties
- Progressive weakness in the hind legs
- Lesions in the epithelial tissue and increased susceptibility to infections, especially in the reproductive tract
- Skeletal abnormalities due to impaired deposit of mineral into bone (not positively identified in horses, but shown in other species)
- Respiratory problems

Vitamin A Excess

This condition does not happen naturally, although a horse fed exclusively on alfalfa may be near the limit. All cases that have occurred were induced experimentally or through mistaken over-supplementation (usually injections). The maximum recommended level is 16,000 IU/kg of dry matter in the diet. Horses with long periods of vitamin A overdoses suffer from unthriftiness, hair loss, skeletal problems, increased clotting time, lack of coordination, and depression.

BY AIDING THE synthesis of mucopolysaccharides, vitamin A helps repair the mucous membranes of the eye, including the cornea. In the retina, retinal combines with the protein opsin to form rhodopsin—or "visual purple." This is a light-sensitive pigment that allows the eye to adjust to alterations in light intensity. It enables us to see even in dim light. See, mom was right about those carrots. And your horse likes them too.

ON RARE occasions, injections of vitamin A or beta-carotene may be given intramuscularly. It is sometimes done to increase the reproductive efficiency of mares. This treatment should be done only on the advice of a veterinarian, since too much vitamin A can be toxic, and the storage capacity of the liver is rather quickly filled.

HORSES CAN manufacture B vitamins using the clever microbes in the large intestine. Only horses undergoing extreme stress or that have a very heavy workload need supplementation.

THIAMIN WAS discovered, so to speak, on the island of Java, of all places. Inhabitants suffering from beriberi were cured when they began eating unhusked rather than polished rice. The husks contain thiamin.

Vitamin B complex

The water-soluble B vitamins are all grouped together because they are found largely in the same foods. Originally, it was thought that all the B vitamins were different forms of the same thing, but now we know that significant differences exist between them, both in their structure and in their function in the body.

Vitamins B_1, B_2 and B_6 work together synergistically; that means they are more effective collectively than separately. Because they are water soluble, B vitamins are not stored in the body. This does not mean that all B vitamins disappear from your horse's body after 24 hours. It does mean that there's no large store of B vitamins available to replace those that gradually "wear out" and need to be replaced. All water-soluble vitamins, should be supplied daily.

Luckily, B complex vitamins are both made in your horse's body and found in green forage and brewer's yeast. Thus it is rare for a horse to suffer any B vitamin deficiency. Still, some situations warrant a course of B vitamin (especially B_{12} or folic acid) supplementation. The B vitamins

- Help the immune system and may fight allergies and infections
- Maintain nerve function
- Preserve muscle tone
- Help metabolize fats, proteins and carbohydrates, thus helping to produce energy
- Are essential for red blood cell function
- Ameliorate the effects of stress
- Stimulate the appetite

B_1 (thiamin)

This is a precursor of thiamin pyrophosphate (TPP), which is needed in the citric acid (Krebs) cycle, the principal energy-producing pathway in the body. So we can say that thiamin helps produce energy; if a horse doesn't get enough thiamin, he just won't be able to utilize his food. Thiamin appears to be a conditionally essential vitamin for horses. In other words, although his intestinal bacteria can produce a good amount of the stuff, new studies indicate that horses benefit from additional thiamin from their diets.

Source:

In addition to the amounts horses produce themselves, thiamin can be found in green forages, whole grains, brewer's yeast and wheat germ. In fact, thiamin is found pretty much everywhere, but in rather low concentrations. It should be noted that heating and cooking destroy thiamin, while long storage depletes it. Feed stored for more than three months would have about 50 percent of its original thiamin remaining. Most vitamin/mineral supplements contain thiamin, but you can also buy thiamin-only supplements.

Function:

Thiamin affects all tissues, but especially nerves, stomach and heart, and helps in protein metabolism.

For most horses, including pregnant mares and growing colts, the thiamin requirement is 3 mg/kg DM. However, hardworking, performance horses need more, about 5 mg/kg DM.

Deficiency

Horses can develop a thiamin deficiency if they eat bracken fern, yellow star thistle, or horsetail which inhibit its absorption. Certain parasites such as coccidia and strongylids devour thiamin and thus make it less available for horses. Otherwise, this deficiency is very rare, seen only in experimentally induced cases, or perhaps when a horse is subject to a long-term course of antibiotics. Symptoms of thiamin deficiency include:

- Ataxia (failure of muscle coordination)
- Extremities intermittently cold to the touch
- Nervousness
- Weight loss and poor appetite
- Dull haircoat
- Arrhythmia and bradycardia (irregular or low heartbeat, respectively)
- Muscle contractions

Excess:

Excess thiamin is excreted rapidly in the urine. It is thus pretty non-toxic, but excess amounts could theoretically produce:

- Decreased blood pressure
- Bradycardia
- Respiratory arrhythmia

B$_2$ (riboflavin or Vitamin G):

Riboflavin is component of two coenzymes, flavin mononucleotide (FMN) and flavin adenine dinucleotide (FAD); these coenzymes help release energy from foods. Riboflavin is necessary for the metabolism of vitamin B$_6$ and niacin. Unlike thiamin, riboflavin can handle heat well, although light and irradiation degrade it. Riboflavin

IT WAS FORMERLY believed that lack of riboflavin caused periodic opthalmia. No one thinks this any more.

- Aids in the metabolism of carbohydrates and fat
- Helps in the desaturation of fatty acids
- Helps the nervous system function
- Aids cellular growth

Dietary Source:

Yeast and fresh green forage are good sources. In fact, fresh forage contains between 5 and 20 mg/kg DM. Cereals are low in riboflavin, containing only 1 to 3 mg/kg. Horses can manufacture some riboflavin on their own, using those clever bacteria in the large intestine, although not quite enough for their needs. Since the body doesn't store riboflavin well it should be a daily part of the diet; horses need only about 2 mg/kg riboflavin DM in their diet. Good quality hay contains twice that amount, and grain contains enough as well. The riboflavin requirement is also partly dependent on the ambient temperature; when it gets colder, horses need more riboflavin. Luckily, riboflavin is pretty resistant to oxidation, moisture and heat. Its concentration decreases during storage, but only at a rate of about 3 percent a month.

Deficiency:

Riboflavin deficiency has never been noted in horses on a natural diet. However, experimentally induced riboflavin deficiency resulted in:

- Inappetence and wasting away
- Scaly skin and rough coat
- Inflammation of the tongue
- Conjunctivitis and tearing of the eye
- Ulcers in the colon
- Diarrhea
- Light sensitivity
- Rear end weakness
- No heat cycle in mares

Excess:

Toxicity resulting from excess riboflavin has not been reported; any excess is rapidly excreted in the urine.

Niacin

Niacin, a B vitamin closely associated with riboflavin, is a component of two coenzymes, nicotinamide adenine dinucleotide (NAD) and nicotinamide adenine dinucleotide phosphate (NADP). These enzymes help metabolize foods. Niacin is taken into the body as nicotinic acid and converted into the active form nicotinamide. This is a very stable vitamin, resistant to heat, moisture and so on. Niacin is well absorbed through the gastric and small intestine mucosa.

Dietary Source:

Niacin sources are plentiful in cereals, yeast, legumes and oilseeds. However, your horse can synthesize it himself in his very own hindgut, and doesn't need it in his diet *if* his has enough tryptophan, an essential amino acid. As rule, the more protein your horse gets, the more tryptophan he gets, and the easier it is for him to synthesize niacin. Horses also need sufficient amounts of another B vitamin, pyridoxine, to synthesize niacin.

Function

- Important in the oxidative process of all tissues
- Promotes cellular respiration and metabolism to generate energy
- Processes amino acids, carbohydrates and glucose
- Aid in the biosynthesis of long-chain fatty-acids

Deficiency:

A dietary requirement for niacin has not been established in horses; for most animals it is between 5 and 10 mg/kg. Cats are an exception, but then they so often are, aren't they? No deficiencies in horses have been reported.

Excess:

Niacin is pretty nontoxic, but excess could theoretically lead to:

- Dilation of the blood vessels and bloody feces
- Itching
- Convulsions

It has never been shown to do any of this stuff in horses, but it does in people.

B₆ (Pyridoxine)

Pyridoxine is one of the three forms of vitamin B₆. All three forms are equally good for horses.

Source:

Whole grains, and high-quality forages are good sources of pyridoxine.

NICOTINIC ACID (niacin) bears only a slight chemical resemblance to nicotine, despite the similarity in names.

The vitamin is fairly stable to most storage conditions except light. About 70 percent remains after storage for one year. Your horse can synthesize this vitamin for himself in his cecum and colon, but it is mainly absorbed from the small intestine. The exact requirements for pyridoxine have not been determined.

Function:

Pyridoxine is a precursor of coenzymes involved in the metabolism of several amino acids. In addition, pyridoxine:

- Helps metabolize glycogen and fatty acids
- Helps synthesize hemoglobin and several neurotransmitters like adrenalin
- May have anti-allergy effects
- Helps the immune system
- Is necessary for the conversion to tryptophan to niacin
- Helps in heme synthesis
- Helps process hydrochloric acid
- Helps process magnesium
- Aids in the production of antibodies
- Aids in taurine and L-carnitine synthesis

B_6 interferes with niacin, but is necessary for its metabolism. As with all B vitamins, very little pyridoxine is stored in the body. No reports of niacin deficiency or toxicity have ever been reported in horses.

Pantothenic Acid (Vitamin B₃)

This vitamin is found just about everywhere, as the Greek prefix "panto" suggests. It occurs in all body tissues, and is necessary for the incorporation of iron into hemoglobin. It also helps produce energy. Pantothenic acid exists in two forms, D and L, but the only one that has nutritive value is D-pantothenic acid. It is suggested that 15 mg/kg DM in the diet is adequate, although no one really knows the dietary requirement.

Source:

Pantothenic acid is found in all food, but primarily in rice and wheat bran, brewer's yeast, legumes, alfalfa and peanut meal. Good-quality hay contains nearly six times the needed amount of pantothenic acid. Pantothenic acid is relatively stable; properly stored feeds retain about 75 percent after one year. Grain is a bit deficient. Your horse can synthesize some for himself by means of his clever bacteria.

Function:

Once absorbed, pantothenic acid becomes a component of coenzyme-A, which is involved in releasing energy from fats, proteins and carbohydrates within the citric acid cycle. In addition, pantothenic acid

- Helps synthesizes steroids, cholesterol, and the adrenal hormones
- Helps metabolize fat, proteins, and carbohydrates
- Is necessary for growth

Deficiencies are practically nonexistent, and toxicity has not been reported.

Folic Acid (Folacin or Folate; sometimes called vitamin B$_c$ or Vitamin H)

For some reason, folic acid doesn't get a number (neither does niacin), but it's important for all that. Folic acid is a precursor of tetrahydrofolic acid (THF), a carrier of methyl groups in transmethylation reactions. It is made up of para-aminobenzoic acid (PABA) and glutamic acid. It is involved in the synthesis of thymidine, a component of DNA. It is closely linked with vitamin B$_{12}$, folic acid.

- Helps synthesize purine and pyrimidine nucleic acids
- Help metabolize protein, fats and carbohydrates
- Helps methionine synthesis
- Is necessary for reproduction
- Aids in development of red blood cells
- Builds antibodies
- Aids DNA synthesis

Source:

Grass and yeast are good sources. Like other B vitamins, your horse has friendly bacteria in the cecum and large intestine to synthesize it. The exact amount of folic acid needed in the diet has not been determined. However, folacin is plentiful in pasture and green leafy hay.

Where Stored:

Folic acid is not stored in the body, and must be supplied every day in the diet or by microbial manufacture. Heating, prolonged freezing, and storing in water also destroy this vitamin. One half the original amount of folic acid remains after one year of proper storage.

Deficiency:

Folic acid deficiency is not common, but a supplement of 20 mg per day may benefit stabled performance horses without access to green grass.

Excess:

There are no reported cases of folic acid toxicity for any species.

Biotin (sometimes called vitamin H)

Another numberless B vitamin, biotin is a component of four important enzymes involved in metabolism. It is involved in the synthesis of fatty acids, nonessential amino acids, and purine. It is a coenzyme for carbon dioxide fixation. Your horse can synthesize some biotin for himself; the exact amounts needed have not been determined, and there is currently a great debate as to whether
horses need a biotin in their diet—in addition to what they can make for themselves.

Function:

- Crucial to cellular metabolism
- Processes fat and protein
- Processes vitamin C
- Good for bone marrow
- Good for glands
- Helps metabolize fats and amino acids
- Helps hoof growth and development
- Good for the heart
- Helps connective tissue stay healthy
- May help hoofs retain or regain resiliency

Source:

Biotin is well supplied by most plants. Commercial biotin supplements are frequently touted as being good for the skin and hoofs, and this may well be true. At least it has been shown to be true for swine. Why researchers know more about pig hoofs than horse hoofs is a mystery to me.

Deficiency and Excess:

There are no reported cases of biotin deficiency or toxicity.

B$_{12}$ (Cobalamin or Cyanocobalamin)

B$_{12}$ is the largest and most complex of the B vitamins, but it was only discovered in 1948. It is singular among vitamins because in nature it is synthesized not by plants but only by beneficial microorganisms. In the horse's case, these bacteria are found in sufficient supply in the horse's colon, from which the vitamin is absorbed. Vitamin B$_{12}$ is also the only vitamin to contain a metal atom (cobalt) at its core, and the only B vitamin stored in the body. In many ways, B_{12} acts like folic acid, which is found in forage. For optimal absorption of B_{12}, a sufficient amount of B_6 is needed. Vitamin B_{12}:

- Helps form red blood cells
- Metabolizes fats, protein and carbohydrates
- Synthesizes myelin, the fatty covering of nerves

The exact amount of B_{12} needed has not been determined, but horses seem to be able to make enough on their own. No deficiencies or toxicity have been reported in horses.

Choline

Choline isn't really a B vitamin, although it is often treated like one. In fact, choline is technically not a vitamin at all, since it can be synthesized in the body by all animals—it doesn't have to be added in the diet or produced by microorganisms in the intestines.

Source:

Kelp, yeast, wheat germ, legumes and seeds. All natural fats contain choline. The exact amount of choline needed has not been determined, but how much choline your horse needs in his diet depends upon how much methionine he is getting. If a horse is getting sufficient amounts of methionine, he can make his own choline in his liver. The dietary requirement has not been determined; it is assumed that horses that get sufficient methionine get enough choline.

Function:

Choline is not needed for metabolism, nor is it part of any enzyme or co-enzyme. It is a structural component of fat and nerve tissue and a precursor of acetylcholine (a neurotransmitter), and is a component of lecithin and beta-ine. Choline is also a donor of methyl units for certain metabolic reactions.

- Synthesizes acetylcholine in the nerves
- Transports fat from the liver to other parts of the body
- Aids in the metabolism of fat and cholesterol

Deficiency

Choline deficiencies have not been reported in horses, but it is added to most vitamin supplements anyway.

Excess:

None recorded in horses, but it may acidify the liver, causing liver problems or diarrhea. It therefore should not be supplemented.

SOME HISTORIANS
*believe that the
16th century proph-
et/astrologer/physi-
cian Nostradamus
achieved better cure
results than his com-
petitors because he
incorporated vitamin
C-rich rose petals
into his concoc-
tions. I suppose it's
possible.*

Vitamin C (Ascorbic Acid)

Vitamin C has a chemical structure remarkably similar to that of the mono-saccharide sugars such as glucose. Vitamin C is easily destroyed by heat, light, copper, iron, oxidative enzymes and alkalis. It retains more of its activity if kept in an acid environment at low temperatures. Horses can make their own ascorbic acid. Most animals can do this, although humans, apes, monkeys, guinea pigs and the Indian fruit bat cannot. I thought you might want to know about the fruit bat. I suppose that's why it eats fruit.

Sources:

Fruits (especially citrus), dark green vegetables, kelp. Horses can make it themselves from glucose in their livers.

Function

- As an antioxidant, vitamin C destroys nitrosamines and many free radicals
- Helps develop collagen, the basis for connective tissue. Vitamin C is necessary for the cross-linking of hydroxyproline, the most common amino acid in collagen.
- Helps tissue growth and wound healing
- Aids in the development of bones and teeth
- Helps utilize the B vitamins
- Aids immune function
- Aids exercise stress recovery
- Fights osteoarthritis
- Acts as an anti-inflammatory
- May fight cancer

Deficiency and Excess:

Horses can synthesize their own vitamin C, so a deficiency is unlikely. No vitamin C needs to be added in the diet. On the other hand, vitamin C excesses have not been reported, which is a good thing, since some people insist on supplementing their horses with it. Some reports, however, suggest a benefit to sick or heavily worked horses.

Vitamin D

Vitamin D is a group of sterol compounds which regulate calcium and phosphorus metabolism. The precursors of vitamin D are ergocalciferol (D_2) found in plants and 7-dehydrocholesterol, a fat-like substance in the skin of animals. Cholecalciferol (vitamin D_3) is produced from the precursors by exposure to ultraviolet B in sunlight. D_3 itself is found in animal products like fish oils and in the skin after exposure to sunshine. Most mammals, including horses, can produce cholecalciferol this way. Vitamin D is therefore not called the "sunshine vitamin" for nothing. (This process works best in animals with light hair and thin coats—the same animals that are most likely to suffer from sunburn.) Horses can make vitamin D even on cloudy days, by the way; it just takes longer. However, ultraviolet rays do not penetrate glass, so if you keep your horse under glass you'll need to supplement. (The same would be true if your horse stayed in the barn all day long without sun-cured hay—or refused to leave the shade of the apple tree long enough to get his vitamin D by sunlight.)

Horses also can get a big chunk of vitamin D from sun-cured hay; this results from exposure to the ultraviolet irradiation of ergosterol, which is found in plants. Interestingly, vitamin D is not found in living plants—only plant products like hay. Living plants seem to have too much chlorophyll—this screens out the light. Only when the plants have been cut and exposed to sunlight does vitamin D develop. Thus vitamin D has the interesting distinction of being the only vitamin which is more abundant in hay than in fresh forage.

Cholecalciferol is an inactive storage form of this vitamin; it is activated when it's transported through the bloodstream to kidneys where it is converted to one of several metabolites.

The functions of vitamin D include:

- Promoting the balance, absorption, transport, and metabolism of calcium and phosphorus, and enhancing their absorption in the intestine. This helps harden or "mineralize" the bones and teeth and prevents leaching of calcium from the bones.
- Synthesizing insulin
- Aiding the immune function

Vitamin D is stored throughout the fatty tissues. It's also found in the muscles, lungs, kidneys, liver, aorta and heart.

Deficiency:

This is so rare as not to occur unless experimentally induced. In that case, lack of vitamin D produces:

- Reduced growth rate
- Loss of appetite

SOME EXPERTS prefer to call vitamin D a hormone rather than a vitamin because of the regulatory functions it performs in the body. In fact, one of its metabolites is calcitrol, which is usually classed as a hormone.

CALCIUM, phosphorus, and vitamin D are all complementary; they work together and need to be kept in balance.

RICKETS DEVELOPS *in most species who are deprived of vitamin D. Horses appear to be somewhat of an exception, but young, vitamin D-deprived horses do show decreased growth and certain bone irregularities. So, even though it is not officially rickets, it might as well be rickets for all intents and purposes.*

HORSES SUFFERING *vitamin D toxicosis are taken off vitamin D, phosphorus, and calcium supplements and given a high-grain diet. Plenty of water should be made available to the horse, and strenuous exercise avoided.*

- Poor eruption of the permanent teeth and other dental problems
- Deficiency or imbalance of calcium and phosphorus

Vitamin D supplementation is not necessary for most horses, unless they are kept in the dark on a diet low in sun-cured hay. These horses should receive 300 IU/kg DM for maintenance and 800 IU/kg DM for other horses. Researchers haven't determined the minimum amount of vitamin D needed by horses who get daily sunlight, but apparently they get enough. The NRC has given the maximum long-term safe level for vitamin D as 1,000 IU per pound (or 2,200 IU per kg of diet DM). That is equivalent to 44 IU/kg body weight daily for an 1,100 pound horse.

Excess:

This is the most common of vitamin overdoses, but it usually occurs only when you over-supplement. When excess vitamin D is given, it does everything it normally does—only more so. Over-supplementation can cause:

- Blocked calcium assimilation
- Hypercalcemia (excess calcium in the blood) which can be deposited in the soft tissues
- Anorexia and weight loss
- Fatigue
- Lameness
- Diarrhea
- Heart murmurs
- Severe dehydration

Vitamin E

Vitamin E is one of the two vitamins your horse cannot synthesize on his own (the other is vitamin A)—he must have it supplied in his diet. It comes in several forms, including alpha, beta, gamma, and delta tocopherols, but it is alpha-tocopherol (technically known as d- or dl-alpha tocopherol) that provides most of the dietary benefits for horses.

Vitamin E is synthesized only by plants, primarily leafy green plants and green forages. Thus, legume hays like alfalfa and clover have more vitamin E than grass hays. (Unfortunately, between 30 to 80 percent of the vitamin E can be lost during the cutting and baling process.) Various cereal grains and polyunsaturated vegetable oils like wheat germ oil, corn oil, sunflower oil and soybean oil, and seeds also contain it. (This figure applies to the oils only, not to meals. Most meals have very little vitamin E.) The best vegetable source is probably cold-pressed safflower oil, which contains the very active alpha-tocopherol form of vitamin E.

Green forage of average quality contains 100 to 450 IU/kg DM, but the amount decreases as the plant matures. Grasses can lose up to 90 percent of their vitamin E by maturity, and alfalfa can lose up to 65 percent. Grass hays contain only 10 to 60 IU/kg, but alfalfa ranges a bit higher; 10 to 80 IU/kg. Cereal grains range between 5 and 30 IU/kg.

This is how vitamin E works. In normal metabolism, cells produce oxidative waste products. If the lipid peroxides had their way, they'd destroy the structural integrity of the body's cells, and they would no longer function normally. Vitamin E acts as an anti-oxidant, preventing this oxidation of polyunsaturated fatty acids (PUFAS) found in cell membranes, thus helping the cells stay in good health.

In addition to acting as an antioxidant, the body uses vitamin E to help produce prostaglandins, which in turn regulate blood pressure, muscle contraction, and reproductive functions. (The name tocopherol is from a Greek word meaning childbearing. Vitamin E is necessary for healthy reproduction by both males and females.) Iron and chloride can reduce its availability. Vitamin E

- Stabilizes cell membranes by scavenging free radicals (ions with unbalanced electrons)
- Is essential for the cell nucleus; involved in DNA synthesis
- Is important for growth and developmental of the muscular system
- Promotes good circulation (acts as a vasodilator)
- Improves the immune system
- Reduces signs of zinc deficiency
- Helps keep connective tissue elastic
- Protects against harmful effects of lead and mercury
- Improves the skin
- Improves absorption and storage of vitamin A
- Is involved in oxygen transport
- In addition, vitamin E is a natural preservative, keeping fats from going rancid

Although the minimum requirement for vitamin E has not been established, the National Research Council recommends 50 IU/kg and 100 IU/kg for performance horses and pregnant or lactating mares. This level, however, may be much too low. Some experts recommend a much, much higher level for equine athletes—up to 2000 IU of vitamin E per pound. There is little research to support this claim; however, it is probably not possible to overdose on the stuff, although it is very possible to overdose on selenium,

VITAMIN E HAS a complex (but completely legal) relationship with the trace mineral selenium. Selenium is a cofactor for an enzyme (glutathtione peroxidase) that helps reduce the number of peroxide molecules formed during fatty acid oxidation. To some extent, vitamin E can substitute for selenium. Since selenium works so much like vitamin E, animals that have selenium in their diet are less dependent on vitamin E as an antioxidant.

FERROUS SULFATE, a common iron supplement, can reduce the effects of vitamin E.

vitamin E's partner. It is possible, also, that very large doses of vitamin E may induce blood coagulation problems by interfering with vitamin K. It could theoretically interfere with the absorption of some other fat-soluble vitamins. For this reason, some conservative equine nutritionists recommend that horses receive no more than 1000 IU/kg in the diet.

Vitamin E's role as a vasodilator is important to exercising horses. The dilation of the blood vessels allows the blood to circulate more easily, which helps oxygen and other nutrients get to where they're going more efficiently.

The absorption rate of vitamin E is 35 to 50 percent. It undergoes very little metabolism. Vitamin E is stored in small amount throughout the body, but the highest concentrations are in the liver, fatty tissues, heart, muscles, testes, uterus and blood.

Horses on a high-fat diet (more than 10 percent) will also need more vitamin E, which is necessary as an antioxidant for the dangerous metabolic products of the oils.

Deficiency:

Vitamin E and selenium deficiencies result in similar symptoms. To some extent, the two substances can make up for deficiencies in the other. Vitamin E deficiency occurs when a horse takes in less than 10 IU per kg of diet DM. (Your vet can check for deficiency with a blood test.) Symptoms include:

- Muscle weakness and fragmentation caused by damaged cell walls
- Ataxia
- Joint swelling
- Wobbler's syndrome (associated with EDM—see chapter 15)
- Signs suggestive of muscular dystrophy
- Progressive retinal atrophy
- Blood disorders
- Weakened immune system
- Equine motor neuron disease (see Chapter 15)

Vitamin K (Quinones)

This fat-soluble vitamin was the last vitamin to be discovered. It comes in two natural forms: vitamin K_1 (phylloquinone), which is found in fresh or dried green plants and vitamin K_2 (menaquinone), which is produced by bacteria in the large intestine. Very little vitamin K is stored in the body.

(This is true not just of horses, but of all animals.) In addition, several synthetic forms of the vitamin exist, primarily vitamin K_3 (menadione). Both vitamin K_1 and vitamin K_3 are available commercially.

Although the exact amount of vitamin K needed for horses has not been settled, it is apparent that they don't need vitamin K added to their diet; they can make enough of it through bacterial synthesis in their cecum and colon. The liver can also turn vitamin K_3 into a nutritionally usable form. However, when the animal is on a course of antibiotics, it's sometimes wise to add vitamin K to the diet as antibiotics kill off some of the normal intestinal bacteria necessary for vitamin K_2 synthesis.

Dietary sources: Phylloquinone is found in leafy green plants like spinach, kale, cabbage and cauliflower. Since horses are unlikely to dine on cabbage, it should encourage you to know that good pasture and high-quality hay have plenty of the stuff. It is found in alfalfa and kelp, but watch out for the excess iodine also found in kelp. The absorption rate is 40 to 70 percent.

Function

- Helps blood to clot by helping produce prothrombin, the clotting protein, in the liver
- Participates in the activation of proteins throughout the body
- Cofactor for the synthesis of the bone protein osteocalcin that regulates calcium/phosphorus incorporation in growing bone

Deficiency:

Vitamin K deficiency is extremely rare, but can result from consuming moldy sweet clover hay. It results in bleeding disorders like increased clotting time or even hemorrhage. Vitamin K deficiency can also occur from anything that injures the gut bacteria which make the stuff. This can include anything from antibiotics to colic.

Excess:

None is recorded, but too much may produce anemia. Vitamin K excesses produced experimentally have resulted in acute renal failure. These horses were given shots of the synthetic form. Oral forms of the vitamin appear more benign.

WHEN A combination of selenium and vitamin E deficiency occurs, horses can develop progressive emaciation, painful subcutaneous swelling, rough coats, and stiffness.

ALTHOUGH vitamin K is a fat-soluble vitamin, it is converted to a water-soluble form before it is stored in the horse's liver. Thus it is easily excreted, and doesn't tend to accumulate.

In Praise of Pasture

PASTURE IS EVERYTHING TO A HORSE:
living room, play room, gym and dining room.
Horses are grazers (not browsers) by nature.
Although they may take an occasional nibble on
leaves or twigs (sometimes to their detriment),
nothing suits them better than walking quietly
along in a pasture munching grass for most of their
waking hours. Horses especially enjoy pasture if
they can share it with other horses. They are herd
animals and like to be together.

One word often used for pasture-derived food is
"forage." Technically, forage is any plant material,
other than seeds and roots, grown for feeding her-
bivores. This definition includes pasture grass, hay
and silage. It includes perennial and annual grasses

as well as legumes (alfalfa and clover). All forage material share the qualities of being low in calories and nutrition and are so lightweight that they "float" through the intestinal tract.

There's no doubt about it—a good green pasture is a horse's paradise, and in theory, ordinary horses require nothing more (other than water and some salt) to live a comfortable life. Horses not only prefer grass and hay to all other food sources, but it is necessary for their health. It is the safest and most natural food for your horse. Forage not only provides nutrition—it also helps horses feel full; the bulk in the diet helps the digestive system move along its merry way. Without sufficient forage, horses are prone to many more illnesses, and more stable vices as well. (A good green pasture should

Horses especially enjoy pasture if they can share it with other horses. Helen Peppe photo.

be an owner's paradise as well—it's a lot cheaper and more work saving—than hay and grain, especially if you don't count the fencing.)

Of course, most modern horses don't lead this kind of life. Instead they are stalled for much of the day, and to "make up" for being deprived of their natural pasture, fed meals of grain and hay. (They also eat out of sheer boredom.) When stalled horses run out of their high-energy food, they often begin to gnaw wood, which is usually the nearest plantlike material available.

To me, a pasture is very much like an animal itself: it is composed of organic and non-organic components, and it varies with season and climate. If you think of your pasture as a living thing, rather than as a place like a parking lot, you and it will get along much better.

Seasonal growth is one factor that affects nearly every pasture. Even if you live in a spot where the climate varies little, the plants themselves still have a specific growth cycle. For example, as most plants and grasses mature, they develop more and more lignin, a kind of woody fiber that is indigestible to horses. This is one reason why horses prefer immature grasses. Legumes, too, develop more lignin as they grow and get "stemmy." More stem and less leaf means more lignin and lower quality forage. Straw, which is the stem material left behind after harvesting grain, has the highest lignin content and is consequently the least digestible of all forages. In this country it is used mostly for bedding, but in other parts of the world straw, especially oat straw, is used as a hay. It is low in digestibility and protein and high in fiber, but properly supplemented it can make an adequate food for horses.

So a general and common sense rule is that pastures contain a much higher level of nutrients early in the season than they do later on. Even though an autumn pasture may look rich and green, it doesn't contain the same food value that a spring pasture does. (However, as we see below, the higher moisture content of a spring pasture can also mean diluted food values.)

So much research has been done lately on pasture that there is simply no reason to have a bad one. Manufacturers are even working on developing grasses that are particularly suited to the smaller-sized pasture found more commonly today. (Not all of us have 700 acres or so!)

A poor pasture is more than a bad dining spot—it can pose positive dangers as well. It harbors parasites—and worse. As we all know, lawns and pastures devoid of rich grass seem to have no trouble at all growing vigorous and often-poisonous weeds. Your poor horse, while wandering about in a fruitless attempt to find proper nutrition, often ends up desultorily nibbling on toxic

COWS CAN GET along on a lower quality forage than horses can; this is because, as ruminants, they are much efficient as squeezing every last ounce of nutrients from their food.

IN CERTAIN PARTS of the world poor-quality hay or straw is sometimes chopped up and fed as "chaff". Often the chaff is mixed with molasses to make it more palatable. This chaff is not usually considered a prime source of energy, but rather something to keep an idle horse occupied and chewing without his risking getting fat.

IF HORSES AREN'T *given sufficient time to adapt to lush pasture, they can develop muscle spasms, sweating, and other symptoms of low calcium and magnesium levels in the blood.*

A HORSE HAS TO *eat up to five times as much (pound-wise) green pasture as hay to get the same caloric benefit.*

IF YOU LIVE IN *a low selenium, acidic soil area, it may help to lime the pasture or add phosphorus and selenium to the fertilizer. See your county extension agency to learn the exact type and amount of fertilizer you need. Be especially careful and don't add selenium unless you're sure you need it.*

plants—simply because nothing better offers itself. If a poor pasture is all you have, set out some good hay; horses much prefer it to poisonous weeds.

However, if you have a prime pasture, bluegrass for instance, a pound of forage provides your horse with about 950 calories, 79 grams of protein, 2.25 grams of calcium, 2 grams of phosphorus, 13 mg of zinc, and 7.1 mg of copper.

Even a lush green pasture may be deceiving, however. The word "lush" really means "soft and tender,", that is, full of liquid. (That's why we call a drunk a "lush.") Grass that is full of liquid has a lower concentration of nutrients. It may also, especially in the spring, be low in fiber. (Horses evolved in dry regions where this wasn't a problem.) Thus, a lush green pasture may have almost as few nutrients as a dried up winter one, and a horse must eat a lot more of it to "keep up." It's a strange world we live in.

For the same reason, because grass has more water than hay, a horse must more grass than hay to get the same amount of nutrients. And while good pasture is adequate for mature idle or light-working horses, it must be managed carefully. A pasture not in good condition cannot maintain a horse in good condition. And that's a rule.

So it's a good idea to provide your horse with hay even when the grass is richest. Don't worry—if the horse is getting enough fiber from his pasture he won't eat the hay. The same holds true for a very fibrous, late-summer pasture. Some nutritious hay along with the grass will ensure your horse's digestive health.

Pasture Size

Your horse can use up half a ton of forage a month. Of course, he doesn't eat all of it. He tramples some, rolls on some, and poops on some. But so far as you're concerned—it's gone one way or another.

The basic rule is that each horse needs two acres of good pasture to prevent over-grazing. Cows may be able to get by on less, but horses have bigger, harder hooves, and more efficient teeth that can do

Even a lush green pasture can be deceiving, however. Helen Peppe photo.

considerably more damage. It possible, with very careful management and very high-quality pasture, to get by on as little as half an acre per horse, but you're taking a risk, even with today's better grasses. Weanlings and yearlings can get by on somewhat smaller acreage. Of course, the number of acres required by horses also varies with the season. A rich, but not overly lush, early summer pasture can support a horse's lifestyle better than an end-of-summer burned over one. And if you live out West, where the ground and pasture are poor, a single horse may need as much as 60 acres to survive.

If your pasture is very small, you may just think of it as a place to exercise your horse rather than as a place to supply his primary nutritional needs.

Pasture Growth

Pasture grows according to its own rhythms, rhythms which depend upon temperature, season and latitude. It doesn't spring up all once on the Spring Equinox, primed and ready to go after a winter's sleep. In general, it takes about 12 weeks for a pasture to attain its mature growth, with the most rapid growth occurring in the first four weeks. These young grasses are full of digestible energy, and so are favored by horses, but they are also very fragile. It's easy for a greedy horse to destroy the young grasses in a short period of time. It's a lot easier to prevent pasture damage than to try to fix it later.

Another reason to watch out for your horse's eating habits during this period is that he can easily overfeed, especially on some types of forage. Don't turn your horse out in a young pasture, especially a small one, for more than a half-hour or so. You can gradually increase his pasture time as the season wears on.

Pasture Preferences

Horses enjoy a mixed pasture rather than a monoculture; clover seems to be a particular favorite. The expression "rolling in clover" had to come from somewhere. (It has a completely different connotation from "a roll in the hay…")

Horses seem to like clover/grass pastures best, with a definite preference for young growing plants as opposed to tough old plants. (I imagine it's kind of like asparagus.) As grasses mature they can lose half their trace mineral and salt content, while the calcium/phosphorus ratio increases slightly. Weeds are often distasteful and lacking in nourishment for horses.

Areas that horses prefer to graze on are called "lawns," while the less favored areas are known as "roughs." Horses tend to eat the lawns down to the bare ground and defecate on the roughs, allowing worms and other undesirables to gain a foothold, as it were. Worms don't usually have feet, but I think you

IT SHOULD BE noted that some kinds of sweet clover can, when moldy, contain dicoumarol, which, if ingested for several weeks, may cause a vitamin K deficiency and blood coagulation disorders.

know what I mean. To keep the pasture more evenly grazed you will have to keep the roughs picked up and well trimmed. If you don't clip these areas, weeds will take over and the horse will be even less inclined to graze there, since horses prefer short grass. Tall grass pastures are generally not properly utilized.

Siting the Pasture

If you have any choice about the matter, choose a pasture site that is flat, but not low. Low-lying pastures often have poor drainage and make ideal homes for insect pests (like mosquitoes) that will torment your horse and carry disease. A fairly dry pasture is both pleasanter and healthier than a wet one. Sloping areas aren't very good either. Not only do horse not enjoy standing at a slant all day, but also hillsides tend to have thinner soils that support only poor plant growth. Horses over-graze them quickly, and, with the plants gone, the soil begins to erode even further. Before you know it, you have a rutted, barren, washed out gully.

Sandy soil is also a poor substrate for good pasture; horses invariably tend to eat the sand along with the grass, which can put them at risk to impaction of the colon and rectum, chronic diarrhea, sand colic, and weight loss. If you have no choice in the matter, a supplement of psyllium and trace mineralized salts with equal parts of bone meal may ward off some of the bad effects. It's also a good idea to give your horse plenty of extra roughage to prevent over-grazing on sandy soils.

Pasture Maintenance

Planning is the not-so-secret ingredient to good pasture management. Injudicious applications of fertilizers and even improvements you may make in pasture drainage can seriously affect mineral availability. It takes about a year for a pasture to become established after first planting.

- A good first step is to have your soil tested by county agents. The test should be repeated every two years. Only in this way can you know your soil type and acidity, and thus know what kind of grasses will be best to plant and to help you decide what kind of fertilizer your pasture needs. Some counties even offer classes on pasture keeping!

- For grass to be keep healthy, it needs to be maintained at a certain length—preferably at least three inches. If you allow your horse to graze down the grass below this length, its capacity to re-grow will be impaired. It doesn't do your horse's teeth any good either. In addition, you'll be opening the door to parasites, which climb the damp glass blades and are ingested along with the grass. The ideal pasture grass is neither too long nor too short.

- Nearly all pastures have some rate of decline because of climate, hoof wear, disease, eating preferences, erosion, or lack of fertilization. If you have the space, the simplest, most economical, and reasonable way to maintain pasture health is to rotate your horse's pastures every 4 to 6 days. This strategy gives each grazing area a chance to lie fallow a few days, thus allowing the food source to go much further. (This doesn't mean you should ignore the fallow pasture—it still needs maintenance and care.) Sow one pasture with a more expensive, more nutritional seed, like Kentucky bluegrass, which withstands long periods of close grazing. Several small pastures are usually better than one large one—unless it is really, really large. Rotation has an additional benefit—it helps break the life cycle of parasites, which is always commendable.

- Don't allow manure to pile up. Remove it (my preference) or drag it at least once a year. Do this when it very hot or when a frost is due—the strongyle larvae are susceptible to temperature extremes.

- Top dress your pasture with fertilizers to maintain and promote pasture growth. Use the right kind of fertilizer for your area and the pasture you are trying to maintain. As a general rule, grass pastures need nitrogen fertilization, and some need additional minerals. Legume pastures generally contain enough nitrogen, due to the nature of the forage, but most need other minerals. The wrong kind of fertilizer is worse than none at all. Check with your agricultural agent if you are not sure.

- Keep your horse off pasture immediately following rain or irrigation. If you let the pasture dry out first, damage to the plants will be reduced.

- Keep weeds down. Non-nutritive weeds simply rob the soil and your horse of food. Fortunately, most toxic weeds are apt to be eaten only if all the "good stuff" goes first.

- Make sure your pasture is free from junk like old tires, rusted tractors and Aunt Emmaline's busted hairdryer. Stumps should be removed.

- Fence your pasture safely and securely. Please don't use barbed wire. Barbed wire may be all right for cows, but horses tend to crash into the stuff and rip their chests or flanks open. Use a wood or similar safe fencing material. It is more expensive, but you'll save on vet bills.

- To help save pasture grass, feed your horse a good meal of hay before he is put on pasture.

A LEGUME IS a plant which has microorganisms associated with its root system; these microbes are able to grab the nitrogen from the soil and air to produce protein.

TALL GRASSES tend to crowd out short legumes, however, so choose the mix carefully.

Horses are selective grazers. They wander about the pasture choosing the most delectable foods upon which to dine, and leaving the least palatable fare (weeds) for last. Thus, over time, a pasture can become overgrown with weeds.

You have to know your pasture and its grasses like the back of your hand. Some kinds of grasses like smooth brome and crested wheat grass—and the legumes like alfalfa and clover—should not be grazed too much, since it takes these plants a considerable time to recover. On the other hand, Kentucky bluegrass, orchard grass and Bermuda grasses are tough grasses and actually thrive on intensive grazing.

Green Chop

Although we are accustomed to feeding our horses upon either pasture, hay, or hay products like pellets or cubes, there is a food source intermediate between pasture and hay: it's called green chop. Green chop is fresh forage that is cut and fed immediately without drying, curing, or fermentation (ensiling). Green chop has a lot of advantages: its fresh taste is extremely palatable—almost as good as grass itself. You can also chop less favored grass into small bits so that the horse will actually eat it rather than ignoring it as he would normally do. It is one way to get extra use out of a small space.

But green chop has one big disadvantage—you have to cut it fresh every single day. Grass that is allowed to wilt is very dangerous. Cutting fresh grass every day is time consuming (if you do it yourself) or very expensive (if you have to pay others). It is most commonly done in areas where people have plenty of time, or else a cheap source of labor—like South America. Green chop is also very nice for older horses with poor teeth that have trouble with hay.

One caveat: green chop is not lawn trimmings. Lawn trimmings are mown too fine and ferment very fast, and are apt to contain toxins and bits of poisonous ornamental plants. Do not give your horse lawn trimmings and think that it's green chop. If you do give your horse an occasional helping of grass clippings, make sure they are no more than a few hours old and are chemical-free. Don't let them dry out too much, though. They are so fine that they get very dusty and are bad for the horse's respiratory system.

Spread them out over a large area, so that you horse won't gulp them down all at once, but will wander about looking for them. This will help prevent any intestinal distress.

Pasture Plants

Pasture plants come in two main varieties: grass and legumes. Legumes are seldom used alone, as they can't handle the trampling of horses' hoofs. But they make an excellent "fill." Each kind of pasture plant has its advantages: legumes enrich the soil and provide high-quality nutrition; however, the best plan is combine grass and legumes for a tough, high-quality pasture. Allow your horse to sample a smorgasbord of delicacies. The ideal ratio is 40 percent legume and 60 percent grass. (Only one or two grass species should be planted with the legume.) Consider planting vegetation that is native to your area. These native plants have evolved to suit your climate and soil type, and such pastures are generally more easily maintained.

This combination provides good nutrients, a long grazing season, and a long-lived pasture. In addition, the quality of grass is often improved by the legumes. In all cases, it is wise to select compatible grass species for your pasture; some less vigorous but nutritionally important plants can be crowded out if not managed carefully.

Common varieties of forages and grasses include:

ALFALFA (*Medicago sativa*): This is a deep-rooted legume that does best on a soil with a pH of 6.5 or higher. When conditions are right, alfalfa is a tremendously nutritious plant, but it is generally better as a hay because of its fragility and high management needs. Alfalfa can be grown almost anywhere in the United States, as long as the soil is fertile and non-acidic.

ALSIKE CLOVER (*Trifoium hybridum*): This thin-stemmed plant does well in a cool wet climate. It can handle a clay soil well. Unfortunately, horses aren't particularly fond of this kind of clover; it can also cause photosensitization if it is the sole forage source.

BAHIAGRASS (*Paspalpum notatum*): The main advantage of this grass is that it can be grown where a lot of other species can't—including drought stricken and sandy soil. Its disadvantage is that it cannot take the least bit of cold, and it is difficult to establish.

BERMUDA GRASS (*Cynodon dactylon*): This common warm-season grass does well on sandy soil and tolerates heavy animal traffic. It grows well even in the hottest months, but is not tolerant of cold. One variety, Coastal Bermuda Grass, is more nutritious than other kinds and makes a good hay. One good thing about this grass is that it makes several cuttings—each more nutritious than the last. This grass should not be allowed to over-mature or it loses a lot of its nutritional value.

BLUEGRASS (*Poa pratensis*): This world famous cool season grass is not limited to Kentucky; it can grow in most areas, and is also highly nutritious and palatable. Because it forms such a dense sod that can handle heavy traffic, both human and equine, it is not only an excellent choice for small pastures, but also a particular favorite of lawn gardeners.

SOME PARTS OF your pasture, notably around gates and troughs endure heavier hoof traffic than other parts. It's smart to plant these areas with tall fescue. First, horses don't favor fescue, so they won't be inclined to gulp it down, and second, it's a mighty tough grass that will endure the hoofs better than some other choices. Many older varieties of fescue, however, are subject to an internal plant fungus that is harmful to pregnant mares. Select a new, safer variety from your garden center.

KENTUCKY bluegrass can be improved by the addition of lime and fertilizer, but make sure you have a soil test done first. In any case, don't expect instant results; it takes a least a year and more likely two or three to get your pasture in shape.

One disadvantage of bluegrass is that it is a low-growing plant and hence does not make good hay. It doesn't handle drought well, turning a nasty brown if not sufficiently watered. This grass combines well with white clover or birdsfoot trefoil, a legume.

BROMEGRASS (*Bromus inermis*): One main advantage to this long-lived plant is that it can handle wet soils. It is very hardy and mixes well with alfalfa. Since it is a perennial, it does not require replanting every year, but does need a fertile soil. Its palatability seems to vary with individual horses.

CRIMSON CLOVER (*Trifolium incarnatum*): This cool season legume serves well in the southern U.S. as winter grazing. This is a great advantage, since not many legumes can be grazed in the winter, even in the south. It is not fussy about soil, and is similar to red clover in nutrients. However, this clover cannot be grazed during the summer months—it just shuts down.

LADINO CLOVER: This large clover, a variety of white clover (*trifolium repens*) is the most nutritious of all clovers. It is easily established, and grows quickly. However, it cannot take long dry summers. It is also not a tough plant—continuous grazing can shut it down, although a short rest will revive it.

TALL FESCUE (*Festuca arundinacea*): This is a tough, nutritious, cool season plant that, unfortunately, is not a favorite with horses. It is an easily established perennial that can take summer heat (although it prefers cool) and heavy horse traffic. It is a very aggressive plant that can take over a pasture. Curiously, horses like it best after a frost has fallen—apparently this causes the sugar content of the grass to rise. Fescue combines well with clovers.

The really big danger of fescue is that it can become infected with an endophyte fungus (*Acremonium coenophialum*) and the associated toxins can cause death and serious reproductive problems for brood mares. Although new fungus-resistant and fungus-proof varieties are being developed, the grass is naturally present in many pastures. Brood mares should be removed from tall fescue areas at least three months before foaling. (Among its many other effects, fungus-infested fescue can cause delayed gestation—up to 13 or 14 months. Learn to identify tall fescue in your pasture; you can ask your county extension agent for help. You may be asked to bring samples in to the office—get several from different areas of the pasture. Tall fescue is easiest to identify in the spring months when it is growing most rapidly.

LESPEDEZA (*Lespedeza spp*): This inexpensive legume grows well on poorer soils, but is not as nutritious as other legumes. Like other legumes, it is useful for improving the soil.

ORCHARD GRASS (*Dactylis glomerata*): This fast growing cool season grass can handle a fair amount of shade (hence its name)—but it is a sensitive soul that can readily succumb to overgrazing. If used for hay, it needs to be cut early. It will not tolerate drought, and is not very palatable to horses. This is a good plant to combine with ladino clover or lespedeza.

REED CANARY GRASS (*Phalaris arundinacea*): Horses will eat this cool season grass readily in its growing and immature stages; however, as the grass ages it becomes coarse and tasteless. Its big advantage is that it can withstand both very wet and drought conditions; it is winter hardy as well. Warning: this plant can contain hordedine when it is mature: this can be detected in a drug test and may disqualify a performance horse.

RED CLOVER (*Trifoium pratense*): This widely grown, fast-growing clover has a low resistance to various diseases and pests, including a mold called black patch (*Rhizoctonia leguminicola*) that is poisonous to horses. It causes a nasty condition called "slobbers," which is just exactly what is sounds like. When grown as a hay, red clover can yield one or two crops a season. It is high in nutrients.

RYE GRASS (*Lolium spp*): Ryegrass is the most commonly used cool season grass for horse pasture. It comes in both annual and perennial versions. It is nutritious, especially early in the season, and horses seem to like it well enough. Rye grass can become infected with a bacteria causing rye grass toxicosis, although this problem occurs much more frequently in cattle and sheep than in horses.

SWEET CLOVERS (*Melilotus officinalis and M. Alba*): These clovers grow fast, and are drought-and cold-resistant. They need a well-limed soil. However, many older varieties contain coumarin, which can be converted by a mold to dicoumarol, an anti-coagulant. Sweet clover does not make good hay—too many stems and not enough leaves. Some horses have to learn to like it.

TIMOTHY (*Pheum pratense*): Timothy is a rather picky cool season grass. It grows best in non-humid, cooler areas, but doesn't like drought either. Timothy seems to do best in the north and mountainous areas. Like alfalfa and so many other hays, timothy presents a challenge to the commercial grower. It is most nutritious early in its cycle, but it produces higher yields per ton when in full bloom or later.

WHITE CLOVER (*Trifolium repens*): This legume grows best in cool damp areas; it is a common component of many pastures and lawns. Although this is a fine pasture legume, it is sensitive to drought and has low yields.

SUDANGRASS
and its hybrids
contain compounds
which are very
dangerous to
horses. Do not use
as horse feed.

Starting Over

If you have the time and money, the best way to improve your pasture may be to start from the ground up. This means removing all the existing plants, and planting more desirable grasses. If you are interested in getting the very best pasture and the highest yield per acre, this is the method of choice. Do a soil test to find out exactly what plants would thrive best in your pasture. Take into consideration the lay of the land and its drainage, too. Consult a specialist if you have any questions; there's no point in doing it wrong.

Several months before you plan to reseed, apply any needed lime; it's best to disk or plow it right into the soil. Kill of the old grass by means of some of the great new herbicides, and then reseed. Water the seedlings well and frequently. If you do it right and control the weeds, your new pasture will be ready for grazing in one year.

The Hayfield

If you have enough land to grow your own hay, you're lucky. You will have a lot of control over the quality of what you feed your horse. If you have the option, select a simple mixture of one legume like alfalfa and one grass like timothy. This is preferred over a monoculture.

Fertilize your hay pasture every year. It's best to do a soil test but if that is not practical, a good rule of thumb is to top dress legumes annually with at least 50 pounds of phosphate and 150 pounds of potash (0-10-30 or equivalent) per acre. If your pasture is mostly grass, you can add 60 pounds of nitrogen per acre in late winter or early spring.

Hay

"…Good hay, sweet hay, hath no fellow…" *Midsummer-Night's Dream*

Hay, of course, comes from pasture. Technically, it is dried forage and most modern horses depend upon hay to live. This seems too bad, since hay is bulky, relatively expensive, difficult to store and handle, and is low in nutrient value. In fact, hay contains between 28 and 38 percent crude fiber, most of it insoluble and non-nutritious. It is high in calcium and low in phosphorus. (Grains, on the other hand, are high in phosphorus and low in calcium. This is why feeding both together helps insure a balanced diet.) Most hays are good sources of potassium, and vitamins A, E and K, while grains tend to be low in these nutrients. (The amount declines over time with storage.) If the hay is sun-cured it also has a lot of vitamin D, although sun curing reduces the amounts of other vitamins. The amount of protein and digestible energy varies with the type of hay.

Hay also varies wildly in the amount of water it contains (the more water per ton of hay, the less nutrition). Still, hay has a role to play in your horse's diet by absorbing water and "rehydrating" in the gut, thus pretending to be grass. (This is why it is very important to provide a stalled horse with lots of fresh water.) The amount of water a bale of hay contains obviously affects its weight. In fact, a small square bale of hay can weigh anywhere from 40 to 100 pounds. The giant round bales you see in the fields can weigh anywhere from 500 to 2,000 pounds. Most of the time these bales are left in the field and animals are permitted to simply nibble on them. This saves a time and effort, especially if you are feeding a bunch of horses—but the hay loses a lot more of its nutrients. Wrapping the bales in plastic or spraying the bales with warm liquid that hardens into a water repellent wax may help stem the loss.

One the most difficult problems about hay is assessing its quality. When you buy a can of Campbell's soup or even a package of properly labeled dog food, you sort of know what you are getting. Not so with hay. It might be anything. The nutritional quality of hay is so variable that the horse owner faces a new predicament every time she goes out to buy some.

One simple rule is to buy local hay if possible. It will be fresher and less expensive than hay brought from afar.

Cutting and Baling

One real concern is the nature of the growing season—and the economy. Hay harvested early in the season is the best so far as nutrition goes. However, early summer yields (tonnage) tends to be low. As summer wears on, the tonnage goes up—but the nutrient value of the product decreases. If a farmer waits until he can harvest the most hay, its quality will be correspondingly low. First cuttings also tend to be high in weeds, especially if the field is not carefully tended. The actual number of weed present in hay depends both on the kind of weed in question and the way the field is maintained. Properly maintained hayfields do not have weeds. For alfalfa hay, the first cutting is least likely to contain the deadly blister beetle.

After the first harvest, you can re-cut four to six weeks later. The warmer the climate, the more cuttings you can get—as many as seven in the south if rainfall and sunshine cooperate. Second cuttings often have fewer nutrients. Sometimes quality returns to autumn hay, so the worst hay is generally that cut in the heat of midsummer.

To make things even more problematic, the digestible protein of hay can vary enormously, depending largely upon when it is cut. Only 50 percent of the protein in late-cut hay, for instance, might be digestible.

Most hay is best if cut right before mid-bloom, or early maturity stage, when its quality and digestibility are highest. After that, most hay loses nutritional value, especially protein, since a lot has gone into making seed heads and baby hay.

THE MAIN disadvantages of hay concerns the horse owner. Hay is bulky and hard to deal with. Its nutrient content is highly variable—not only between different kinds of hay, but between one cutting and another of the same kind of hay.

COUNTERintuitively, baled wet hay is a fire hazard. That's because it generates heat in a process akin to composting, and when stored in a hot, poorly ventilated barn, can initiate chemical reactions and oxidations that raise the temperature to a point where the hay can actually catch on fire. The interior temperature of hay bales should be checked frequently, and hot bales should be carefully removed from the barn. Bales that feel unnaturally heavy may also be moist inside and should not be stored.

IF YOU ARE baling your own hay, you should know that a number of substances like propionic acid are available which, if applied correctly at the time of baling, make it possible to bale and store hay safely even when it has a moisture content of up to 30 percent. Propionic acid is entirely safe for horses; in fact, it is normally found in the horses digestive tract. Propionic acid doesn't hurt horses, but they prefer untreated hay. You can also add drying agents like potassium carbonate to the hay. All of these things increase hay costs by 5 to 10 dollars a ton.

EATING MOLDY hay can gives a horse heaves, among other things. Once a horse gets heaves, he can seldom be restored to complete good health.

For grass hays, the best time to cut is when the grass heads begin to show through the sheaf. Legume hays like alfalfa should be cut just before flowering. After harvesting, hay should be sun-cured until its moisture level is reduced to about 20 percent. Rain at the wrong time can reduce the leaf content of hay bales, destroying much of its value. Hay can be dried artificially, but this is not as nutritious.

During the hottest part of the summer, hay grows the fastest. However, this fast growth produces more stems and fewer leaves; thus the quality is lower.

Hay that is too moist is usually at risk of spoiling or contamination from dangerous molds. But the naïve horse owner can be at the mercy of unscrupulous dealers in this regard—obviously, wet hay is heavier than dry hay, and if you are buying hay by the ton rather than by the bale you might be paying for a lot of water that not only doesn't increase the nutritional value of the product, but may actually harm it.

Still, hay can't be completely dry at harvest, or else it won't process correctly as it is moved through the baling equipment. Alfalfa, clover, and other legume leaves can "shatter" under such conditions.

Rain is the enemy of cut hay. If it rains immediately after a crop is harvested, and the hay is allowed to dry out thoroughly afterwards, little damage may be done, but the later into the curing process the hay gets wet, the more nutrients are lost. Rain-damaged hay can lose well over half its nutrients. On the other hand, a blazing hot sun can destroy 80 percent of the vitamin A content of cut hay in 24 hours. Sometimes you feel as though you just can't win.

Storing Hay

Hay should be stored indoors, or at least under cover and off the dirt or floor. You can usually get pallets free from wholesale lumberyards and other places. If you cover the hay with a tarp, create a space between the top level of hay and the tarp so that moisture doesn't collect underneath to spoil the hay.

Rats and mice should of course be encouraged to live elsewhere; your friendly barnyard cat and non-venomous snakes will be glad to help you out. Well-stored, high quality hay can last a year.

Grass Hay

Grass hays are identifiable by their tall slender stalks, and long, slender, non-branching leaves. Major kinds include timothy, brome and orchard grass. These hays are easy to establish, often tolerate cold weather, grow actively in the spring, and are safe to feed; they are also less dusty but more bulky than legume hays.

Your location largely determines what kind of grass hay is available to your horse, since different areas of the country foster different sorts of vegetation. Some grass hays, like timothy, don't handle temperature extremes very well, while brome-grass, which does, isn't very palatable to horses when fed alone.

Cool season forages (which means forages that tolerate cold) include tall fescues, annual and perennial rye grass, timothy, smooth bromegrass, orchard grass, millet, sorghum, clover, wheatgrasses, oatgrasses, Kentucky bluegrass, Canada bluegrass and redtop reed canary grass.

Warm season forages (forages that tolerate heat) include Bahiagrass, Bermuda grass, switch grass, bluestem, buffalo grass, Grama grasses, Indian grass, love grasses, panic grasses, Johnson grass, limpo grass, digit grass, and various kinds of wheat, rye, indigo, clover, millet and sorghum. Don't worry if you have never heard of most of these. You're not alone. Many are annual grasses that don't make very good pasture, anyway. The perennials, however, like Bermuda grass and bahiagrass, are satisfactory.

Grass hay is high in fiber, which is critical to the horse's digestive system. The high fiber practically eliminates the possibility of founder or colic. Grass hay quality varies, but many kinds, including timothy, brome, orchard grass, prairie grass and tall fescue, make adequate hay. Timothy, orchard grass and coastal Bermuda grass vary in protein levels from 7 to 13 percent, while brome varies even more—from 5 to 14 percent, depending largely on when it is cut and baled.

On the average, though, a diet of bromegrass does not provide enough calories, protein, calcium, or zinc to maintain even a layabout horse. Horses fed largely upon grass hays may need a daily supplement of a grain like oats (about three pounds) for energy and soybean meal (about a pound) for protein.

Here is a broad breakdown of some important nutrient levels of various grass hays. However, this table is for general comparison only. The wide differences between individual samples needs to be take into account.

IF THE ONLY KIND of hay you can get is low quality (not moldy, of course, but just lower in quality), you will have to feed your horse more of it. And there is a limit to how much even a horse will eat.

ONE GREAT advantage of grass hays is that they don't harbor hideous blister beetles; see page 105.

NUTRIENT	BROME	TIMOTHY	ORCHARD
DE (Cal/lb)	850	800	880
Protein (g/lb)	58	39	52
Calcium (g/lb)	1.13	1.9	1.08
Phosphorus (g/lb)	1.13	0.9	1.36
Zinc (mg/lb)	11.8	17.3	16.3
Copper (mg/lb)	10.0	6.4	7.6

ALFALFA, LIKE other legume hays, is low in phosphorus compared to calcium, although it has plenty of both in absolute numbers. Thus it may be wise to include a phosphorus supplement if you are feeding largely alfalfa. This is especially important when you are feeding young, growing horses who have less tolerance to wide calcium/phosphorus margins. In some cases, however, the amount of calcium in alfalfa is limited by the presence of oxalic acid.

Legume Hay

Working horses, growing horses and mares that are lactating or in the last three months of pregnancy need more than a diet of grass hay. As a rule, legume hay contains two or three times the protein and calcium of grass hay, more beta-carotene, more calories, and more soluble carbohydrates. However, it has less digestible fiber, which is also important to horses.

While some horse owners supplement with grains and other concentrates, others may change to top-quality, high-calorie legume hay like alfalfa. Other legume hays include clovers (alsike, sweet, crimson, red and ladino), trefoil, soybeans, cowpeas, vetch and lespedeza. Lespedeza is widely grown in the south, and can handle both drought and poor soil. However, it is lower in minerals than many other legumes.

Legume hays have rather coarse, branching stacks and easily detachable, fragile leaves. These leaves contain about two-thirds of the nutrients of the plant; that's why cutting alfalfa at the right time, treating it correctly, and feeding it in tub rather than a rack that could drop the leaves is critical.

Alfalfa (*Medicago sativa*)

For as long as we have been feeding horses, we have been feeding them alfalfa. (The first recorded use goes back about 2500 years.) But nowhere in the world grows more or better alfalfa than the United States, mostly in the west. (In Europe and elsewhere alfalfa is known as lucerne, which was not named for the Swiss city, although I wish it were. It's a lovely place.) The word alfalfa is Arabic, although you certainly can't grow any of the stuff in Saudi Arabia. (I'd like to go into this further, but it's not that kind of book.) At any rate, America produces enough alfalfa to export it world wide, largely to the racehorse industry and breeding farms. About half the hay we harvest in the United States is alfalfa or an alfalfa/grass mixture.

Alfalfa hay has three times as much protein as grass hay. In fact, fresh cut alfalfa can be as high as 20 percent protein. Not only that, but its level of digestible protein is also high. For instance, alfalfa hay that is 18 percent crude protein may contain 13 percent digestible protein. Grass hays cannot match that level. The crude fiber level of alfalfa is about 21 percent.

In fact, alfalfa hay is so rich in nutrients that with the exception of being a bit low in zinc (true of most hays, in fact—timothy is the best) it provides practically complete nutrition for your horse. It not only provides plenty of protein, but large amounts of vitamin A, calcium and phosphorus. However, it should be noted that alfalfa hay does contain a binding substance (antagonist) that can decrease the utilization of vitamin E by as much as 33 percent.

To make things worse, alfalfa can lose up to 65 percent of its vitamin E when it is harvested late, and 40 percent from hot sunlight when it is being cured.

Although it is more expensive than grass hay, alfalfa is widely available all over the country (unlike many other legumes), and its use can cut down on the amount of even more expensive grains. It is especially good for young horses, and pregnant or lactating mares.

However, alfalfa is not without its detractors. It has been accused of causing kidney problems, and of being more susceptible to molds. Alfalfa, however, does not cause kidney problems, and molds come from poor processing, not from the hay itself. Early harvested alfalfa may be hard to cure properly, especially if there has been a wet spring, and for that reason alone, some owner prefer more mature alfalfa.

Properly cured alfalfa is at no more risk of mold than any other kind of hay. It is true, however, that alfalfa increases urination (it's the protein). The urine of alfalfa fed horses has a stronger ammonia smell to it (the protein again) and contains crystals of the excess calcium also contained in alfalfa.

While none of this should be of concern if your horse has normal kidney function and access to plenty of water, I would not feed alfalfa to a kidney-impaired horse.

The Curse of the Blister Beetle (*Epicauta spp.*)

Some southern-produced alfalfa hay contains blister beetles. These nasty bugs come in 300 varieties, but the worst of a bad lot are the black ones with the orange stripes. Or maybe they're orange with black stripes. It's hard to

Blister beetles can be deadly. Pam Tanzey.

GREEN-GROWING alfalfa has been known to cause bloat in ruminants. It does not have this effect in horses. However, excessive consumption of lush alfalfa grass can cause colic.

THE EUROPEAN version of the Blister Beetle is the infamous Spanish Fly. I thought you'd like to know.

WHEN BUYING commercial alfalfa, only buy a product that is certified free of blister beetles.

tell. They might even be an invisible bug painted black and orange for all I know. They range from about a quarter inch to one inch long. Their special weapon is cantharidin (which for once is more potent in males than in females). This stuff is deadly.

Their preferred habitat is alfalfa hay. The worst kinds live mostly in the southern part of the country, and cannot stand cool weather.

If your horse should be unfortunate enough to eat infested hay, an irritant in the filthy beetle can cause an injury to the digestive and urinary tracts which can kill a horse. In fact, it takes only a child's handful of the bugs, dead or alive, to be lethal. Even the remains of last years' bugs are killers. The only way to be sure your horse won't be affected is to avoid feeding alfalfa; however, you can examine the hay carefully, bale by bale as you feed it. I talk more about blister beetles in Chapter 14.

Clover

Clover is another legume hay that is highly favored by horses. It tends to cure darker than many other hays. Many different sorts exist, but the best is probably Ladino clover. It is a good choice to add to any pasture mixture. Ladino clover by itself, however, is a low-growing plant that doesn't make good hay.

Hay Preferences

Given their druthers, most horses seem to prefer clover or alfalfa hay to other sorts. This seems to be true even if the legume hay is of poorer quality than the grass hay. When different qualities of the same kind of hay are offered, horses unerringly head for quality: namely hay that is low in dust, mold and weeds. They also like hay that is higher in protein and energy, and lower in fiber content. Of grass hays, timothy seems to be the favorite, with Bermuda grass liked the least.

It has also been noted that once a horse gets accustomed to a particular kind of hay, he is often loath to change to a different kind. This can create problems in a world when you are never sure just what kind of hay is available form one month to the next.

Cereal Grains Hay (*Gramineae* family)

Technically, there is a third source of hay: cereal grains. Unharvested wheat, oats, and barley can also be turned into hay if they are cut while the plants are still green. So with cereal grain hay, you are using the entire plant. Normally what happens is that the heads are used for grains, and the rest of the plant becomes straw and is used for bedding or chaff.

Cereal grains are similar to grass hays in nutritional value. These hays are seldom fed in North America, mostly because of the expense. However, most of them (except rye) are quite palatable to horses. Most cereal grains are used to feed human beings.

Selecting a Hay

No matter what grass, legume, or grain you choose for your hay, pretty much the same criteria apply when choosing a bale.

- High leaf-stem ratio and quality. Look for lots of leaves; there should be a low percentage of bloom (indicating older hay). What stems are present should be fine, indicating a younger, more nutritious plant. Prominent, thicker stems are a telltale sign that the plant is older. Alfalfa hay leaves should be soft and hang on the stems in clusters.

- Touch. Hay should feel firm, but not stiff to the touch. Squeeze it. Stiff, sharp hay is probably from a late cutting.

- Color. Good grass hay is usually very light green; good alfalfa may be a brighter green, while clover may be darker. Don't select bales which are "striped," a sign they may have been rained on.

- Sweet smelling. Use your nose. Fresh, fragrant hay is less likely to be contaminated by dust, mold, or other foreign material.

- Dry. Wet hay is dangerous.

A good sample of hay. Helen Peppe photo.

IN MANY CASES, the ideal solution is to grow or buy "mixed" bales, part grass, part legume, thus getting the best of all worlds.

IF YOU HAVE your hay analyzed by a laboratory, an acid detergent fiber value of over 35 percent indicates a past-bloom hay.

- Consistency. The inside of the bale should exhibit the same qualities as the outside. Ask the seller to take apart a bale of your choosing (or have him use a "hay probe") to get a look what is inside. Many an innocuous bale has a moldy, wet core. Hay should not contain weeds, which are low in nutrients and may even be poisonous.

- Small bales are likely to store better than the cheaper large round ones (which are usually kept outdoors).

- Mold free. Mold often appears as mat-like areas in the hay.

- Dust free. Try dropping a flake of hay and see how much, if any, dust rises from it.

Hay is expensive. Nowadays many people have a sample of hay analyzed for its nutritional value before they spend several hundred dollars on several hundred bales. Several different kinds of tests (including the excitingly named near-infrared reflectance test) are available for a reasonable fee ($10 to 35 dollars). The lab can sample your hay for moisture, total digestible nutrients, crude and digestible protein, calcium, phosphorus, magnesium, relative feed value (RFV)—just about anything you need or want to know. The relative feed value is a measurement originally used in the dairy industry. It compares the price of the hay with the feed value it contains.

Of course, it not practical to use a lab analysis if you must buy hay in small lots from different people. But it is worthwhile for buying in quantity, or if you harvest your own hay—so you will know what you need to improve. On the other hand, it is worthwhile to purchase the largest amount of hay you can conveniently use, feed, and store. It is not only cheaper and labor and timesaving, but it also provides your horse with a nutritionally consistent food source. Of course, this is an advantage only if the hay is high quality in the first place.

Storing Hay

Hay gradually loses its nutrients during storage, but the earlier it is cut (and baled after cutting) the better.

Silage or Haylage

Silage is readily available in some parts of the country, especially in places where it rains so much that haymaking, which requires dry weather, is risky. When grass is cut and stored wet in a silo, it's called silage or haylage, in which grasses, legumes, or grains are stored in airtight, high moisture conditions. This kills molds, yeasts and aerobic bacteria. Any kind of plant can be ensiled, but in this country the common ones are alfalfa and corn. (Usually grains are called silage and legumes and grasses are called haylage, but it's basically the same thing.)

The resulting fermentation action can improve the quality of the forage and makes a suitable horse feed, if it is mold-free. In fact, haylage is quite suitable for horses with respiratory difficulties. Its nutritional values are similar to those of hay, but silage should probably not comprise more than half the roughage a horse eats. It is also important to note that haylage or silage destroys almost all the vitamin E of hay, so horses on haylage need to have this vitamin supplemented. Its only other downside so far as vitamins are concerned is its lack of vitamin D.

Good haylage smells nice (a little sharp), and is greenish or brownish, not too dark. If it smells bad, it is bad. Silage normally has a damp feel, but it's not slimy. It pH value should be between 3.5 and 5, a number that can be checked with a strip of pH paper. Once horses get used to silage, they seem to prefer it to regular hay.

However, moldy silage is extremely dangerous to horses, and can cause sudden death. For example, poorly cured silage can contain botulism. Never use silage if the plastic bags in which it is contained are open for more than three days. Moldy silage often goes undetected, because the bad silage can be mixed in with the good—and it doesn't take much to kill a horse. Since silage can only be used fresh out of the silo and doesn't transport well, it is not a convenient food source for most horse owners, anyway, especially those living in warm, humid areas.

Cubed and Pelleted Hay

Although we commonly think of hay as being stored in bales, or perhaps in haystacks (needles notwithstanding), there's no rule about it. In fact, there's much to be said for grinding hay and making it into pellets or compacting it into cubes. Hay cubes and pellets are less wasteful, produce less manure, and are easier to store than baled hay. They are easier to transport and create a lot less dust, too. Horses may have to learn to eat them, but once they do, they gobble them right down—although that is not necessarily a good thing!

One study showed alfalfa pellets with high leaf content have nearly a third higher nutrition value than natural-form hay. Most hay pellets are made from alfalfa, and often contain 17 percent protein. Pelleted hay, however, can be made from almost any type or combination of grasses or legumes. One big advantage of pelleted hay is that it contains a nutritional label, something not true with baled hay.

The downside of pelleting is that the contents move more quickly through the digestive tract that does hay in its more natural form; this untoward speed may lower its digestibility. This can be gotten around by chopping hay and mixing it in with the pellets, thus slowing down the pellet's rapid transit through the digestive tract. Another disadvantage is that pellets and cubes are much more expensive that regular hay.

Pelleted hay is finely ground, then artificially dehydrated. (Most hay cubes are sun-cured.) Hay cubes are made by simply chopping sun-cured hay (usually alfalfa) into small pieces, adding moisture and heat, and forcing it through a cube die. The resulting product is very easy to store and measure, so you will have less waste. (You also avoid the problem of having the horse turn the hay into his mattress.) The major difficulty with cubed hay (aside from the fact that most horse have to learn to eat it) is that it's not possible to check the quality of the hay after it has been processed into cubes. You have to take the manufacturer's word for it. In general, hay cubes are superior to pellets—offering most of their advantages, and few of their disadvantages. However, hay cubes ought not to be fed to horses who bolt their food, as this can lead to choke. ▬

Hay Pellets. Helen Peppe photo.

After they learn to eat them, most horses love cubed hay. Helen Peppe photo.

Grains and Oil Seeds: The Energizers

ALTHOUGH PASTURE SHOULD BE ABLE to support a horse, at least in theory, it doesn't always work that way. Pregnant and lactating mares, growing horses, and performance horses need more than pasture, and in much of the country, good pasture is a seasonal event. And perhaps just as important, most pastures, unless carefully managed, don't provide all the nutrients your horse needs.

That's why grains are often added to horse feed. They are the most convenient way to add calories and proteins to your horse's diet. Yes, but just what is grain? Technically, grains are the dry, one-seeded fruit of cereal plants like corn or oats. Grains are members of the grass family Gramineae, which gives them at least a nodding acquaintance with grass. Each individual grain consists of the seedhead of the plant, which contains the nutrient for the plant embryo. The seedhead has a coat, starchy endosperm, and finally the germ or embryo itself. Certain grains (like barley and oats) have in addition, a husk that provides more fiber, while others like corn do not.

Grains are four to eight times heavier than an equal amount of baled hay and have about 50 percent more calories than moderately good hay. Almost all grains are suitable for equine consumption, but each grain has its special attributes.

Technically grains can be considered "concentrates," a digestible and heavy supplement to the diet. Grains are primarily digested in the stomach and small intestine, as opposed to hay and other fibrous material which are digested in the large intestine. Horses are not "natural" grain eaters, since they would not get much of it in the wild, but they readily adapt to eating grain (especially if its flavor is "improved" by the addition of molasses or other sweeteners).

An idle horse may not need grain at all, but it is essential for most riding, growing, and breeding horses. However, excess energy in the form of grain is more dangerous than excess energy from grass forage. The reason may be that grain energy comes from starch, not the volatile fatty acids that grass produces (via the good microbes). Starch stimulates insulin production, which may in turn result in bone problems like osteochondrosis. One rule-of-thumb to follow is never feed your horse more than five pounds of grain at any one meal. Most horses need much less.

As a horse owner, you pretty much get to decide what type of grain to feed your horse. This is of course less true with hay, which you must to some extent buy as available and which is largely subject to local weather conditions, and even less with pasture, which you are pretty much stuck with. Therefore, grain becomes a critical item in your horse's diet. One of the great things about grain is its consistency in quality. Corn is pretty much corn, and barley pretty much barley. Although there are some differences from crop to crop and field to field, these differences are very much smaller than with pasture and hay.

You can confine your horse to eating one kind of grain or you can select a specific mix. And of course, many people decide to buy a commercial, already mixed food with various supplements. (We'll discuss these in a later chapter.) For now, let's just talk about the various commonly fed grain and their virtues. Nearly all grains provide plenty of energy and are high in phosphorus. Grains are generally pretty low in fat—usually between 1 and 5 percent, with oats near the top of that figure and wheat near the bottom.

Many grains are low in protein, but if the protein is of high quality horses can make do with a relatively small amount. Even when grains and manufactured feeds contain substantial amounts of protein, however, the amino acid availability can be damaged by heat and improper drying techniques. The length of storage can also reduce the amount of available proteins. This is why many companies fortify their feeds with the essential amino acids lysine and methionine.

The digestibility and palatability of many feeds can be improved if the feed is rolled, ground, or crushed. This is because crushing sort of "pre-chews" the feed, making it more available for the microbes and enzymes to get to work on. That doesn't mean that crushed or rolled grain is always the correct choice, however. The very process that makes it easier to chew and digest also leaves the grain more vulnerable to oxidation and decomposition. This is especially true of grain that must be stored for a long period. Unless you have an aged horse with poor teeth, or a foal that is just learning to chew, certain whole grains, especially oats, are often the wisest (and least expensive) choice.

Grain Terminology

Grains can fall into the following categories:

- Whole unfortified grains: These include the entire seed head harvested and stored. In most cases, whole unfortified grains are not as digestible as the processed forms. (This is obviously in the evolutionary best interest of the plant, if not the horse.) The starch in most whole grains is less digestible than in processed grains. Oats, however, are somewhat of an exception on both counts.

- Processed unfortified grains: Processing refers to cracking open the hard seed shell to make the inside more available for digestion. Depending on the procedure and grain, processing can increase digestibility up to 30 percent

- Processed fortified grains: Fortified grains have been supplemented with vitamins and minerals. They are also usually a combination of two or more grains. Mixing grains improves the amino acid profile of the feed, although this is not a major concern with horses so long as they are getting enough lysine and methionine.

Processing Grain

Although grains can be processed in a number of ways, most are sun-cured first. Grains must be dried to a moisture level of 13 percent (20 percent is good enough for hay), because grains ferment a lot more easily. If the moisture level goes below 10 percent, it will also stop the growth of most insect pests. The only problem is that when moisture falls below 12 percent, the

MANY CEREAL grains and grasses have inadequate amounts of phosphorus, calcium, protein, and lysine.

GRAINS ARE sometimes categorized by the presence or absence of hulls; grains without hulls include corn, wheat, rye, and sorghum. Grains with hulls are oats and barley.

grain kernels often start to break, and that can increase the risk of mold and lowered nutrition.

Processing can take the form of cracking, crimping, rolling, steam rolling, popping, micronizing, extruding, pelleting, flaking, or grinding. It can be done hot or cold, with hot processing being more expensive. Some grains are better processed by cracking, others by rolling, and so on. While processing large kernel grains like oats, corn and barley doesn't improve their feeding value much, grinding corn and barley is important for reducing diarrhea, colic and laminitis. Small kernel grains like rye, wheat and milo (or sorghum) must be processed in order for the horse to chew them. In general horses prefer all grains processed as far as taste goes, and good arguments can be made for processing all grains except probably oats, which are palatable enough to horses eat whole. And no grain should be finely ground; fine grinding causes more problems than it solves.

The main disadvantage of processing grain is that you vastly increase the risk for mold contamination, bacteria growth, and breakdown of important nutrients. Their storage life is greatly shortened by processing, even when storage temperature as cool as 41 degrees F.

Buying Grain

Always look for U.S. grade No. 1 grains, although No. 2 is adequate for most horses. If the grain is not graded (all too frequently the case), get a money-back guarantee from the seller should it prove to be unsatisfactory. Look at the grain carefully before you buy it; a visual inspection can tell you a lot. In general, kernels should be plump, clean, and well formed. They should not stick together—a sign they are too moist. The grain should be dust-free, mold-free, and bug-free. Corn is always the most dangerous feed—inspect it carefully.

Storing Grain

Grain needs to be kept free of insect pests like weevils and mites. Rats can get into grain as well, not only devouring the product, but also leaving their excretions in the food, making it both unpalatable and unhealthy. Remember that this can have happened before you even buy the grain, which is why purchasing from a good source is so critical.

This feed bin will keep out insect pests and mice and rats. Courtesy Dan's Saddlery.

Store grain in a cool, dark spot with good ventilation. If you can keep the grain room at a uniform temperature, all the better. Containers should be very clean and tight. An unused chest freezer, which is dark and well insulated, makes an excellent grain bin; it's also easy to clean.

Grain Preferences

Horses seem to like oats best of any grain, followed by corn, wheat, barley, rye and crushed soybeans, pretty much in that order. Oats are indeed a sensible choice for horses, since it is the safest of all grains and the least likely to cause digestive upset. Nowadays, however, horses are more likely the get the cheaper, but distinctly second favorite corn. Interestingly, horses, who are conservative by nature, tend to stick with the grain they are used to and are loath to test a new variety. This is surely an evolutionary adaptation. If grains are switched suddenly, the horse does not have enough of the proper intestinal bacteria to process it properly; this can lead to a lactate buildup and lower the pH value in the intestine.

Corn

Corn is, in one way the gold standard of grains. It's cheap, and it produces more energy per unit of cultivated land than any other crop. It also has the highest energy value of any grain—about twice as much as oats (by volume). So, as far as calories go, corn gives you the biggest bang for your buck. Corn is native to the United States, and we grow a lot of it all over the country. Because it is so widely grown, corn is readily available and inexpensive in

Cracked corn. Helen Peppe photo.

FOR REASONS too odd to go into, wheat is called corn in England. In Scotland and Ireland, corn is oats. Corn is corn in Australia, though. Corn is really maize, which is Indian corn. I hope this is all clear.

most localities. It is fed to animals more than any other grain; in fact, corn presently comprises about 80 percent of the grain fed to animals in this country. Corn contains 7.5 to 12 percent protein, which is about what you may find in high-quality hay. The protein found in corn is considered low quality because it lacks the essential amino acid lysine. It is the also the only grain that has a really significant amount of vitamin A.

Corn has a lot of starch and only 2.2 percent fiber, making it a rather dangerous feed for horses. For example, while about 98 percent of ground oats are digested and absorbed before reaching the ileum (the end of the small intestine), only about 60 to 80 percent of ground corn is. As a result more starch enters the horse's cecum—and horses have a hard time digesting starch. Starch buildup causes more volatile fatty acids and lactic acid, a lowered cecal pH—this can lead to increased risk for what is called cereal acidosis.

Some kinds of processing like popping or to a lesser extent grinding, substantially improves the starch digestibility of corn. Cracking, on the other hand, doesn't have much effect. However, this processing has its downside: processed corn is much more susceptible to mold, a number of which produce aflatoxins that can cause potentially fatal poisonings in horses. (Many people use a 50:50 mixture of oats and corn to get the greatest benefit from both.)

You can feed whole corn, but if you do, it should be dampened before feeding so that the kernel is soft by the time the horse eats it. Horse also enjoy eating corn on the cob, as long as the kernels aren't too tightly packed together. This promotes salivation; it's also not easy for a horse to bolt down corn on the cob and risk colic.

Another downside to processed corn is the rapid deterioration of its vitamins and oils. Within three weeks after processing, the feed value of processed corn can decrease significantly. Vitamin E, for example, is rapidly lost when grain are ground or cracked, due to exposure to air. It is usually not necessary to grind corn; the cracked variety is sufficiently processed and it won't deteriorate so fast. If possible, it's best to crack corn freshly only a few days before feeding. Store the feed in a tightly sealed container away from air, heat, and light.

Corn is evaluated on its moisture content and the percentage of unsound kernels. U.S. grade No. 1 weighs 56 pounds per bushel; it contains no more than 3 percent damaged kernels, and 2 percent broken corn and foreign material. The grading levels go down to U.S grade No. 5, which can contain up to 15 percent damaged kernels and 7 percent broken corn and foreign material.

The corn primarily used for horses is called "dent corn," because the mature kernel has a dent in it when dry. Both white and yellow corn are of high

nutrient value, although yellow corn has higher levels of beta-carotene; corn is the only grain that contains significant levels of this important precursor to vitamin A.

Choose corn that is plump, firm (not hard) and dry. Moist corn can contain toxic molds like fusarium that cause liver and brain damage.

Oats (*Avena sativa*)

"Truly a peck of provender. I could munch your good dry oats…"
Midsummer-Night's Dream

Oats, a cereal grain, are mostly cultivated in the northern part of the country. Of all grains, they are the most digestible, mostly because oat starch can be readily digested in the small intestine. Oats also have more protein, minerals and fat than other commonly fed grains. Oats used to be the staple of horse feeds, perhaps a leftover from the early days in England, where corn (more properly called maize) was not available. Nowadays, its use is decreasing, principally because it is such a bulky feed, weighing a little over half as much per unit as corn or milo. (Bulky means that is has a high volume in proportion to its mass.) Horses like oats, and they are one of the few grains to which you don't need to add a sweetener like molasses to tempt their taste buds. (It's an odd thing that horses seem to prefer a bale of dry hay to rich, flavorful grains, but there you are.)

Whole oats. Helen Peppe photo.

Oats are often fed whole; I personally prefer this method. Whole oats keep better, and retain more of their inherent nutritive value. Unlike most other grains, whole oats can be chewed readily by horses. Still, they can also be rolled, crushed, or crimped to break the seed coat. Processing oats this way make more sense for an older horse, or a horse with bad teeth, than for a young sound-mouthed horse. Processing oats improves their digestibility only slightly—5 to 10 percent. Processed oats can be kept longer than other pro-cessed grains, but not as long as whole oats.

Although the bulkiness of oats is a disadvantage in some respects, it has its benefits. For one thing, a horse is less likely to overfeed on oats than on most other grains; its high fiber content (11 percent) makes it a safer food. Because of the fibrous hull, horses fed on oats are less likely to suffer colic and laminitis.

On the other hand, if a horse is eating large amounts of oats (ten pints or so), rolling, crushing, or crimping may be valuable, since some of the oat kernels are otherwise passed undigested. One downside of oats is that their quality seems to vary more than in other grains. This is largely due to the percentage of hulls in the sample. In buying oats for a performance horse, look for "heavy oats," which weigh 42 pounds or more per bushel. The aver-age weight of oats is 32 pounds a bushel; anything lower than this suggests a too low proportion of kernel to hull.

In America we grade oats according to several factors. U.S. No. 1 oats are 97 percent sound, weigh at least 36 pounds a bushel, with no more than 0.1 per-cent heat-damaged, no more than 2 percent foreign material, and no more than 2 percent wild oats. (Although you are allowed to sow all the wild oats you like, only 2 percent can get into U.S. No. 1 grade oats.) U.S. No. 2 oats are still good; they weigh 33 pounds a bushel, and contain 94 percent sound oats. No more than 0.3 percent can be heat-damaged, and no more than 3 percent foreign material and 3 percent wild oats can be present. The grading continues downward to U.S. No. 3 and 4. These last two have a higher per-centage of weathered oats. Get the best quality oats that you can afford.

Oats are typically white, but can be gray or black, depending on where the oats are grown; this doesn't affect the quality—unless the oats you're looking at are white oats that have "gone bad." Some distributors bleach naturally dark oats in the hope of making them look more appealing, but this inter-feres with the natural goodness of the grain. The kernels should be fat, clean, dust-free, and of uniform size.

One danger is that newly harvested oats, with a moisture content of more that 13 percent, can harbor dangerous molds. (If they are harvested when fully ripe, the moisture content is about 10 percent.) However, in general, oats are fairly immune to mold growth.

Oats contain between 9 and 14 percent protein. Their carbohydrate content is about 60 percent. They also contain about 70 percent total digestible nutrients. They are low in calcium and fairly low in phosphorus. They have no beta-carotene, and are a poor source of B vitamins as well. Oats have only about 85 percent of the energy of corn per pound and only 50 percent of the energy per volume. (This is one reason why all feeds should be compared by weight, not volume.) But—oats produce 130 percent as much protein per pound! The average sized, moderately worked horse (1,100 pounds) will eat about 4 1/2 pounds of oats per day, in addition to plenty of forage.

Because oats generally have to be shipped to where the horses are, they can be the most expensive of grains.

Barley (*Hordeum vulgare*)

Barley is the most widely cultivated grain in the world; it doesn't need much rain or a long growing season. It even grows in Tibet, and that's saying something. However, it's not especially popular in this country, where we prefer corn. (We grow only 5 percent as much barley as corn.) The best quality barley grown in the U.S. is produced on the East coast; it has a TDN (total digestible nutrients—a term I explain more fully in the next chapter) of 78 percent. However, barley is somewhat more popular in parts the West, although it isn't as good. It stands between corn and oats as far as energy provided, and sort of looks like little oats. Like oats, most types of barley contain hulls, but the percentage is lower; barley is thus considered a "heavy" grain. In fact, barley is quite similar to oats, but the grains are smaller and heavier.

Altogether, barley can be an excellent horse feed, supplying nearly as much energy as corn and somewhat more protein, between 11 and 13 percent. It also is a good source for niacin, and contains more lysine (that essential amino acid) than most grains. Because of its high protein count, barley is sometimes added to the feed of brood mares, foals and performance horses. The low fiber content can make barley more dangerous to horses than oats. When used, barley is usually added to a sweet feed mixture. It is sometimes cooked also, to make its starch more digestible.

Horses don't really like the taste of whole dry barley, so it is usually crimped or steam rolled, which softens this hard grain and improves its digestibility by about 5 percent. (Whole raw barley contains sharp awns which are unpleasant to eat, as well.) However, the improvement in taste may

ALTHOUGH WE think of oats as a grain crop, they can also be cut for hay, in which case they are cut earlier.

OATS MAKE AN excellent winter-warmer for non-working horses. (That's because they are so fiber-filled.) Add about 4 ounces to the diet for every hundred pounds of horse. Working horses, however, may benefit more from the extra energy of corn.

**ROLLED BARLEY
and corn can
replace the tradi-
tional oats dinner.
Use slightly less
(about 4 pounds).**

be somewhat offset by the vitamins lost during the cooking process. Still, cooked or boiled barley, unlike the raw stuff, seems a positive treat for horses; it is especially nice for foals, brood mares, and aged, or ailing animals, often serving to pick up a fading appetite You can cook the stuff in a crock pot overnight.

The top grade of barely weighs in at 47 pounds per bushel. This is U.S. No.1 barley, and it contains 97 percent sound kernels. Only 2 percent of the kernels are damaged, 0.2 percent heat damaged, and contains no more than 1 percent foreign material, 4 percent broken kernels, and 10 percent "thin" barley. In the lowest grade, U.S. grade No. 5., 75 percent of the barley is "thin." When choosing barley, select grains that are heavy, ripe, and free of weed seeds.

Grain Sorghum or Milo (*Sotho maili*)

The term "grain sorghum" can actually refer to a number of different grains, including hegari and feterita, but it most commonly means milo. It is very hard to chew and needs to be cracked, crushed, or steam-rolled before serving, so that the horse gets the utmost energy from the product. Cracking grain sorghum can increase its digestibility by up to 15 percent. It is not commonly fed to horses in North America, but in some parts of the world, milo is a staple of the horse diet. Milo is grown in poor soil and dry areas of the Midwest and Texas, areas not suited for corn.

There are actually two varieties of milo, yellow and brown. The yellow kind is best, because it is low in tannin, which decreases digestibility and palatability. Unfortunately, yellow sorghum is hard to distinguish from the brown kind. In fact, yellow sorghum also contains white and red kernels. This is not helpful, but it's what happens when one enters the wonderful world of sorghum.

Milo is a small, round, yellowish, hard, drought resistant seed that matures early. It is less digestible than oats, but more digestible than corn or barley. In addition, a lot of improvements have been made in this grain which have enhanced its nutritional value. It is a frequent addition to many mixed-grain feeds, although its tannin gives it a rather odd flavor. A batch of milo can easily be tested for tannin content by applying bleach to a small sample and heating the kernels, then rinsing. When dry, the kernels will be white if no tannin is present. The more tannin, the darker the kernels.

Milo contains somewhat more protein and 90 percent as much energy as corn. Like corn, therefore, milo is considered a high energy feed that needs to be fed with care in order to avoid laminitis and colic. It should not comprise more than one-third of the grain portion of a diet.

Wheat (*Triticum aestivum*)

This cereal grass is grown mainly for human use. In some respects it might be considered a good livestock feed, having about the same energy and protein content as corn. It is considered a heavy feed, weighing about 60 pounds a bushel. It contains about 80 percent total digestible nutrients, and 11 percent protein.

Unfortunately, however, wheat has serious problems as horse food. For one thing, it is very expensive, since nearly all wheat products go to feed humans. Too often, the wheat available for stock feeding is considered "distressed," another way of saying that it is moldy or infested with weevils.

Even more important, whole wheat may swell up in the digestive tract and cause colic, so it must be rolled or cracked before being fed. On the other hand, if it is rolled too fine or ground it may be digested too rapidly and cause another entire set of digestive problems. Ground wheat releases the gummy wheat gluten inside, which becomes a sticky mass. Finely ground wheat also increases dust content leading to respiratory allergies and heaves. Wheat is best given in small amounts only—as in a piece bread now and again.

Other wheat products fed to horses include wheat bran and wheat middlings. Wheat bran is the coating of the kernel; it contains about 67 total digestible nutrients, and is sometimes used as a laxative—although there's no evidence to show that it really has this property. Nor does it prevent colic.

However, horses find it palatable, and it is sometimes given as a treat to pick up the animal's appetite. It contains lots of protein (15 percent), but its calcium/phosphorus ratio is so unbalanced in favor of phosphorus that it becomes downright dangerous as an only feed. It is high in fiber, bulky, and slowly digested. However, when wheat bran is used in conjunction with soybean meal, the availability of zinc and copper may be reduced. If bran is fed in any large amount, it must be balanced with added calcium.

Wheat middlings are the middle (hence the name) layer of the kernels—just inside the outer bran covering. It is heavier than bran and of higher nutritional value. In some parts of the country, notably the Midwest, it is an economical food. Middlings contain about 16 percent crude protein, and have a TDN of 77 percent. They tend to be fine and powdery, and many experts feel they tend to pack up in a horse's stomach and cause problems.

Rye

Like wheat and grain sorghum, rye is considered a "hard" or a "rough grain." It is mostly grown in poor, sandy soils, and is more often used as a pasture than as a grain. To improve both its digestibility and palatability, it must be processed by cracking or steam rolling before serving. Since rye is largely used in the flour and whiskey business, not much is left over for horse use except in milling areas. This is probably a good thing, since horses are not partial to rye flavor. Since most horses don't like the stuff much, it is added to other grains rather than served solo. Most commonly rye is added in the form of rye middlings (the part of kernel left after the grain has been milled). The middlings themselves have to ground fine in order to be used in feed. Rye should not comprise more than one-quarter of the grain ration. Rye contains 72 percent TDN and 17 percent crude protein. The digestible protein is between 12 and 13 percent.

Rice (Oryza sativa)

It may sound odd, but rice can be fed to horses. After all, it is one of the most important grains in the world, and in its rough or unpolished state is extremely nutritious. Its energy content is similar to that of corn by weight (but not volume), but it is low in protein.

Like wheat bran, rice bran has a phosphorus calcium imbalance. It is sometimes added to feeds as a fat supplement. However, the fat in rice is unsaturated and becomes rancid in the presence of heat and damp. It is possible to buy rice bran with most of the fat removed.

Mixing Grains

Each of the commonly fed grain has its advantages; no one of them is perfect. For most owners, the best solution is to choose a judicious mixture of grains suitable for your horse. If you really do your homework and carefully study the properties of each grain, your can custom design a blend that is perfect for your own horse. However, unless you are willing to spend an awful lot of time and effort in learning what you need to know, the simplest plan is to buy a commercial feed that is correctly balanced for your horse's needs. With a vast assortment of special mixes from which to choose, it's a buyer's market, and though you still need to understand what your particular horse needs, the job of finding just the right mix is easier now than ever before.

Oil Seeds

Oil seeds are grown primarily for vegetable fat production. Some oilseeds include soybeans, cottonseeds, peanuts, flax, linseed, sunflower seeds, canola (rapeseed) and coconut. After the oils are extracted, the remaining protein-rich (35 to 50 percent) meal is dried. The oil can be removed by simply pressing it from the seed, a fairly inefficient method that leaves some of the oil in the meal. (This was a bonus for horse owners, since the resulting oil-containing meal was beneficial to the coat.) Nowadays, most oil is extracted by using solvents. This takes out nearly all the oil from the meal, but the residue is even higher in protein than was obtained by the older method.

Oilseed Meals

After the oil is extracted, the remaining part is called oilseed meal, which contains proteins, carbohydrates and minerals. In fact, many of these meals contain as much as 50 percent high quality protein (although a few are deficient in certain essential amino acids). Their main drawback is that they are more expensive than grains and are hence used in much lower quantities. They are also low in fiber. Because of their low fiber and high protein, oilseed meals should be introduced gradually into a horse's diet, and should never be a major feed source.

Soybean Meal

Soybean meal is the most commonly used oil seed meal. It is palatable, digestible, and inexpensive. It also contains the highest quality protein of all plant sources, with a crude protein value of about 44 percent and 79 or 80 percent TDN. (Actually the crude protein of the soybean is very high—53 percent; however, ground soybean hulls are added in the amount necessary to produce the desired protein content.)

Soybean meal contains the valuable amino acids lysine (2.9 percent), methionine (0.6 percent), and threonine (1.7 percent). These are of special benefit to growing horses.

Cottonseed Meal (*Gossypium spp.*)

Cottonseed meal is another common protein source for horses, with a crude protein content varying between 34 and 50 percent (depending on what is wanted by the consumer) and 72 to 75 percent TDN. Its values are thus somewhat lower than in soybean meal, and cottonseed meal is becoming more expensive due to less extensive cotton planting. Cottonseed meal also is low in the essential amino acid lysine. However, horses prefer cottonseed meal to soybean meal. Cottonseed meal should probably not be given to young horses because of the possible risk of gossypol toxicosis, a condition caused by the pigment found in most cotton plants. Older horses are quite safe from this condition, and even young horses have been fed a fair amount of cottonseed meal without harmful effects, but the possibility of injury remains.

Linseed Meal (*Linum usitatissimum*)

Linseed meal comes from flax which is used to make both linen and certain drying oils. The crude protein content of linseed meal is only about 35 percent, although its TDN is 81 percent. It contains digestible protein, calcium

DON'T FEED your horse whole soybeans—only the meal. Whole soybeans contain a trypsin inhibitor that severely decreases protein utilization by the horse. The cooking of soybeans, which accompanies the extraction process, destroys the inhibiting factors.

and phosphorus. Linseed meal is expensive and low in lysine and certain other essential amino acids; it is also low in carotene and B-complex vitamins. However, linseed meal does wonders for the coat, giving it a special bloom. It has a laxative effect, and horses find it fairly palatable.

Sunflower Meal (*Helianthus annus*)

This meal contains between 41-45 percent crude protein; however, it has only half the lysine needed by growing horses. (Most oilseeds except soybean have the same deficiency.) If the hull is not removed, it is high in fiber (25 percent). If the hull is gone, the fiber content drops to about 12 percent. It is less expensive than many other protein supplements, and is used widely around the world.

Canola Meal (*Brassica napus* and *B. campestris*)

Canola used to be called rapeseed, but this unfortunate name is no longer in common use. (The name "Canola" was adopted by the Canadian government in 1979 to describe safe rapeseed.) Older varieties were not safe to use as supplements, since they contained high levels of glucoinolates that interfere with the thyroid gland and cause goiter. New varieties are safe. Canola contains between 36 and 43 percent crude protein, and 2 percent lysine, which, while lower than that in soybean meal, seems to be safe enough for growing horses. Canola is also higher in calcium, phosphorus, magnesium, manganese and selenium than soybean meal. Canola is considered equal to soybean meal as a supplement for mature horses, and as adequate for growing horses.

Other Oils

Nowadays we are seeing a variety of previously little used oilseed meals as feed supplements. These include oils from peanuts, coconuts, safflower, and cull peas. Since not much research has been done on their properties as feed supplements, most experts recommend no more than a third of a horse's protein source come from these meals until we know more about them.

Hulls

The outer covering of grains and seeds are called hulls. Hulls are sometimes added to feed to replace some or all of the hay or forage for mature (not growing) horses. Hulls have no carotene, and some kinds can be dusty, which is bad for horses with respiratory problems. They are a nutritionally safe feed: high in fiber (50 percent more than grass), and low in energy (50 percent less than grass). They are cheap and can be useful for feeding a horse that needs to lose a few pounds, or to entertain an idle stall-bound horse. But I wouldn't put a three-day eventer on a diet of them.

Soybean, sunflower and almond hulls are commonly fed. Sunflower hulls are the highest in both fiber and digestible energy. Many hulls can be bought in pelleted form.

Commercial Mixed Feeds

Although some people still prefer to mix their own feeds at home, or order custom mixes from the mill, the vast majority of horse owners prefer to simply buy a commercial feed to supplement their hay and pasture. This way, they don't need to figure foods out by a complicated formula, and can rely upon the expertise of the manufacturer and distributor. Even with this advantage, however, your work as a horse owner is not over. With the great variety of feeds on the market, it is your job to make sure that what you buy is meeting the needs of your particular horse.

In the United States, all commercial foods must be registered with the state agriculture department, and most conform to the guidelines of the Model Feed Bill, which was developed by AAFCO, the Association of American Feed Control Officers. AAFCO, formed in 1909, sets nutrient standards and provides model regulations for state legislation. It also sets standards for substantiation claims by manufacturers. AAFCO is a non-profit trade organization of state and federal livestock and companion animal food regulators. Its power is advisory only, but its stated goal is to insure that all pet foods are nutritionally adequate and are uniformly (if somewhat confusingly) labeled. The labeling guidelines have not changed in nearly 40 years—a scandal considering how much more we know about equine nutrition than in days of yore.

Labeling

Much of the information you need to make a good decision is on the label, known in the horse business as the "feed tag." This tag must be attached to each bag of feed. Its job is to identify the feed by brand and product name, give the net weight, provide instructions for use, and supply the name and address of the manufacturer or distributor. They must also provide a guaranteed analysis of ingredients, and list the common name of each ingredient used. It is the custom (and the law in some states) to list ingredients from greatest to least percentage; however, no federal law requires manufacturers to do so.

Manufactures have the choice of using two kinds of formulations: fixed and variable. This means that instead of listing each grain separately, they can simply call the ingredient "plant protein." This saves them a lot of time and money. For example, let's say the manufacturer has been using a certain grain, Grain X, as a protein source. All of a sudden the price of Grain X skyrockets due to drought or some market fluctuation. The manufacturer can then switch to grain Y without having to change the feed tag. There are limits to all this, of course. The guidelines stipulate that if the label lists "plant protein," it must be just that—plant protein, not fishmeal or some other animal product. When the label reads "processed grains" (instead of specifically

IF YOU WANT TO be fancy, and order a custom mix, you have several ways of doing so. You might choose to custom mix grain—say ordering a mix of 80 percent cereal grain, 12.5 percent soybean meal, and so on. Or you might specifically order a mix containing a certain percentage of protein or calcium.

MANY LABELS bear the word "All natural." This means that the product contains no non-protein nitrogen, which is suitable for cattle, not for horses.

NEVER FEED A horse a commercial food formulated for another species! Besides the inherent imbalances likely to occur, many of the feeds are contain growth stimulants or antibiotics which can be toxic to horses.

NEVER ALLOW your horse to bolt his grain. Mix it with hay, if you have to, or place a large stone or brick in with the feed to force him to eat more slowly.

what kind of grain) or generic "plant products," you know that a variable formula was used.

Unfortunately, some manufacturers resort to weasel words like "processed grain byproduct." A by-product is what is left over from processing the food for its main (usually human) use. While some by-products may be perfectly acceptable for horses, others can be really trash. And there's no way to tell by the label alone which is which. You will have to contact the manufacturer directly, or check out his advertising. This all seems very awkward, of course, but that's the way it is. Part of the problem seems to be that the government wants to look out for the farmers as well as for the consumer. Those leftover floor sweepings have to go somewhere, and apparently one of those places is your horse's belly.

The guaranteed analysis indicates the minimum crude protein, minimum crude fat, and maximum crude fiber present in the food. (This is true for all animal feeds, including dog food.) The crude protein level is the trickiest. Recall that all protein is not equal, and the guaranteed crude protein analysis does not show the quality of the protein contained. The crude fat requirement is not very important for horses, which don't need much fat in their diets. However, the maximum crude fiber analysis is something else. While horses do need lots of fiber, they obtain it best and most economically from their hay, not grain. A feed that contains lots of fiber (seen most often in ground and pelleted rations) may be cheating your horse of important nutrition—and cheating you of your hard-earned money.

Other terms of nutritional interest including ash (percentage of minerals in the feed) and nitrogen-free extract (sugars and non-nitrogen organic acids). Total digestible nutrients or TDN are usually not listed.

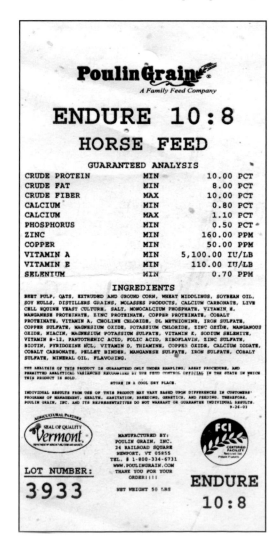

A feed bag's label contains a wealth of information. Helen Peppe photo

Sweet Feeds

One popular form of processed feed is the so-called sweet feed, which has, in addition to its other components, a helping of molasses and often a very light spraying of vegetable oil. Sweet feeds are more palatable than plain grain, and they have an enticing smell to the horse owner—something which has not escaped the manufacturers' notice. As far as nutrition goes, sweet feeds are no better for your horse than the regular kind. Most have a shelf life of about six months. When you buy sweet feeds, choose one that smells good, and whose grains are plump, and not completely soaked in molasses. (Molasses should not comprise more than 10 percent of a sweet feed, and in a humid climate, the percentage should be about half that to prevent mold.)

Depending upon the ingredients, the fiber level of sweet feeds can vary from 8 to 20 percent.

Pelleted Feeds

Another form that feed can take is pellets, which may be round, oval, or cylindrical. Some pellets are comprised of forage only, some of grain, and some are mixes (called complete feeds). Alfalfa pellets are quite common. Almost anything can be turned into pellets: corn cobs, peanut hulls, straw, grape pulp and chicken manure. In fact, one enterprising group of folks fed horses pellets containing 25 percent computer paper. They then added appropriate amounts of vitamins, minerals and protein, and proclaimed the resulting product equal to alfalfa hay (without the blister beetles). At one point they had considered using newspapers but decided that the large amount of ink (not to mention the news) might give horses indigestion.

To make pellets, the manufacturer grinds and wets the feed, steam heats it to about 185 degrees, and pushes it through a die mold under low pressure. Then the stuff is cooled, dried, sifted, and bagged. Grain, complete feeds, hay and supplements may all be put into pellet form.

Pellets are usually glued together with a "binder" like wheat, barley, or molasses. The amount of molasses must be carefully calculated. Too much and the pellets are mushy; too little and they become dry and brittle.

Some pelleted feeds use artificial binders like lignin sulfonate, sodium/calcium bentonite (a kind of clay), or hemicellulose extracts.

Pelleted foods are almost dust-free, a great advantage for horses with respiratory problems. They are easy to measure for horses that need a very specific, measured quantity of food. They are much easier to eat than regular grains or hay, so they may be the food of choice for older horses, or horses with dental

---

THE HORSE food industry calls sweet feed "textured rations." It's the same thing.

THE HEATING process is not really cooking, which would destroy most of the vitamins; the purpose is to break down the starches and improve digestibility.

PELLETS CAN BE all grain, but many kinds include hay—or might even be all hay. Check the label. Some pelleted feeds combine hay and grain to make a "complete" food. Complete it may be—natural it is not. Some horses fed pellets develop colic.

IT IS BEST IF the grains used in pellets are coarsely, not finely ground. Finely ground grains are more dusty, less palatable, and possibly more like to cause gastrointestinal problems than coarsely ground grain.

IN EUROPE, pelleted feeds are known as "compounded nuts." Don't you find that charming?

PELLETS COME in various sizes, but as far nutrition goes, the size doesn't seem to matter. Smaller pellets do tend to be eaten more slowly, which is an advantage.

problems. Pellets also produce less waste (and less manure). Whether this is a good or bad thing is under debate. The passing of waste is a natural part of the digestive system, after all.

Also, because they contain much less molasses, pellets don't freeze in the winter as sweet feed sometimes does. Another advantage is that since they combine their ingredients in an indivisible whole, picky eaters cannot select their favorite grains and thus avoid getting complete nutrition. This is especially good for performance horses, which may need fats in their food. Horses don't naturally take to fat, so disguising the stuff in pellets is a good way to get it down painlessly.

However, it should be kept in mind that pellets are much more expensive than hay or grain. When buying pellets, deal with a source you trust. It's a lot easier to sneak bad ingredients into pellets than into grain or hay. In fact, one tempting use for bad ingredients is to put them into pellets. Horses also eat pellets faster than either traditional feeds or extruded feeds; this is especially true when horses share feed. It's better to feed pellets to horses kept separately.

Extruded Feeds

Another form of horse feed is "extruded," a process invented in 1957 by the Purina Company. (Nearly all dry dog food is now extruded.) As with pellets, grains, complete feeds, hay and supplements can all be extruded. Extruded food is actually cooked; it thus stores very well, and has a higher quantity of fat than pelleted feeds. Most reputable companies also steam-condition the feed at temperatures which are low enough not to destroy all the vitamins. Those that are destroyed must be added back by the manufacturer.

Extrusion decreases protein digestibility, although it improves the all-round digestibility of grain mixes (as opposed to complete feeds). One big advantage to extruded foods is that horses chew them much more slowly than pellets—this is a good deal for horses that bolt their food.

Extruded feeds are put under much higher pressure than pellets are; this

Extruded feed.
Courtesy Purina Mills.

is what causes them to expand. Since extruded foods are "puffed," they are about half the weight of pelleted feeds, although the companies often charge the same price per bag. In effect, you'll be paying more for less. Some horses don't like extruded foods at first, but once they get sued to them, they seem to do very well on them. They are very useful for horses prone to bloat or colic, since they have to be more thoroughly chewed than pelleted feeds.

Complete Feeds

Complete feeds, which include both forage and grain, are valuable under certain conditions, and for certain kinds of horses—notably hard keepers or horses with certain kinds of health problems. However, it is such an unnatural way to feed a horse that many horses on this diet eventually develop stable vices out of sheer boredom.

Kinds of Commercial Feeds

Every kind of concentrate you can imagine is available. For example, let's take the Purina Company. Purina produces numerous kinds of feed, including:

- Horse Chow 100—a complete mix for the recreational horses and to manage obesity. Also for ponies, miniatures and draft horses.

- Horse Chow 200—a complete mix for breeding stallions and pregnant mares

- Omolene 100—for the active pleasure horse. Also for draft horses.

- Omolene 200 Performance—a sweet feed for high-performance, pregnant and lactating mares, yearling to two-year-olds, and breeding stallions

- Omolene 300 Growth—a sweet feed for nursing foals, weanlings and yearlings

- Strategy—an all pellet feed for high performance, pregnant and lactating mares, nursing foals, weanlings to yearlings, yearlings to two-year-olds, and breeding stallions. Also for draft horses.

- Equine Junior—a complete mix for weanling to two-year-olds.

- Equine Adult —a complete mix for the recreational horse. To help manage obesity. Also for ponies, miniatures, and draft horses.

- Equine Senior—a complete mix for the older horse.

- Complete Advantage—a complete mix for high performance, also for allergy-prone or allergic horses.
- Athlete—an extruded particle supplement.

This is just one company's offering, one which is pretty typical. As you can see, you have many choices to make! Nearly all commercial grain mixes and complete feeds contain additives. These additives are put in to increase feed utilization and storability. Most also contain by-products like beet or fruit pulp, bran, hulls, molasses, or straw. Some of these are useful. Some aren't. ▪

A few of the offerings available through Purina Mills. And this is just one company! We consumers have a wide range of targeted selections for our horses. Courtesy Purina Mills.

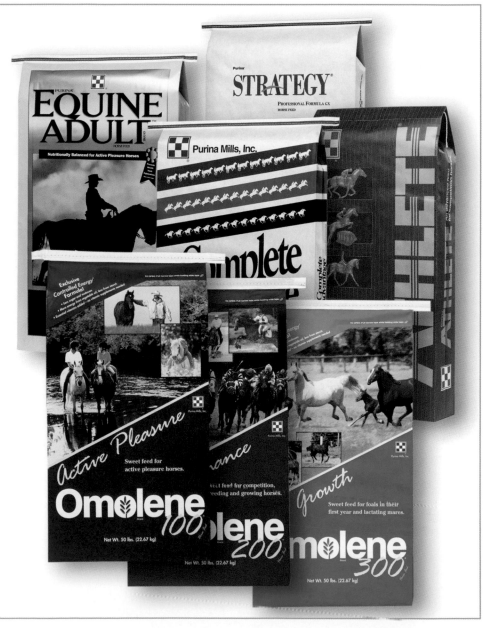

9

Feed Management

NOW THAT WE KNOW WHAT THE
basic ingredients in food are, it's time to look at
how much of it horses need—and how to give
it to them.

Amount

It seems so simple, but it's easy to forget. Your
horse must receive an adequate amount of each
critical nutrient and he must receive sufficient
energy. For example, if he doesn't get sufficient calcium, nothing can make it up. He'll suffer harmful
effects. The same is true if he doesn't get enough
protein. Or enough vitamin E. And so on. This is
called the principle of limiting nutrients. If minimum levels of these nutrients are not met, nothing
can take their place. Think of it as a chain: unless

LIKE HUMANS, horses tend to eat more in cold weather, especially more pasture grass and hay, whose fermentation produces a great deal of heat. They may even eat more than they need for their energy requirements, and in consequence of overindulgence, develop digestive or metabolic difficulties. Conversely, in hot weather, horses often prefer grain to forage, apparently not desiring the hot sticky feeling that comes with fermentation. This is especially true for working horses.

MOST NUTRITION charts divide horses into one of three broad categories: pleasure horse, working horse, or reproducing horse. Each of these requires somewhat different types and quantities of nutrients, but again, these are only general guidelines.

every link is strong, the chain breaks. The same is true for energy. If your horse doesn't get enough calories, he will gradually starve. This seems so obvious as to be not worth mentioning, still—one never knows.

How much your horse needs to eat depends upon his individual energy requirements. These requirements can vary enormously from animal to animal, depending upon size, health, ambient temperature, exercise level, breed, temperament, and a myriad of other factors. Although there are hundred of charts designed to help you figure out the specific nutrient requirements for your horse, the variables are so many that any chart can serve only as the broadest guideline.

The knowledge of what best suits your particular horse is something that only you can know. Some horses are "easy keepers," while others seem to require much more food. For example, draft horses and warmbloods are easy keepers compared to hot-blooded Arabs and Thoroughbreds.

My Morgan mare thrived on a diet that would have starved my similarly exercised Thoroughbred. No one really knows why this is so; however, it is suggested that it has something to do with glucose/insulin response which tends to vary between horses and ponies and among breeds.

On average, a horse eats between 1.5 and 2.5 percent of his body weight dry matter (DM) daily, although this can increase to up to 3.3 percent with continually pastured animals. This translates roughly to this: the average horse (average size, average workload) needs about 20 pounds of dry matter per day. This usually means something like 20 to 25 pounds of hay (90 percent DM) or 65 pounds of fresh grass for an 1,100 pound horse. (Larger horses need proportionately less food than smaller ones.) Of course, we're assuming here that the pasture has adequate nutrients; some mature hays are low in phosphorus or protein.)

At least half of what your horse eats every day should be forage (hay and pasture), and never less than one pound of forage per 100 pounds of body weight. Providing your stalled horse with hay also helps prevent boredom and concomitant stable vices like cribbing and weaving. (Horses really should be outside as much as possible for their own benefit and health. Horses kept stalled for long periods are miserable.)

So the best plan when developing a diet for your horse is to begin with the forage portion, and then add the grain part (if needed). Idle horses usually need no grain at all. Horses doing moderate work, including dressage and pleasure riding, can get along with 30 percent grain. Only hard working horses need as much as 50 percent of their calories provided by grain. These last can also benefit from a little added fat.

A low-maintenance horse of the standard weight of 1100 pounds (this standard is common because it converts easily into 500 kilograms) needs about 16,500 calories a day, 650 grams of crude protein, 22 grams of calcium, 14 grams of phosphorus, 8 grams of magnesium, 400 milligrams of zinc, 80 milligrams of copper and 15,000 IU of vitamin A.

Horses who exercise lightly have improved digestive efficiency, since exercise reduces the rate of passage through the digestive tract. This slower passage gives the system more time to digest everything thoroughly. On the other hand, hard exercise tends to depress the appetite.

The daily grain portion should be divided into two or three equal portions, with no more than half a pound per 100 pounds body weight per feeding. This will help prevent excessive gas production, laminitis and colic.

Measuring Amounts

The nutrient values of any given feed are listed as "dry matter basis" or "as fed" basis. The problem with "as fed" comparisons is that they don't allow for the different amounts of water present in the various foods. This is a much more important problem for dog owners, of course, since a can of dog food can contain over 75 percent water. All horse food is pretty dry, at least for my taste.

The dry matter count is important because when we compare nutrients, we want to discount the amount of water in the feed. The dry matter of most grains is about 90 percent. It's about 80 percent for most hay, while the dry matter content of lush grass can be as low as 20 percent. To convert as fed to dry matter, just divide the stated value of the target nutrient by the percent dry matter of the feed.

- Corn, for example, is 86 percent dry matter and 10 percent crude protein on a dry matter basis. To convert dry matter protein content to "as fed" for corn, multiply 0.10 (the decimal equivalent of 10%) by 0.86 (the decimal equivalent of 86 percent) to get 0.086, or about 8.6 percent crude protein as fed.

- To convert as fed to dry matter basis, divide by the percent of dry matter; if oats are 11.8 percent crude protein as fed and 89% dry matter, divide 0.118 by 0.89 to get 0.133, or 13.3 percent crude protein by dry matter basis.

Evaluating Your Horse's Condition

Horse weight/condition is generally graded according to a scale that goes from "very poor" to "obese"; however, these scales are only useful in a general sense. A hardworking thoroughbred is going to be thinner than a pleasure

IN A NORMAL, healthy horse, it takes a long time for a nutrient deficiency to show up. In underweight animals, however, the dangers of poor nutrition will make themselves known more quickly, since the horse has no reserves of body fat to draw upon.

THE NATIONAL Research Council publishes complete tables of various horse feeds and the nutrients they contain. If you are interested in a scientific approach to this subject, you can get a copy of this information through your county extension agent or equine veterinarian.

STRICTLY METRIC units, kilojoules, are sometimes used to report food energy. To convert kilojoules to kilocalories, divide the number of kilojoules by 4.18.

horse of a different body type. Show horses typically weigh more than endurance horses of the same breed.

A lot depends on your own eye and your riding purpose. Be honest. Does the horse look too fat or thin for his function? No horse should have bulging fat around the tailhead or withers; likewise no horse have his ribs sticking out. If you're not sure about your own horse's condition, check with an equine veterinarian or a knowledgeable friend.

A horse at proper weight and in good condition will have clear, bright eyes and a well-filled out neck. The withers will meet the back smoothly, and the spinal column should not be visible below the withers. The hips will be well rounded, and you should be able to feel, but not see the ribs. A cresty neck, especially with pony breeds, suggests that your horse is seriously overweight and at risk of founder.

How to Weigh a Horse....

Well, first you step on the bathroom scale, holding your horse carefully in your arms, then, put the horse down and weigh yourself, and then subtract— wait a minute, that won't work. Unless you have a fairly small horse. Let's think of something else.

Of course the simplest method to weigh your horse is to stick him on a livestock scale and note the result. Oh. You don't have a livestock scale. Never fear. You can trot down to the feed store and buy yourself a weight tape. This handy little device measures around the horse's girth and then allows you to figure out about how much your horse weighs based on his measurements. The result will only be approximate, but that is good enough for most feed calculations. A more cumbersome measurement that will get you more accurate results involves measuring the horse's girth at the widest point (the heart girth), then measuring the length of the horse from point of chest to point of croup. (Use inches.) Multiply girth times girth times length. (For the mathematically inclined, that's the girth squared times the length.) Then divide by 300. Then add 50. (OR you can divide by 330 and forget about adding 50 pounds. See how much fun this is?) That's the weight in pounds. One hopes.

If possible, monitor your horse's weight by repeating the above steps every few months. You will find this to be very helpful.

So Where Does a Horse Get All His Energy?

Like the rest of us, horses need energy to go about their daily business. Energy is a mysterious, almost magical substance. It has no structure, mass, or dimensions, but it is the lifespring for all living creatures. The sun is the ultimate energy source, naturally, and plants capture the sun's energy and by clever tricks like photosynthesis, change carbon dioxide and water to carbon compounds like carbohydrates and fats. Plants then draw up nitrogen from the soil. (Nitrogen was originally floating around in the air too, but has been changed to a usable form (fixed) in the soil by lightning and certain bacteria.) The nitrogen helps the plant make protein. Horses then eat the plants.

Energy is supplied by the three classes of nutrients: fats, carbohydrates and protein. That's it. Digestion breaks down the chemical bonds that hold the nutrients together, and releases energy in a form the animal can use. The magical compound is adenosine triphosphate: ATP. ATP is present in all cells (plant and animal) and it stores energy temporarily in the form of high-energy phosphate bonds. ATP is the usable form of energy for body cells.

Horses can turn food into ATP through both anaerobic and aerobic respiration. Anaerobic respiration (meaning that the process doesn't need oxygen) is quick, but not very efficient. It makes use of glucose, providing quick energy for a sprint. Aerobic respiration, while slower and requiring oxygen, can make use of fats and proteins—not just glucose. It takes longer to get going, but provides more total energy. So endurance horses can benefit more from the energy provided by fats and protein than sprinters can.

As you probably recall, energy is measured in calories. A calorie is the amount of heat energy necessary to raise the temperature of one gram of water from 14.5 degrees Celsius to 15.5 degrees Celsius. This is such a tiny amount that it's not very useful, so we usually talk about kilocalories (kcal) for gauging nutritional requirements. A kcal equals 1,000 calories. In this (and most other books on nutrition) calorie equals kcals.

The "energy density" of a food refers to number of calories in any given weight or volume of food. When a horse gets too much or too little energy in comparison to what he needs, an "energy imbalance" is created.

It stands to reason, of course, that the bigger the horse, the more he needs to eat. Other factors being equal, a half-ton horse needs about twice the calories of a quarter-ton horse. In addition, a running horse uses up twice as many calories as a fast trotting horse, and five times as many as a walking horse. Still, there are exceptions. Draft horses require 15 percent less energy to maintain their condition than would a "light breed" at the same weight. One reason is that draft horses are more tranquil in nature and have a lower metabolic rate generally.

The more fiber a food contains, the less digestible energy it has. Average quality feed has a DE of about 65 percent of the GE. That's a pretty generally rule. And the ME of most feeds is about 90 percent of the DE.

THE FIRST LAW of Thermodynamics reminds us that energy, slippery as it is, can be converted into heat (and thus measured.) The total amount of energy in food can be measured when a sample of the food is burned. This value is the "gross energy" (GE) of the food. Some food is not digested or absorbed by the body. This energy is left over in the feces. The amount absorbed, therefore, is the GE minus the amount remaining in the feces. This is called the "digestible energy" (DE). (Notice it doesn't take into account the energy lost in the urine or gastrointestinal gases.) The body, however, cannot make full use of all the energy it absorbs from the digestive tract, particularly the protein. The urea and other end products of protein metabolism present in the urine (and gas production) are higher in energy than the end products of combustion. Metabolizable energy (ME), therefore, is the energy available to the

...continues on next page

body after unused energy present in the feces and urine has been subtracted from the GE. This value is the one most frequently used when talking about the ingredients in feeds.

The ME value of any food source depends upon both the nature of the food itself and the animal who is eating it. Horses can get more energy from grass than dogs or people can, so the ME of grass is greater for horses than for either people or dogs. The FINAL number is the net energy (NE) which is the amount of energy available for the horse after all the above process and the amount of energy he needs to metabolize the food in his body. Your horse lives and works upon his NE.

Another energy term applied frequently to horses and other large animals is the "total digestible nutrients" (TDN). TDN is a measure of digestible energy expressed in units of weight or percent. TDN is the sum of digestible

...continues on next page

Protein Amounts

Pregnant mares, breeding stallions, and hardworking horses require more protein in their diets than the stall and pasture potato. In fact, well-conditioned horses in general need more protein in their diet. Partly this is because they simply have more muscle mass, and partly because that mass probably contains increased muscle protein. Working horses also lose nitrogen in their sweat (as much as 1.5 grams of nitrogen per 100 kg of body weight.) This loss may require an increase in crude protein of up to 0.5 percent (DM) in the diet. Since most working horses are on a high-energy diet, it's important for owners to make sure that the horse's diet contains enough extra protein. The horse would have to eat whole lot of hay to get the required amount of protein, probably more than he needs so far as energy is concerned. So most owners for practical reasons prefer to give their working horses a high-energy diet with increased protein instead.

(However, one study showed that growing horses getting regular exercise are better able to utilize protein and can get along with a lower protein level than their non-exercising companions, so long as the protein is good quality.)

Fat Amounts

Horses can actually thrive on a diet of 20 percent fat, but it's certainly not necessary—the average working horse does very nicely on a diet of 12 percent. As an energy supply, eight ounces of polyunsaturated oil equals about a pound and a half of whole oats or a pound and a quarter of cracked corn. The fact that fat packs more energy per unit becomes an important factor to consider when you need to increase the energy output of a small-framed horse, or one whose appetite is depressed by hard work.

If you need to use more fat and less grain as an energy source, you should also provide a calcium supplement. (This is because while cereal grains contain calcium and phosphorus, fat does not). For each half cup of fat you substitute for grain to the diet, include a tablespoon of dicalcium phosphate to help keep Trigger's phosphorus and calcium at the correct ratio.

Frequency

Because a horse's stomach can hold only between two and four gallons of material, including saliva (of which the horse produces a vast amount to cope with the dry hay he eats), providing your horse multiple feedings, rather than trying to cram it all down in fell swoop, is a good idea. If the stomach is packed, the sheer volume forces the food into the small intestine before it is sufficiently broken down. Then you get more problems. The digestive system works best when the stomach is about two-thirds full.

There's another reason to feed your horse small frequent meals. The upper part of your horse's tummy consists of non-glandular, squamous cells; these cells are particularly sensitive to the hydrochloric acid secreted by the stomach. A moderately full stomach tends to absorb the hydrochloric acid and keep it away from this sensitive area. A horse fed less often will have periods when his stomach is empty and is much more prone to stomach ulcers.

In short, feeding more frequent, smaller meals are vastly beneficial to your horse's digestive system, because it is more natural. Every horse should eat at least twice a day, for both physiological and psychological reasons. Infrequent feedings can also disrupt the life cycle of beneficial intestinal bacteria, which are designed to have a constant supply of food. Without the right bacteria, your horse's supply of B vitamins is reduced, and he will not be able to digest fiber.

Regularity

Horses like to be fed on time. They like it so much that they begin snorting, neighing, stamping and pawing at their stall doors if it is late. (Consider how difficult it is for a hoofed animal to paw at all. Only hunger could drive him to such a feat. Ahem.) Regular feeding not only makes your horse happy, however. It is good for him. In fact, it has been estimated that regular feeding of grains can increase its digestibility by 40 percent. That's nothing to snort at. Irregular feeding also leads to wood chewing, weaving, and other stable vices. If possible, the feeding should be done at equally spaced intervals. Feeding horses in a quiet atmosphere will reduce the chances of digestive upset.

Hay or Grain First?

You will hear arguments on both sides of this issue, but it probably doesn't make much difference. However, the hay-first advocates point out that hay fills the stomach more quickly than grain does. This stimulates the digestive enzymes, which will be thus be in full "battle gear" to deal with the less natural grain. It is true that if your horse is a bolter, feeding hay first may make him less hungry. But maybe not. Studies seem to show different results about this issue. So, you may be pleased to know that hay and grain can probably be fed together. It's certainly easier that way. However, studies do indicate that if you are giving your horse an essential amino acid supplement, he can utilize it better if it fed after the hay portion of the meal has been consumed.

In any case, be sure the horse has clean fresh water available at all times while he eats.

Changing Your Horse's Diet

The big rule is: Not too fast. It takes about three weeks for the horse's cecum to build up enough of the right microbes to handle a new food. (Not every microbe likes every kind of grain.) If the food is not properly digested, a

carbohydrates, plus digestible protein, plus digestible fats times 2.25. TDN is not as accurate a gauge as net energy or metabolizable energy, but is a number readily available for horse feeds and for many years was the most commonly used term. However, more accurate measurements are now available.

DM REFERS TO dry matter, the amount of all material a horse consumes except water. For convenience's sake, we often talk about measuring food in the "as fed" form, which, of course, includes the water normally present in grains and grasses. However, this is unscientific, since every batch of grain or grass differs in the amount of water it contains. So for technical purposes, we use the term dry matter to talk about the contents of a feed. Obviously, moist grass contains so much more water than hay that a larger amount of it must be eaten to get the same nutrition. In a similar way, horses fed on a diet of hay need more water than those eating grass.

compaction will result, and your horse can come down with colic. So, to be perfectly safe, you should take about a month to change over the grains. Replace about a quarter of the old feed with the feed each week until by the end of the month, the horse is on the all-new diet.

Handling and Storing Horse Feeds and Supplements

Oils

Most oils are subject to rapid oxidation and become rancid quickly. They should be sealed, kept away from light and heat, and not shaken up before adding to food. (Shaking increases the amount of oxygen that gets into it.)

Grains

Unprocessed grains can last a good while—say about a year if they are properly stored. Processed grains, whose seed hulls have been cracked, are much more perishable, especially if they include molasses. Products with molasses generally last only about three months. You can expect a shelf life of twice that with dry processed grains, especially those in pellet or extruded forms. Products with added fat also have a short shelf life. Remember that fats are unstable and spoil faster than anything else. Most grains have a "fed by" tag. Pay attention to it.

Hay

Hay is pretty durable stuff, and if properly cured, baled, and stored, it will last inside a barn for a good year. However, vitamin depletion will continue during storage. Keeping hay in the dark helps preserve its vitamin content.

Feeding Methods

Although horses naturally graze with their heads down, it is common practice to attach a feed tub at about chest height in the stall to make cleaning easier. Feed tubs should be non-breakable, non-porous, and easy to clean. They should have rounded or rolled edges to prevent injury. A deep feed

tub is less likely to spill. Higher feed tubs are also less likely to become contaminated from urine or manure, and are in less danger of being tipped over. They are usually safe enough, although horses with a respiratory tract infection should be allowed to feed with their heads down so that the nasal passages can drain naturally during feeding.

Belmont Tubs. Courtesy Dan's Saddlery.

Horses are herd animals, as we all know, and studies have shown that horses who eat in the company of other horses—or at least who can see them while they eat—dine more happily and less stressfully. They also seem to drop less feed.

Many people like to put their horse's hay in a rack and have the horse pull the hay down. It's very true that horses won't be able to soil the hay when using such a contraption, but it forces them to eat at an unnatural angle. Any dust or other irritants in the hay also will go directly into the horse's eyes and nose. Horses who are confined to their stalls for long periods should be fed dampened hay and feeds to reduce the dust problem, which can cause all kind of respiratory ailments. A water/molasses mix not only dampens, but sweetens feeds. As for hay, you can stick the horse's hay supper in a dampened burlap bag for a couple of hours before dinnertime to reduce the dustiness. This is one time when stemmy hay is preferable to the leafy kind—less dust associated with it. If you do use a hayrack, place it so that the bottom of the rack reaches about the point of the horse's shoulder.

Horses with dinner companions—the company of other horses—dine more happily and even seem to drop less feed. Helen Peppe photo

DON'T FEED your horse large amounts of feed before exercise. Hay especially can make a horse feel full and cranky.

BE SURE TO thoroughly clean any trough that has held cattle feed. Cattle feed often contains ingredients which are toxic to horses, and even a residue could cause serious harm.

NEVER STORE dampened feed for more than 12 hours; it can go moldy in that time.

TO AVOID wasting hay, try chopping it up. This keeps a horse from picking and choosing his favorite parts (usually the seed heads) and letting the rest fall to the ground. In any case, a hay tub is the answer to fighting waste. Hay that might otherwise fall uneaten to the ground will simply end up in the bottom of the tub and be taken in with the next mouthful.

ONCE AN OLDER horse begins to lose weight, it's really hard to put it back on.

When mixing feed, be sure to do a thorough job of it. Mixing carefully will prevent a horse from simply selecting the morsels he likes and ignoring the others.

Feeding Outdoors

Place the feed tub well away from any gates, especially if you have more than one horse. The last thing you want is bunch of hungry horses charging at the gate as you arrive with their dinner. Sooner or later they'll be out and all over the neighborhood.

If possible, situate the feeding tub out of the wind. This only makes sense, but it's amazing how many people forget.

Just because you feed your horse outdoors, doesn't mean you can forget about cleaning and taking care of the feed tub. This may require some scraping, especially if you use sweet feed. It's also a good idea to make slit in the bottom so that the rainwater can drain out of it. If it does rain on the feed, clean it out and provide fresh food for your horses.

If feeding more than one horse, spread the hay out in separate piles so than fights don't break out. It's especially important to provide special places for new horses to feed. (New horses should also be quarantined in a separate paddock for a few days in case they have worms that you don't want dropping in your good pasture.) You can introduce one of your older horses in with the new horse; when they make friends, the new horse will have a "buddy," who, even if he won't protect him, will at least provide a little moral support.

Special Cases

Geriatric Horses

Geriatric horses need special consideration. Their teeth are often in poor condition, especially if they have been grazing on sandy soil. They also

lose teeth as they age. Old horses even lose elasticity in the lower lip, which makes it more difficult for them to obtain food. If they are ill or arthritic, they may not feel like eating as much. Cold and hot weather also affects them more severely than it does younger animals. When it becomes a great deal of work to eat, many older horses just don't want to go to the trouble.

A fence feeder. Courtesy Dan's Saddlery

And because their digestive systems aren't as effective as they used to be, older horses need 10 to 20 percent more calories just to sustain their weight. They also need more protein, more calcium, and more phosphorus than young adult horses.

Pamper your older horse with food he loves, and take good care of his teeth and joints. He has served you well—now it's your turn. If your older horse has trouble eating, ground or pelleted food can make things easier for him. You can add molasses to it to make help soften the stuff and make it even easier to chew. Add vegetable oil for extra calories. Hay should be cubed or dampened. If the hay you are feeding is not alfalfa, and the horse's grain diet is low in protein, add soybean meal as a supplement. And it may be a good idea to feed your older horse separately from aggressive younger ones to make sure he is getting his full share.

In cold weather, many old horses can benefit from some (not too much) extra fat in the diet. Adding a lot extra all at once can induce diarrhea. You might also consider adding some cooked barley to the feed.

Weight Watchers for Horses

It's pretty easy for a horse to become overweight. They are programmed to eat pretty much all the time, but in the natural state they walk around a lot munching on low calorie grasses. The combination of diet and exercise kept them thin. Today, however, many horses are stalled for a good part of the day, and fed high-quality hay and grain. The combination of smorgasbord, lack of exercise, and boredom is a sure recipe for weight gain. In fact, many people supply extra hay just to keep the horse from getting bored and chewing his stall door to pieces. It's not an especially good trade.

Fat is as dangerous in horses as it is in human beings. Fat horses are ill suited to work and prone to more diseases, including founder and fatty tumor in the abdomen which can twist around the intestines. Obese horses have higher heart rates, higher respiratory rates, and recover more slowly from exercise than normal-weight horses.

The only practical and safe way to reduce the weight of an obese horse is through a combination of diet and exercise, just as with people. When a horse exercises as well as diets, he increases his energy expenditure, making weight loss easier. Even when he is resting, a well-exercised horse will continue to expend energy at a higher rate than a horse that just stands around most of the time. Moderate exercise actually decreases the appetite, so even a pastured horse will tend to eat less. A well-exercised horse won't lose bone or muscle during his diet, something you really have to worry about with a non-exercising horse. In fact, it is actually dangerous to starve an obese animal, particularly a pony, into thinness. Sudden weight loss can provoke

DON'T TRY TO put a mare on a diet within a few weeks of the breeding date; it can affect her fertility.

ADDING OAT OR sunflower hulls to the diet is an excellent way to increase bulk without adding extra calories.

severe metabolic problems like hyperlipidosis (excess fat in the blood serum or tissues), especially in ponies.

Some people actually suggest muzzling a horse on pasture. Wire-mesh muzzles are available that restrict, but don't entirely prevent, a horse from grazing. The horse must nibble the grass through the muzzle, which obviously cuts down on the amount of feed that he can consume. This has always sounded inhumane to me, although I confess I had a friend who tried it on her Quarter Horse with great success.

Horses are smart, however, and most seem to automatically increase their physical activity on their own (if possible) when they are over-fed. People and dogs aren't like that! That's why a horse fed a high-energy food prances, bucks, or runs away. Hence the expression—feeling one's oats. Oats in particular seem to produce this effect in horses. (You never hear about feeling one's pizza.) More ominously, overfed young horses can develop orthopedic problems relating to faster-than-normal bone skeletal development. If a horse gets too much nutrition all at once, (from overindulging in the unlocked grain-bin, say) of course, he's also in trouble. Such a horse can develop colic, acute laminitis, or severe diarrhea. If the horse eats too much over a long period instead, he will accumulate the excess as body fat (just like we do).

If a horse overeats enough to be become actually obese, his health is at risk. It may interfere with proper gaiting and locomotion, optimal function of the respiratory and cardiac systems, and a reduced ability to fight infectious diseases. Exercise your overweight horse gently at a walk or trot while your are reducing his caloric intake to about 50 to 75 percent of what he would need if he were at his ideal weight.

Underweight Horses

Horses don't have to be emaciated to be underweight. And underweight horses, even if they are not starving, are not in good condition. Because they don't have enough body fat to serve as reserve energy for prolonged activity, they have lower muscle glycogen and decreased performance.

If your horse needs to gain weight, it usually means that grain has to be added to the rations, for the simple mechanical reason that a horse can only eat so much hay, which is very low in nutrient value. Grain is much richer and can be taken in a much smaller volume to supply the same number of calories. However, grain should be increased only gradually to prevent intestinal problems.

- The horse must be free of any mechanical problem that prevents proper digestion. Dental problems are a likely cause.

- The horse must be free of any psychological stress that prevents proper digestion.

If a horse is inadequately fed, he begins to draw on its own reserves of carbohydrates (e.g. glycogen), fats and proteins in that order. Inadequate protein results in decreases of liver and plasma proteins, degeneration of the gastrointestinal tract, loss of immunity, breakdown of the respiratory system, impairment of the heart, and degeneration of the skeletal muscles, pretty much in that order. None of this is pretty. Feed your horse correctly!

In trying to rebuild an emaciated horse, it's a good idea to add salt to his feed. Not only does he need it, but also it will make him thirsty. This is a good thing because a starved horse may eat enough dry food in a hurry to cause an impaction. Sufficient water removes this risk. And of course, it is wise to increase the amount of food gradually to avoid diarrhea and colic as well. Feed the starving horse small meals at least four times a day. He should get as much calories from grain as from forage at this stage.

To increase a horse's weight, you'll have to add concentrated calories in the form of grains and even fat, remembering, however, that half the diet should remain forage for his intestinal health. Do not, however, pour molasses or other sweeteners in his food. You may be thinking you are helping, but such an unaccustomed loading of sugar can send an emaciated horse into "sugar shock," and throw him into a coma.

Try giving him a food formulated for broodmares and growing horses. If he is in very poor condition, it is wise to feed him only one-third the amount he would need if he were at his best weight. This seems cruel, and one's instinct is to stuff the horse, but this would be a big dietary error. Stick with one-third the amount divided into four feedings for the first week. You can then gradually increase it until the horse is getting twice the maintenance-at-ideal-weight amount. Then reduce to the amount over a week or so to the optimum.

All of us have seen our share of starved and underfed horses. While I am sure no one reading this book has allowed her own horse to get in that condition, many of us have rescued such animals from abusive and neglectful homes. It is a tough challenge. It can be more difficult to put weight on a horses than to take it off, and it does take time to build up an emaciated horse. In fact, on the average, a horse can safely gain only about a half pound a day (that is only about 21 pounds in six weeks), so patience is required.

Many horses are underweight not only because of poor feeding, but also because they may have a heavy parasite or worm infestation. Obviously, you'll need to take care of this problem first, before you can address the weight problem.

ALTHOUGH legume hay is full of good nutrition, it may give a horse loose bowel movements if he is not used to it. In that case, cut back on the legume and replace with high-quality grass hay.

SINCE MANY emaciated horses lack the intestinal flora to manufacture B complex vitamins on their own, it may be wise to feed a supplement. The same can be true with fat-soluble vitamins; after all, if a horse has no fat tissue, he is going to have a hard time storing fat-soluble vitamins.

DR. RAY GEOR, a diplomate of the American College of Veterinary Internal Medicine, and a nutrition consultant, suggests increasing the both the quality and quantity of roughage, and then adding fat. Insufficient roughage in the diet can lead to gastric ulcers, colic, and other digestive problems. (The constant chewing horses do while eating roughage produces saliva that helps neutralize stomach acid.) Since horses eat grain about twice as fast as they heat, they only produce half as much saliva.

In addition to abused horses, heavily exercised horses may also have trouble keeping flesh. Sometimes they need twice as many calories as an idle horse. You'll simply have to provide enough to keep your performance horse fit. Older horses also generally need more calories to maintain condition.

The key is patience. A horse doesn't lose condition overnight, and you can't restore him to the proper weight and condition in a week or two. Feeding a horse too much too fast can turn a horse "hot," and unmanageable. If your horse turns "hot" with more food, you'll need to provide him more exercise (both more work and more turn-out time). Not enough exercise to make him lose the weight you want him to put on, but enough to take "the edge" off. It's a delicate compromise, but it can be done.

Supplemental fat is also a good idea for this type of horse. Fat cannot be used as readily as carbohydrates for immediate energy, so the horse can gain more weight without getting overly hot. (Unfortunately, the hot that tends to get hot is usually the same horse that is difficult to keep weight on. Part of the blame lies with inherited temperament and can't always be controlled by diet. Some people get great results by adding beet pulp to the grain ration.

Greedy Horses

Let's face it, some horses are just pigs. Instead of munching daintily on tender bits of grass as they stroll sedately about a lush meadow—they tear chunks of hay from a bale and devour them as if they were wolves ripping flesh from a carcass. Not only is such behavior unattractive, it can be dangerous. For one thing, horses that are ripping and tearing are not chewing. Swallowing grain whole makes it unlikely that the stuff will ever get digested properly. And on a more mundane level, a piggish horse can end up choking on his food.

To slow down a gobbling horse, intersperse grain with hay, which perforce takes longer to chew. As I mentioned earlier, you can also put a big clean chain or large smooth rocks in among the grain; the horse will have to take the time to eat around it. It may also be a good idea to feed bolting horses extruded foods rather than grains or pellets; they chew them more slowly, and so are less likely to get colic.

Picky Horses

The opposite of a greedy horse is picky one. Sometimes horses have a perfectly good reason not to eat. Perhaps their teeth hurt, or there's a sore in the mouth. Perhaps the sudden loss of appetite is due to a food change, or a change in surroundings. And of course, ill health, especially upper respiratory problems that affect the sense of smell, often leads to lack of appetite. Lonely or depressed horses seem to lose interest in their food. Other times, it just seems to be a whim. (Fillies in particular tend to be picky eaters.) You might want to try these dandy taste-enhancers if your horse seems to go off his feed:

- Bits of cooked barley or other grain sweetened with molasses
- Salt
- Peppermint

Although sugar such as found in molasses is a treat to many horses, this isn't always the case. About 20 percent of horses, undoubtedly for health reasons, do not deign to eat sweets at all.

Feeding for Breeding

Before Breeding

Technically, mares about to be bred don't require more or different nutrition than do horses not destined for breeding. Still, you can increase the chances of success if you step up her nutrition a month or two before the breeding. Better early nutrition helps both the estrus cycle and the chance of the breeding to "take." (In nature, most horses come into estrus in the early summer when the grasses are at their peak nutrition.) It has been shown that inadequate nutrition is one of chief causes of infertility in mares.

It doesn't make much sense to spend thousands of dollars on a valuable mare, only to skimp on her nutrition to save yourself a little money.

When feeding grain, many experts recommend that the grain be whole, heavy oats rather than corn. This traditional feed is very safe. Barley is another good choice. If you decide to feed corn, use a half corn/half oats mixture.

Feeding Level for Pregnant Mares

It is very important that early-stage pregnant mares have good nutrition; in fact, proper feeding in the 18th to the 35th day of pregnancy prevents early embryonic death. Mares on low-quality diets are much more likely to re-absorb the fetus. If the deficiency continues throughout the pregnancy, the mare is not only more likely to have a smaller foal, but one suffering from skeletal deformities, a reduced immune system, high risk of disease, and poor brain development. All this should be enough to convince you not to starve a pregnant mare. Energy requirements, however, do not increase much before the last three months of gestation. This is because during the early months the fetus is undergoing differentiation and not massive growth. In fact, for about the first three months, a pregnant mare needs no more food than a non-pregnant one.

During pregnancy, the average mare will increase her weight by about 15 percent. During eighth or ninth month, as the foal begins to develop very rapidly, the mare's needs rise as well. If these needs are not met, the parasitic little foal will pull what he needs, especially calcium, right from his mother's own bones and tissues. (You certainly don't want that to happen.) A mare in her eleventh month consumes 1.20 times what she needs for maintenance in her pre-pregnant state. (It's 1.13 times during the tenth month, and 1.10 times during the ninth.) In the later stages of pregnancy an 1100 pound mare needs about 19,600 calories per day. One of the reasons for this is that the growing fetus is gaining about a pound a day!

Grain is especially helpful in the later stage of pregnancy, when the fetus is doing about 65 percent of its growth. Feed your late-stage pregnant mare about a pound of grain per 100 pounds of body weight. If necessary, you may have to decrease her hay portion a bit (down to 1 or 1.5 pounds/per 100 pounds body weight) in order for her to have room for the grain. In total, a late-stage pregnant mare ought to be eating about two and half pounds of combined grain and hay per hundred pounds of body weight. Split the grain into a least two servings, and give her free access to good forage or pasture (at least 10 percent crude protein)—that should take care of it. One reason for increased grain is that as the mare's womb expends, there is less room for the long, drawn-out process of digesting fiber.

As the foaling time draws nearer, it often helps to increase the percentage of grain your mare gets to make sure she is receiving sufficient calories. Never forget, though, that grains are low in calcium, which is critical to your mare and her fetus. This is why calcium supplements are important.

During the final three months of pregnancy, mares need to increase their protein intake to at least 11 percent crude protein in the feed. This translates to about 45 grams per 1,000 calories of digestible energy. This is the bare minimum. Choose a concentrate with a protein level of 14 to 16 percent, especially if your mare is pastured on grass or gets grass hay.

Lactation

Due to the demands of milk production, a lactating mare will require up to 80 percent more digestible energy than she did before she became pregnant. (Converting nutrients into milk is not as efficient as you might think.) This is where a lot of owners err—they overfeed a pregnant mare, and underfeed a lactating one. This makes no sense whatever, but people do it anyway.

She also needs 60 percent more protein, and as much as 66 percent more calcium. This is more than a horse doing performance work. In addition, lactating mares need more phosphorus and vitamin A. This requirement can largely be fulfilled by putting mares on high-quality fresh pasture and a high-quality concentrate. Vegetable oil can be added to increase fat.

A lactating mare can easily produce four gallons of milk a day—and a young foal will suckle over a hundred times a day. That's a lot! But if a mare is inadequately fed during this time, she will rapidly lose weight and condition in the three months following foaling. Under-conditioned mares are less likely to make an early return to estrus. Of course, most amateur horse owners don't choose to re-breed their mare right away, but if your mare doesn't go into a foal heat, it's a signal she has not received sufficient nutrition.

Water

Similarly, lactating mares require more water than formerly, since milk is largely composed of water. Light breeds produce milk to equal about 3 percent of their body weight during the first three months of lactation, and 2 percent for the remainder of lactation. Ponies average 4 percent and 3 percent, respectively. All this milk-production requires water, of course. An 1,100 pound mare can produce about 30 to 35 pints of milk a day, an amount which increases her need for water by 50 to 75 percent.

Protein

The mare's greatest protein needs come during the first three months of lactation, when the percentage of crude protein in her diet should be at least 13 percent; in most cases you will need to supplement. Obviously, they need the extra protein to produce milk. A lactating mare can produce 30 pounds or more of milk per day. (For some reason, the milk of large animals always seems to come out in pounds rather than gallons, as one might think. Anyway, there are a little over 8 pounds in a gallon.)

DO NOT OVERFEED your pregnant mare! Obese mares may produce foals with limb problems (not proven, but strongly believed by many); in addition, obese mares are less likely to get pregnant again during the next heat cycle.

A BREEDING stallion needs 12 to 15 percent more food than a gelding, at least 20,500 calories per day. This is especially true if he is around a lot of mares. It seems to make males nervous to be around a lot of females. For some reason. For some stallions, this need continues even after the breeding season. Their diets should include about 800 grams of protein, 25 grams of calcium, 18 grams of phosphorus, 9 grams magnesium, 340 micrograms of zinc, 85 micrograms of copper, and 22,000 IU vitamin A. Older stallions may require more calcium in order to keep up bone density.

CONSTIPATION
*can be problem with
lactating mares. To
prevent this, give
her adequate exer-
cise. Linseed meal
may act as a laxa-
tive in addition to
serving as a protein
supplement.*

ALTHOUGH A
*new mother does
need more grain,
giving an excess in
the first ten days
puts the foal at risk
of milk scours, a
severe diarrhea.*

By the time a foal is three months old and eating solid food more frequently, the protein in a mare's feed can be cut back to normal levels. In rare cases, the mare's milk may be over-rich in calcium, causing epiphysitis in the foal. In such circumstances, the mare's rations should be reduced to slow milk production, or else the foal should be supplemented with phosphorus to correct the imbalance. In some cases, you may have to wean the foal early.

The mare's feed should include sufficient amounts of lysine and methionine, amino acids needed in large amounts by the growing foal. Soybean meal is an excellent source of these essential amino acids. Begin feeding your average-sized horse (1,100 pounds) about a pound (0.5 kg) soybean meal during the last two weeks of pregnancy and 1.5 pounds (0.7 kg) during lactation. You may also choose to use high protein (16-18 percent) pellets.

Fat

One study added a supplement of 5 percent feed-grade animal fat to the diet of brood mares. The result was a higher pregnancy rate and a quicker return to estrus after foaling. It could not be determined, however, whether the higher rate was due to the fat itself, or the extra calories that it naturally supplied. More controlled studies need to be done before drawing any conclusions. It is known that lactating mares that have fat added to their diets have a richer milk, which may in turn make foals grow faster. Whether or not this is a good thing is a matter of opinion.

Minerals

CALCIUM: A pregnant mare in the later stages of pregnancy needs nearly twice the amount of calcium (and hence phosphorus) that a non-pregnant mare does, even though her total energy requirements are increased by only 15 or 20 percent. A pregnant mare in the last stage of pregnancy needs 35-37 grams of calcium per day; this extra calcium goes right to the fetus. If extra dietary calcium is not provided, the fetus will draw what it needs from the mare's bone reserves. Lactating mares need about 56 grams a day during the first three months and 36 grams a day between three months and weaning. At foaling, calcium requirements increase by up to 66 percent above normal in response to the forthcoming lactation. Older brood mares are especially likely to need a supplement, since calcium absorption decreases with age. The ideal calcium phosphorus mix is 0.4 percent calcium and 0.3 percent phosphorus.

PHOSPHORUS: Pregnant and lactating mares also have an increased need for phosphorus, at least by the time she reaches the latter stages of pregnancy. (For the first eight months, her requirements are the same as a maintenance horse.) Towards the end, her requirements nearly double to about 36 grams of calcium and 28 grams of phosphorous per day. A deficiency in phosphorus during the last three months of pregnancy can produce

negative effects on the skeletal development of the foal. Many legume-based pastures (and hence alfalfa hay) are so high in calcium that a relative deficiency in phosphorus results.

When she is nursing, her phosphorus needs depend on the amount of milk she is producing. In general the greatest need is during the first three months of lactation, when the mare needs about 36 grams per day, decreasing to 22 grams a day after three months. Pregnant mares should receive approximately 36 grams of calcium to 27 grams of phosphorus—or thereabouts for a calcium: phosphorus ratio of 0.4 percent calcium and 0.3 percent phosphorus (1.3:1).

POTASSIUM: Mares in early pregnancy require no more potassium than non-pregnant horses, that is about 25 grams per day. However, mares in the last stage of pregnancy require about 31 grams of potassium per day.

A lactating mare needs about 46 grams of potassium, nearly as much as a performance horse. (The difference is that the mare is probably not sweating as much.) However, a mare on forage is getting more than enough potassium, since a pound of grass hay contains about 6.7 grams of potassium. Lactating mares on a high potassium/low magnesium diet are subject to tetany (intermittent muscle spasms).

ZINC AND COPPER: A pregnant mare's need for zinc and copper remain the same as a non-pregnant mare. However, while a pregnant mare doesn't need any extra copper for herself, new studies indicate that a copper supplement is important for the foal, and that this supplement is best administered (if possible) to the mare rather than to the foal.

MAGNESIUM: The pregnant mare's need for magnesium goes up slightly, from 7.5 or 8 grams per day to about 9.4 grams in the last three months of pregnancy.

IODINE (I): Sufficient iodine is necessary for a mare's normal heat cycle. But too much can be a particular problem with pregnant mares. In fact, iodine toxicity has been seen in pregnant mares consuming as little as 40 mg per day. Both mares and their foals have suffered from goiter due to the excess. In many cases, the excess was associated with a large supplement of kelp in the diet. On the other hand, mares who are iodine deficient are likely to give birth to foals who will not survive. Thus it is important to watch the iodine intake carefully. (Some studies indicate that iodine-deficient stallions have low sex drive and poor-quality sperm.)

IRON: Pregnant and lactating mares need about 50 ppm of iron in their diets, as opposed to 40 ppm for maintenance horses. Most forages contain plenty of iron.

SELENIUM: Mares in the last three months of pregnancy and lactation does better with 0.1 or 0.2 mg/kg selenium in the diet. This is twice the amount needed for an idle horse. Of course, this doesn't mean you should start pouring selenium down your mare's throat. The stuff is toxic in excess.

Vitamins

VITAMIN A: A pregnant or lactating mare needs nearly twice the vitamin A as a non-pregnant horse, especially during the last quarter of pregnancy. This is critically important. Not only is it required for the bone development of the growing fetus, it is also necessary for the production of milk. The brood mare can easily use up all her stored vitamin A during this period, since the most stressful period of pregnancy can occur during the winter months, when green pasture is not available in many places.

In addition, beta-carotene, the precursor to vitamin A, is important for ovulation and the maintenance of pregnancy. Studies have shown that mares lacking fresh pasture may benefit from injections (not oral) doses of beta-carotene to improve their conception rate. At least, that's the way it worked with pigs.

B-COMPLEX VITAMINS: It has been shown in human beings that pregnant women benefit from a folic acid supplement. The same has not been shown in horses, which usually get plenty of the stuff in grass; however, it wouldn't hurt anything to add a little to the diet. It is generally included in vitamin supplements, anyway.

VITAMIN D: Although most horses get enough vitamin D if they are in sunlight and eat sun-cured hay, pregnant and lactating mares can benefit from a safe commercial supplement.

VITAMIN E: This is an essential vitamin for breeding horses. It has been established that pregnant and lactating mares need about 100 IU per pound of diet DM per day, and most horse people firmly believe that it helps the stallion as well. The mare can pass along this important vitamin on to her foal. Many commercial supplements contain daily dosages of about 2,000 IU, which is three or four times what a broodmare actually needs. On the other hand, vitamin E is non-toxic, so you can't overdose on it.

Vitamin E supplements may be especially useful for mares kept on dry forage.

VITAMIN K: This vitamin is particularly essential around foaling time, since a lot of blood may be lost. You may wish to supplement if you are not sure your pasture is well supplied with the stuff. ■

11

Feeding the Foal and Young Horse

AT NO TIME IS NUTRITION MORE important to a horse than when he is just a foal. This is only common sense, but it is a fact sadly and often overlooked by many horse owners until the damage done by malnutrition is too extensive to be corrected.

A foal's first food is the highly digestible colostrum, the milk produced during the first day of lactation. It is an important source of vital nutrients, including vitamin A and the protein substances called immunoglobulins (antibodies). Colostrum has twice the calories and five times the protein of mature milk. The average foal will take in between 5 and 9 pints of this invaluable substance within 12 hours after he is born.

Colostrum supplies more than calories; it also provides antibodies that were concentrated in the dam's udder during the last two weeks of pregnancy. This will protect your foal against common diseases for the first few weeks of his life. The mare produces colostrum for two or three days; but most of the antibodies are passed within 12 or 14 hours. After the first twelve hours the digestive tract of the foal changes so he can no longer absorb the immunoglobulins.

The stomach of foals is comparatively larger than it is in adult horses, mostly because the stomach has a big role in digesting milk.

Immature horses have incompletely developed cecal and colonic digestive ability. Before a foal is three months old, in fact, he has very little microbial digestion at all. This is one reason why foals require a comparatively low-fiber diet, one they can easily digest in the stomach, or foregut.

Newborn foals tend to nurse up to five to seven times an hour, usually for short periods, maybe only a minute or so. It is thought that the frequent suckling protects the gut lining against bacterial invasion for the first few days of life. A nursing foal will eat 25 to 30 percent of his body weight a day. After the first week, the nursing frequently goes down to two or three times an hour.

A foal begins to show interest in food other than mama's milk by the time he is a week old, and by three weeks or so, he will most certainly be taking

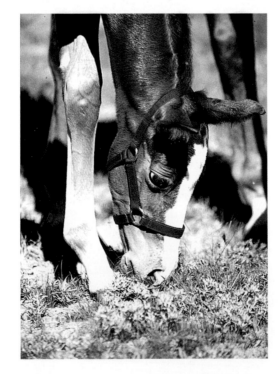

nibbles of whatever he can get. This is a good thing, since mama horse will very soon be running out of the ability to provide complete nutrients for the fast-growing foal. A three-month foal of average size needs a little over 12 pounds of food a day—14,600 calories of digestible energy. A mare's milk supplies only about 6,800 of those calories. Foals also need 730 grams of protein (480 supplied in the milk), 35 grams of calcium (11 supplied in the milk), and 20 grams of phosphorus (7 supplied in the milk). During the first month of

By three weeks of age or so, a foal will be taking nibbles of whatever he can get.
Helen Peppe photo.

life a foal can gain 4 pounds a day!

As far as grain goes, it's better to buy a commercial feed specially designed for foals. These feeds have high-quality protein and are low in fiber. I strongly urge you to do this, since a mistake in feeding foals is often irreversible.

The mare should be on pasture while nursing if at all possible. This will give the foal a chance to explore his grassy new world. He needs both the exercise and the vitamin E of green grass.

Grain for Foals

As the foal grows, he might have to worry about his mother stealing his portion of grain. Horses aren't as moral in this regard as they might be. To prevent this thievery, it's best to install a creep feeder so the foal can get dinner while mother must look on in envy. It's important to make sure the creep feeder is secure from the predatory efforts of the mare. The result might be more than a deprived foal—the mare could develop colic or even laminitis after a sudden unfettered access to rich food. Most experts suggest the creep feed ration be about 20 percent protein. Foals are one of the few classes of horses that can readily benefit from a protein supplement. Replace the feed daily, since you don't want to encourage over-eating: foals allowed to free-feed are at increased risk of developmental orthopedic disease. Besides, feed should not be left there day after day to spoil or get wet in the rain. Figure out want you need to feed your foal, and give him that amount and no more.

It should be stated that some experts object to creep feeding on the basis it that will allow the foal to grow too rapidly; of course, this depends entirely upon how much feed you supply to the foal. One great advantage of early creep feeding concentrates is that it makes the transition at weaning a lot easier; the foal will be less likely to suffer deficiencies that sometimes occur because of a reluctance to eat new food.

What you choose to feed your foal depends largely upon the quality of pasture available. For example, protein supplements can vary from 16 to 30 percent. More protein is not always better—it depends on how

When the mare is on pasture, it gives her foal a chance to explore his grassy new world. Helen Peppe photo.

EACH FOAL HAS an optimum growth rate. However, the optimum growth rate is not the fastest growth rate. Do not try to push your foal into growing faster than his natural destiny calls for. If you do, you are asking for all kinds of developmental orthopeidc problems.

THIS USUALLY means between 5 and 8 pounds of high energy (14.5 to 16 percent protein) feed per day in addition to plenty of good-quality forage.

much protein is available in your horse's forage. You may decide your foal just need more calories, not more protein. No one can make the decision but yourself, based upon what you already know about your pasture and hay.

The greatest danger young foals face, however, is not insufficient nutrition—it's too much. Well-meaning but ill-informed owners tend over feed their foals in hopes of faster growth and stronger bones; what they often end up with is developmental orthopedic disease. It is unwise and dangerous to attempt to improve too much upon nature. You wouldn't stuff your children full of food in a misguided attempt to make them grow faster; the same is true of horses. Respect your horse's natural growth rate and feed him in a way that supports, not forces, that growth. Too many calories might make your foal fat, but excessive caloric intake also contributes to osteochondrosis by reducing bone density and cortical thickness. The scary thing is that it is nearly impossible to see the effects of developmental bone disease until irreversible damage has already occurred.

Vitamins

Vitamin A:

Like all fat-soluble vitamins, vitamin A doesn't transport well across the placenta, so all foals are born with a deficiency of vitamin A. In fact vitamin A deficiency is more common in foals than in any other class of horses. Under normal circumstances, if the mare has been receiving sufficient amounts of fat soluble vitamins, the colostrum will make up for the deficiency, but foals not receiving a sufficient amount of colostrum may suffer diarrhea. Weanlings should receive about 8,000 IU per day and yearlings about 15,000. Over supplementation should be avoided, however, as more than 20,000 IU per day may actually decrease growth in young horses. A diet including green pasture or good-quality hay probably supplies sufficient vitamin A (actually its precursor beta-carotene) for even growing horses.

Vitamin B Complex:

Many experts recommend adding B complex vitamin's to the weanling's diet. They can be added in the form of brewer's yeast.

VITAMIN D:

Although most horses get plenty of vitamin D if they spend time in the sunshine and eat sun-cured hay, young, growing horses can benefit from a safe commercial supplement.

VITAMIN E:

It has been suggested that weanling foals be given a supplement of 250 to 300 IU per day.

VITAMIN K:

Newborn foals are vitamin K deficient. Some experts recommend giving newborns an injection to prevent hemorrhagic diseases.

Minerals

Mineral imbalances are almost always more common, more obvious, and more dangerous in foals than in adult horses.

CALCIUM:

Growing foals need about 36 grams of calcium per day. If the foal receives insufficient milk, he will receive insufficient calcium.

IODINE:

Foals born to mares with iodine deficiency will suffer the same deficiency—in a much more severe form. Affected foals are weak and hypothermic, with a weak sucking response. Most die shortly after birth, and those who survive are subject to bone and joint abnormalities.

COPPER:

If foals don't get a sufficient amount of copper, they may be in danger of developing osteochondrosis. (This is still under discussion.) Copper supplements can be given directly to the foals, or even better, to the pregnant mother. It is suggested that young foals receive 50 mg/kg DM in their diet. (This is about 5 times the amount needed by adult horses.) Weanlings need about 25 mg/kg. In most cases, mare's milk supplies enough copper for her foal; however, weanlings between 3 and 12 months of age may benefit from supplements.

IRON:

The dietary requirement for foals is about 50 mg/kg DM. Iron deficiency is more common in nursing foals than in any other class of horse; this is because of their rapid growth rate. Milk is unfortunately low in iron, containing only between 12 to 28 mg/kg DM; it decreases even more as the weeks go by. This has led many people to supplement, but this too can be a dangerous practice. Iron toxicity can occur in foals that have been given too much iron supplement—usually injected. Affected foals will suffer depression and become dehydrated. In severe cases, the liver is affected and the foal will die. Do not given any iron supplements to your foal unless a confirmed case of anemia exists. Deficits in milk are generally made up for by the usually adequate levels of iron in grain and forage.

ZINC:

Foals need between 50 and 60 mg/kg of zinc in the diet to avoid risk of developmental orthopedic diseases. Some studies that have shown that foals

SOME PEOPLE
attempt to supplement a foal's diet by syringing milk into the foal's mouth. This can be very dangerous, since the milk is just as likely to get into the lungs as the stomach.

FOSTER MARES
usually accept the orphan within a day or so, although she may initially need to be restrained to allow the foal to nurse.

can get along on less, but these studies did not do careful examination for joint cartilage defects. Mare's milk contains about 30 mg/kg DM at foaling, but decreases to 18 by the time the foal is a few months old. Grain and forage consumption make up for much of the difference, but a supplement may be beneficial

SELENIUM:

Foals are more likely to suffer selenium deficits than are mature horses. This deficiency can cause white muscle disease. Affected horses will have dark urine, walk oddly, lose hair, and have difficulty breathing. The symptoms may show up right after birth—or several months later. Death from cardiac arrest is possible. Foals living in selenium deficient areas should receive 0.2 mg/kg in the diet. Sometimes selenium injections are given at birth, then at one, three, and six months of age.

The Orphaned Foal

Although naturally nothing can replace mother's milk, sometimes things don't work out as planned. The mare may die, or reject the foal. She may become too ill to nurse her baby, or may develop of agalactia—the failure to produce any milk at all. In such cases, it is the horse owner's job to care for the baby.

The situation is made markedly worse if the foal did not receive colostrum, or first milk, which contains not only very high levels of calories and nutrients, but important antibodies that protect the foal from bacteria normally found in the environment. A foal that does not receive these antibodies is at a very high risk of infection. If the foal is less than one day old and did not receive colostrum, he should be given it from another mare.

Obviously, the very best solution to the orphan foal problem is to find him a foster mother. This not only provides the correct nutrition, it has the additional benefit of helping the foal naturally socialize with others of his kind. The big downside to fostering is twofold: availability and expense. Not everyone has access to a foster mare, either free or for a fee. And even though it may possible to lease one, the cost can be prohibitive—up to $3,000 and more. Some localities have community colostrum banks; ask your vet in advance of the blessed event. You'll need to give about one pint every hour.

Most of the time you will have to use a milk replacer—buy a commercial one designed specifically for horses. Don't try to make one up yourself; this is not the time to be experimenting. If you absolutely cannot find equine milk replacer, you can use calf milk replacer, but choose one containing only milk (not soy) protein and no more than 0.2 percent crude fiber. Follow the directions on the label carefully.

If you must hand raise the foal, you have two choices: bottle feeding or bucket feeding. It's easier to bottle feed at first, since the foal is naturally equipped to suckle, but you're better off if you can teach the foal to drink from a bucket. (The bucket may begin as a shallow pan.)

This is because bottle feeding encourages a too-close bond between human and foal, a bond that can produce later undesirable and anti-social behavior. You do not want the foal to think of any human being as just another horse. Bottle feeding encourages the breaking of a natural barrier.

Even if you have to start with a bottle, you can usually teach the foal to drink from a bucket by the time it is only a couple of days old. To teach your orphan to drink from a bucket, use warm (about 98 degrees) milk replacer and dip the foal's muzzle gently into it. At first the foal may refuse to drink directly from the bucket, but will suckle your finger. Gradually dip your fingers further into the bucket until the foal is drinking directly from it. This may take some patience. Be sure to keep the bucket very clean and discard any unused milk. It's best to offer the bucket to the foal every hour, if at all possible. (Obviously, you'll need some help.)

When the foal is about a week old, you can start introducing milk-based pellets and some concentrates. Starter feeds are available with the special nutrients a youngster needs—use them. The time the foal is two or three week old, he will begin to graze.

Weaning

A nursing foal requires about 16 percent crude protein in his diet. When the foals reaches four months of age he should be drinking milk only four times a day or so, as well as eating grass, grain, and hay. Feed foals alongside their mothers. This makes them both happy.

Many foals run into serious digestive danger at the time of weaning, which generally occurs between four and six months. Of course, this largely depends on the size and development of the foal, condition of the dam, and on the available pasture. Even though the normal foal will have been experimenting and gradually relying more and more on non-milk sources of nourishment, he will usually still be drinking some milk. The change to a completely new diet is always fraught with some difficulty.

If the weaning is stressful or sudden, the foal may stop eating altogether. When he does begin to eat again, he may eat too much, especially if grain is available. Bacteria in the stomach may start to ferment the grain, producing

IN FOALS ONLY a few hours old, don't feed either water or mature milk until the colostrum is given.

CLEANLINESS IS important at all times, but even more so when foals are concerned. And orphaned foals are in the greatest danger. They are very prone to gastric upset from bacterial infections. Rinse utensils with cold water, then sterilize with boiled water or hypochlorite sanitizer.

too much lactic acid, which can paralyze the pyloric sphincter. (Remember that the job of this muscle band is to release food out of the stomach. The stomach can then rupture.)

Cereal grains may be low in lysine, and other essential amino acids, all of which are required for growth. Lysine is especially critical. A young horse may not have enough of the right microorganisms to synthesize this amino acid. A mostly grass diet may be deficient in threonine as well. Therefore a young horse's diet should contain 0.65 percent lysine DM. This can be provided by adding a protein supplement with at least 5 or 6 percent lysine. These supplements also contain high amounts of other essential amino acids. Sources include soybean, canola, fish and meat meals, and dairy products. However, some weanlings find them unpalatable and have to be gradually introduced to them.

In addition, weanlings who get mostly cereal grains and grass hay may not get enough protein or calcium. If the correct calcium/phosphorus ratio is not maintained, serious orthopedic problems can result.

Weanlings need 700 to 800 grams of protein per day; yearlings need about 850 grams a day. This means that the weanling's diet should contain at least 14.5 percent crude protein, while 15 or 16 percent is better. Remember that protein requirements are calculated for a mixture of hay and grain. So even if the hay is very high in protein, the grain should be at 18 percent. Feed the weanling about a pound and a half of high protein ration per 100 pounds of colt. This should be supplemented with an equal amount of forage.

Six-month old light-breed foals have reached about 46 percent of their mature weight, and 83 percent of their mature height. An average six-month-old weanling needs about 17,000 calories, 900 grams of crude protein, 27 to 38 grams of calcium, 22 to 30 grams of phosphorus, 4.7 grams of magnesium, 375 mg of zinc, 145 mg of copper, and 11,000 IU of vitamin A. Weanlings on winter pastures should probably be supplemented with vitamins A and D. Other trace minerals may also be lacking.

Many people use feeds designed specifically for foals; these feeds often contain milk protein rather than plant protein. Protein derived from animals (including milk) has a more complete amino acid profile. Milk protein is not advisable for older horses, however, because many adult animals (including humans) have a low tolerance for milk, although it's the milk sugar (lactose) rather than the protein that is usually the problem. In addition, adult horses have more tolerance for lower quality protein than foals, since they have finished growing—a primary use for protein.

Young horses benefit from the addition of oilseed meals and alfalfa and clover hay, for these provide good protein. However, the high protein intake is associated with rapid bone growth. This may sound like a good thing, but if your foal's diet lacks the necessary minerals to support this rapid growth, he is at risk of developing altered endochondral ossification and osteochondrosis. The same thing can happen with too much grain. Weigh your foal regularly to monitor his growth.

By three months, the foal should be eating one pound of creep feed, as well as between 1 and 1.5 pounds of hay for each 100 pounds of body weight a day. By weaning, the foal should be eating between 5 and 8 pounds of creep feed per day

Equally important is the fact that many grass forages and cereal grains are low in calcium, phosphorus, protein and lysine. However, don't overfeed your horse on alfalfa, other leafy legumes, or grain; this will result in too high an energy intake. Likewise, these diets may contain an insufficient amount of zinc or copper to support a foal's growth.

Yearlings

The average yearling has achieved 85 to 90 percent of his adult height and 65 to 70 percent of his mature ideal weight. (By 18 months of age, a horse has attained 95 percent of his mature height and 81 percent of their mature weight.)

A yearling needs at least 12.5 percent crude protein up to the age of 18 months, when the protein requirement can drop to 12 percent. If grazing is poor, they need between and 1 and 1.5 pounds of forage and about 1.5 pounds of concentrate per 100 pounds of body weight,

At two years the protein requirement goes down to 11 percent, unless the horse goes into heavy training (which I don't recommend anyway). Remember than an idle adult horse can get along on 8 percent protein, while a horse doing light to moderate work needs 11 or 11.5 percent.

Feed at least three times a day, but feed individually, so that the more dominant ones don't boss the others away. If you want to mix your own feed, you can try the following: Yearlings thrive on a daily combination of corn for energy (4 pounds) and oats for fiber and flavor (3.5 pounds). If oats are expensive or you need more calories in the diet, you can use barley (3 pounds), which has more energy than oats. For more protein, you can add a pound of soybean meal (gradually over a week or two, since horses need to get accustomed to the taste.) Add molasses if you like, salt, and a commercial vitamin/trace mineral supplement. If your horse is on a legume pasture, you may want to add some dicalcium phosphate for both phosphorus and calcium. If your horse is on a grass hay diet, add calcium carbonate for calcium alone.

WHEN FEEDING young horses in a group, try to separate them into subgroups according to age, size, and temperament. This helps ensure that each foal gets enough nutrients.

YOU DON'T WANT a fat yearling! He should be lean, sleek, and gangly in appearance.

Older Colts

Many people work and train two-year olds. Two-year old horses are raced, as we all know. This is an economic decision made by the racing industry on behalf of breeders who want to make money quickly. Why let a young horse hang around and eat without earning his keep? What is good for the horse racing industry, however, is distinctly not good for horses. Horses do not reach maximum bone strength until they are between two and seven years old. Working young horses hard maximizes the stress on developing bone— no wonder racing is so dangerous for both horses and riders. And while some interesting studies have shown that natural exercise serves to increase bone density—forcing a horse to exercise hard or race has precisely the opposite effect. Horses are smart enough to know when to quit.

Magnesium

Magnesium is especially important for young horses. One reason is that if they don't get enough in their diet, can than draw it from their bones— which isn't very good for the skeleton! (Older horses seem to lose this ability.)

Potassium

A foal needs up to 1 percent potassium in a purified diet. That's about 11 to 13 grams of potassium a day. Yearlings need 18 grams daily, an amount usually supplied in the diet, so supplementation is unnecessary.

Variety: The Spice of Life

When your horse is still young and malleable, offer him assortments of different kind of fruits and grains. This will make him more adaptable as he grows older, and less apt to refuse a meal that is even slightly different from the one he was used to.

Feeding for Performance

IF A HORSE HAD THINGS HIS WAY, HE'D never perform at all. Horses much prefer to wander peacefully around munching tender blades of grass and visiting companionably together. Nature, however, who has to look out for predators as well as prey, made horses a juicy treat for some of the larger predators. To get away from them, horses found it necessary to run, jump, twist, and rear. Thus was born the performance horse.

What is a performance horse? For our purposes, we'll use the term to describe a horse that is working beyond the level normally expected of a pleasure horse. Obviously, there is an enormous range here. Is a horse that is shown regularly in Western Pleasure class a pleasure or a show horse? The answer depends largely on the individual case—how much stress is he under? How much traveling does he do? How much work does he get between shows? No fine line exists between a performance horse and other types. And luckily, just as there are infinite gradations between a horse that never leaves the pasture and one who goes on 100 mile endurance races, your feeding options are pretty limitless as well. Everything in this chapter is meant to be a guideline only. You'll need to adjust your horse's food for his own needs and your own goals.

Sprinters and Endurance Workers

Glucose, fat and glycogen are turned into energy by two metabolic processes:

- Aerobic (requiring oxygen)
- Anaerobic (working without oxygen)

Ordinarily, the two processes work in sync. The anaerobic process starts by splitting the glucose molecule in two. This is quick, but produces only a small amount of energy and leaves a residue of lactic acid that saps muscles of their strength.

Aerobic metabolism uses oxygen and the lactic acid leftover from the anaerobic process to produce much more energy. The aerobic process is much slower than the anaerobic, so when a horse is working very hard, the aerobic process can "fall behind" the anaerobic process; it does not use up all the lactic acid that is being produced. Then lactic acid gradually builds up and the muscles get sore and tired. This is the anaerobic threshold where the anaerobic phase of metabolism gets ahead of the aerobic phase. If enough lactic acid builds up in the muscles, it not only fatigues the horse but can also injure muscle fibers.

Different kinds of performance call on different kinds of muscle. For example, sprinting and pulling a heavy load require large muscle fibers; endurance activities require small muscle fibers. Large muscle fibers are called "fast-twitch" fibers. They are strong but can't use oxygen well. This is one reason why sprinters and weight-pulling horses "burn out" quickly. Endurance horses have more "slow-twitch" muscle fibers, which have the reverse capacity. They are not as strong, but they can go on for a lot longer.

A performance horse may need double the calories of an equally sized stall potato. A peak conditioned race horse, for example, would need to eat 36 pounds of alfalfa or 45 pounds of brome grass to stay in shape—and not many horses can eat that much! This is why a performance horse needs to have concentrated food as part of his diet. Of course, this is completely unnatural, but so are steeple chasing, barrel racing, and endurance riding. Horses in nature just don't do things like that.

To keep your performance horse in the best of shape, however, no matter what his sport, you'll need to provide high-quality legume hay, corn for energy, and oats for fiber. (A racehorse can easily consume 7 pounds each of corn and oats, and double that amount of alfalfa.)

Although hardworking horses may of necessity require more concentrates than ever before, remember that this is not a natural arrangement. Under no circumstances should any horse be given less than 1 pound of forage for every 100 pounds of body weight, nor should his diet ever consist of less than 50 percent forage. Serious, perhaps deadly digestive problems can result in horses fed inadequate amounts of forage. And remember that horses on large amounts of concentrates (over 5 pounds) should have the ration divided between at least two meals.

Endurance horses are under tremendous stress, largely due to the loss of electrolytes through perspiration. This must be replaced, or the horse will suffer fatigue, muscle spasms, and dehydration.

Water for the Equine Athlete

Since many equine athletes must travel, they will be exposed to water with an unfamiliar taste. Some horses decline to drink the new offering, no matter how much they need it. To prevent this from happening, try masking the taste of the old water several days before the event; add a bit of molasses, vinegar, or some other flavor. Then do the same with the new water. Chances are, the horse won't be able to tell the difference.

Concentrates for Performance Horses

Most people feed their performance horses a commercial feed designed for such use. If you care to make up your own, you will find that most horses do very well on a 50/50 grain mix of corn and oats. Barley or milo can replace some of the oats if you like. If your horse is on a grass hay diet, you may want to add protein in the form of soybean meal. In any case, an excellent vitamin/mineral supplement is a must for the performance horse, as is an electrolyte supplement.

Although it's a good idea to start feeding your performance horse extra grain for several days before an event, never to feed a horse grain less than three hours before heavy exercise. To do so causes a surge in blood sugar and insulin. (This doesn't happen when horses eat grass or hay.) The insulin is busy trying to store the blood sugar instead of allowing it to be released for use

ALONG WITH their additional needs for calories and protein, performance horses have increased needs for calcium, phosphorus, magnesium, zinc, and vitamins A and E.

WHEN YOUR high-performance horse is resting between events, most experts suggest you omit the corn from his diet, and cut back the oats by half.

during exercise. On the other hand, if insulin levels are low, the glucose that is stored can be easily released.

Sprint athletes like barrel racing horses shouldn't have grain within four hours of exercise during practice rounds. On the day of the competition, withhold grain for eight hours before the race.

Forage for Performance Horses

In general, performance horses should be allowed free access to forage (except for sprinters directly before an event). Performance horses should eat between 1 and 1.5 pounds of forage for each 100 pounds of horse. If the horse doesn't seem to want to eat this much, decrease the amount of grain you are feeding.

For sprint athletes, hay should be withheld 12 hours prior to the event. Hay is bulky enough to make a small difference in timing. Remember that a horse's gastrointestinal tract can hold as much as 25 percent of his body weight! And small differences in timing can make a dig difference between winning and losing.

Endurance horses do not need to be deprived of hay before the event, however, because in their case the benefit of nutrient storage offsets the disadvantage of added weight. The rule of thumb is that if the exercise is gong to last more than several minutes, the horse should be allowed to eat hay beforehand.

Some horses may benefit from the addition of calcium carbonate (one ounce) or dicalcium phosphate (one ounce) for extra calcium and/or phosphorus. Calcium carbonate supplies calcium only; dicalcium phosphate supplies both. Much depends on the kind of hay being given, and how much sweating the horse is doing. Grass hay is lower in calcium than alfalfa. Remember that calcium and phosphorus need to be kept within a vague sort of balance—there should never be more phosphorus than calcium, and no more than six (at the outside) times as much calcium as phosphorus.

It is especially important for endurance horses not to get more grain than forage. Instead of extra grain, make sure they get high-quality hay and pasture, with a protein level of at least 11 percent. You can increase grain by a pound or two and decrease forage by three or four pounds a couple of days before a race. This will tend to "lighten up" the horse.

Protein

As we can see, as horses exercise more, their need for protein increases. This is especially important in early stages of training, since the extra protein

---

SOME FEEDING options seem to be breed dependent. Thoroughbreds, for example, often become extremely difficult to handle a few hours after a grain meal. No one knows precisely why this is, although some suggest that Thoroughbreds have a delayed release of insulin in response to elevated blood sugar levels. The uncontrolled blood sugar level is responsible for the "acting up" of the animal. If your horse is like this, simply don't give him grain on the morning of an event for which he needs to be relatively calm and under your direction. Combined athletes and show horses may benefit from small frequent meals of hay or grass; avoid feeding grain eight hours before the competition event. Endurance horses should be allowed free-choice forage. Skip the grain for breakfast.

helps build muscle and blood cells. Extra protein also helps the day after a day of strenuous exercise, since it will repair the damaged tissue. An 1,100-pound performance horse may need over 1,300 grams of crude protein in a diet of 32,700 calories. This is twice the caloric need of a maintenance horse, and twice the protein. However, extremely high levels of protein have not been found to be beneficial. All it does is increase water intake and decrease the efficiency of digestible energy utilization for endurance horses. Protein levels for performance horses should stay between 10 and 16 percent.

Extra protein can usually be safely added in the form of more grain. In addition, high protein forages like alfalfa contain additional levels of protein, up to 20 percent, although this is uncommon. If you are feeding your performance horse lower quality hay, you may need to add protein in the form of soybean meal, cottonseed meal, or a similar substance. Soybean meal is the best source, since it contains most of the essential amino acids, especially lysine, which are so often lacking in other foodstuffs. Cottonseed meal and linseed meal are also good, although linseed meal is low in lysine.

Some studies suggest that specific amino acid supplementation can be helpful to a performance horse. Research is ongoing.

Fat

"'Twas her brother that, in kindness to his horse, buttered his hay...."
King Lear

However, while extra protein may not prove especially beneficial to a performance horse, extra fat is a different story! For a long time, fats were added to a horse's diet for only one reason—to improve the coat. Performance horses were given energy in the form of carbohydrates. But now we know a lot more about the way the body utilizes fat.

While it's true that carbohydrates provide the ultra-quick energy needed by sprinters, horses doing endurance work benefit most from the addition of fat. Fat provides two and a quarter times the energy of carbohydrates. Consuming fat allows horses to increase their energy intake without increasing the volume of food they eat. (And horses, with their comparatively small stomachs, can eat only so much.) Although fats are more expensive than carbohydrates, there is evidence that horses can use them more efficiently.

And amazingly, horses can digest fat remarkably well, even though they have no gall bladders. (This should not be surprising...I don't have a gall bladder myself, but that minor fact hasn't kept me away from fried chicken and ice cream.) While nobody suggests that horses should go on the 75 or 80 percent fat diet that Iditarod dogs do, it has been ascertained that horses can tolerate a diet of up to 20 percent fat with apparent ease. It is absorbed

FATS DON'T HAVE any vitamins or minerals, so these nutrients are diluted to the proportion that they are added to the diet. Horses on an extra fat diet should have vitamins and minerals to compensate. This is especially important for growing horses.

SOME PEOPLE
like black sunflowers seeds for their fats and oils, while others just pour on eight ounces of corn or other oil. If you use oils in this form be sure to add more of a good vitamin/mineral supplement than you would without the oil.

SPRINT HORSES
are not able to make as much use of fat, however, since fats are digested and absorbed into the system more slowly than are carbohydrates and protein.

almost entirely by the small intestine, so has no effect on the weird mixtures being cultivated in the cecum and large intestine.

A high-fat diet decreases the actual amount of food that needs to be fed while delivering more energy. It has also been shown that if a high-fat diet is continued over a period of time, it will increase muscle glycogen content. Thus, a high-fat diet enhances both aerobic and anaerobic activities and delays fatigue. Controlled studies show that a high-fat diet in the form of added soybean oil worked better than a high protein (25 percent) or a high starch (40 percent) diet for both fast and moderate speed exercises. Add up to 10 percent vegetable oil to the total diet beginning at least six weeks and preferably 10 weeks before the event. You can manage this by adding a cup of oil to every 2 or 3 pounds of grain fed.

One major way that fat helps the performance horse is by pushing back that anaerobic threshold I spoke about earlier. A horse in training will use the stored fat in preference to glycogen. The glycogen stays in the muscles where it does most good for sprint work, and during endurance work, fat-supplemented horses suffered less blood glucose depletion. However, this switch doesn't occur overnight. High levels of fats are not necessary for a horse's natural diet, and it appears that the horse has to "learn" to metabolize this new dietary component. This may take several weeks, so don't expect to see results right away.

Another way that fat helps endurance horses is this: it decreases the energy used for heat production, and makes that energy more available for physical performance or storage. In other words, fats produce lower internal temperatures than does grain or hay. This extra energy becomes available no matter how hot or cold it is outside—and no matter how fat or thin the horse is.

No doubt about it—fats are great for performance horses of all kinds. Fat supplements are more critical to improving performance than adding starch or protein to the diet.

Extra fat is not enough, however. It needs to be supported with good-quality hay and fiber to help keep the electrolytes in balance. Do not make the mistake of throwing away your grain and giving your horse a nice meal of pork chops and oil. He won't like it, and it wouldn't work anyway. As the Buddha said, follow the Middle Path of moderation—that's the way to enlightenment.

The amount of fat a performance horse needs is still under discussion. Many experts recommend a dietary level of about 8 percent for moderately working performance horses, and 10 percent for very high-level work. Even higher levels (15 to 20 percent) have been used for extreme athletes.

Minerals

Calcium

Many performance horses need a calcium boost, especially if they are on a high-grain diet. Not only is grain low in calcium, but calcium is needed to replace sweat losses and maintain bone integrity. If the horse is being fed grass hay as well, calcium supplements become even more important.

Magnesium

Working horses need magnesium above maintenance level, depending up the workload. So while an idle horse needs on 6.8 mg/pound lightly working horse needs an additional 10 percent—a hard working one needs about twice as much as a horse on a maintenance diet.

Potassium

A horse in heavy training requires between 32 and 50 grams of potassium a day. If he is eating plenty of forage, he's getting nearly twice that; however, many such animals are fed heavily upon grain and receive little forage. In addition, these horses often sweat a lot, thus losing more potassium. If your horse is working hard and on a high-grain, low-forage diet, consider a potassium supplement. This is especially true if you are feeding alfalfa, which is lower in potassium than grass hays like orchard grass.

Salt and Electrolytes

What the horse is looking for really, is sodium; 102 grams of salt provides only 40 grams of sodium. We all know that performance horses require more salt than horses on a maintenance diet, primarily because they are sweating more. For example, a maintenance horse may need only 8 grams of sodium per day; a performance horse may need five times that much. To make sure your performance horse gets enough salt quickly, let him have it in loose form; this is much easier for him to eat than licking it, which takes a long time. Commercial supplements like Humidimix are useful for electrolyte supplemention. They encourage horses to drink more water as well, helping to maintain good fluid balance.

SELENIUM: Exercise increases free radical production. This requires more glutathione peroxidase, and selenium is necessary to produce it. A higher amount of selenium for exercising horses is therefore a good idea. Even performance horses, however, should receive no more than a total of one milligram of selenium per kilogram of feed; toxicity has been observed at dietary levels as low as 5 mg selenium per kilogram of feed. Supplementation is tricky because of the wide variation in the selenium content of hay and grain.

IT IS WORTH considering that a horse's natural diet contains almost no fat whatever. Grass has almost none, and even grains contain only 2 or 3 percent fat.

CHROMIUM: Some studies suggest that chromium supplementation is beneficial for highly stressed performance horses. It appears that, through its enhancement of insulin function, chromium reduces lactic acid, which causes fatigue. However, you can't just go out and buy the stuff—it's not available for general consumption. You'll need a prescription from your veterinarian.

Vitamins

B Vitamins

Feeding a horse oral B complex vitamins four to six hours before work may enhance performance by helping to keep the appetite keen. Stabled performance horses may benefit from a folacin supplement of 20 milligrams per day. Thiamin is also useful for performance horses; you can buy commercial supplements. Cobalamin is sometimes given to performance horses in the belief that it prevents anemia; no research supports this wishful thinking.

Vitamin E

Hard exercising horses tend to produce organic peroxides (similar to hydrogen peroxide) in skeletal and cardiac muscle. These oxides can turn toxic if not scavenged by vitamin E. Because vitamin E acts as a vasodilator, many people believe that racing horses and other top athletes can benefit from a vitamin E supplement. It also helps maintain the integrity of the muscles. A performance horse needs about 100 mg/kg DM or 650 to 750 IU per day.

Other Performance Enhancers

Hydroxymethyl Butyrate (HMB)

HMB is a product of the amino acid leucine, and is produced naturally in your horse's body. It increases cholesterol levels and the number of red blood cells; HMB supplemented horses may have somewhat improved performance.

Live Yeast Cultures

Some interesting studies indicate that live yeast cultures (probiotics) may help performance horses by helping to increase their fat utilization. They certainly do no harm. Add about 1 percent of a live yeast culture to the diet.

Carnitine

Carnitine is a non-essential amino acid that may delay fatigue, although this has not been proven. The recommended dose is 5 grams of L-carnitine daily.

Sodium Bicarbonate (Baking Soda)

Baking soda given before sprinting exercises may be beneficial, although it is of no help to endurance athletes. Its purpose is to neutralize the high levels

of lactic acid produced during sprint activity. This is usually done by administering 0.4 to 0.6 g/kg body weight of sodium bicarbonate dissolved in several quarts of water. It is given via stomach tube three to six hours before the event. Horses won't eat it if you put it in their feed.

Other supplements, sometimes given to performance horses, are considered in Chapter 15.

Switching Back

When the competition season is over, you'll probably need to bring your horse down to a lower energy feed. Do this gradually; horses have a more difficult time than most of us in switching from one kind of food to another. Give the animal time to develop the proper bacteria to digest the new food, and make all changes slowly.

This is even more important if you are trying to recondition or rehabilitate a racetrack horse who has been used to a high-grain, low-forage diet. Changes in the digestive tract do not take place overnight, especially when a horse has been conditioned practically from birth to accept a diet skewed in favor of grain. These horses have a shorter digestive tract, one that has not been used to the work of handling a large amount of grass or hay. Allow about six months for the horse's system to return to what is normal. Again, do this gradually. Not only are suddenly dietary changes difficult for a horse to handle, but his appetite may go off as well. You can mix his grain portion into his hay to encourage his return to a more horse-like diet. ▄

CHAPTER

13

Feeding and Disease

GOOD NUTRITION CAN PREVENT, OR
even cure disease. Poor nutrition can not only
open the door to many disease processes, but in
some cases, actually cause the disease. In this
chapter, we'll look at the relationship between
poor nutrition and certain diseases of the horse.

Allergies

Like people, horses can become allergic to things
in their diet. An allergic horse may develop small
bumps, or wheals, all over his body. These may
last just a few hours—or persist for several days.
Technically these are called *urticaria*, but a more
revealing name is "protein" or "skin" bumps. In
most cases, the causal factor is indeed dietary protein, but other agents have also been identified,

- Provide plenty of fresh water
- Provide high-quality, dust- and mold-free hay
- Prevent your horse from grazing in sandy or dusty areas; particles can become impacted and over time cause a blockage
- If you change your horse's diet, do so gradually
- Be regular in the feeding of your horse
- Cool down your horse properly after exercise
- Have your horse wormed regularly. Parasites damage the digestive tract

Horses with colic glare and bite at their flanks, perspire heavily, and roll on the ground. If your horse has colic, call your vet and keep the horse walking.

And although horses don't have gall bladders, they can still get something resembling gallstones that form in the bile ducts and create blockages. There seems to be no end of the problems your horse can develop in his intestinal system.

Colicky horses look at their sides and even bite at them. Call the vet! Pam Tanzey.

Developmental Orthopedic Disease (DOD)

"Developmental" refers to a young horse. "Orthopedic" refers to bone. "Disease" speaks for itself. These diseases can include osteochondrosis, epiphysitis, flexor deformities, and other serious conditions. Many factors play a part in abnormal bone growth. Genetic, hormonal, metabolic, and mechanical problems, and exercise levels can all be responsible. So can nutrition. Both deficient and excessive amounts of certain nutrients can influence bone growth. This is why it is critically import to feed young horses a balanced ration.

Osteochondrosis is one of the most common of the DODs. It is caused by too rapid growth (often a result of overfeeding), mineral imbalance, or, in some cases, a trauma to the affected cartilage. Some breeds, such as the Standardbred and Swedish Warmblood, seem to be genetically predisposed. Osteochondrosis mostly affects the articular (joint) growth cartilage, but in some cases the metaphyseal cartilage is the seat of the disease. The most common symptom can be easily overlooked—a nonpainful swelling of the affected joint, sometimes accompanied by stiffness. Lameness is not usually a symptom in younger animals, unless the site of the disease is in the shoulder. You may, however, notice the limbs of the affected animal being of an unusually upright conformation—the result of too rapid growth. Foals less than six months old are most frequently affected by osteocondrosis of the fetlock, and may spend an unusual amount of time lying down. In older horses symptoms include stiffness, reduced flexion, and some degree of lameness (which often appears at the start of training).

Young animals (under one year) may recover naturally from osteochondrosis, if care is taken to supervise their exercise and reduce their feed intake. In some cases a copper deficiency may be at fault; supplementation may be required. Experts do not agree as to whether correcting the diet can actually alter the course of the disease; however, further damage may be prevented.

Diarrhea

Diarrhea can occur when the large intestine is damaged by ammonia, antibiotics, bacteria, parasites and/or acid. Nervous horses are more prone to it than are calmer animals. A horse can lose up to 40 liters of water and electrolytes, and the bacteria can invade the horse's whole body. It is a symptom of disease, rather than a disease entity in itself. One kind of diarrhea is caused by anterior enteritis, a disease process of the small intestine. Anterior enteritis is often related to high grain, low forage diets, causing inflammation of the gut, which then releases toxins into the system. Other kinds of diarrhea result from problems in the large intestine, often stemming from feed overload, indigestion resulting from overgrazing in rich legume pasture.

Rapid intake of processed pellet feeds may also result in diarrhea. In this case, feed pellets should be reduced and hay supplemented.

Diarrhea also results when a horse consumes excess water; this often happens when a horse is placed on young green pasture. The extra water from the grass combines with the grassy fiber and can move too quickly through the intestine.

Diarrhea can also occur if you change your horse's diet suddenly, without adequate preparation. The new diet and the "old" intestinal flora may not get along, so to speak, and until your horse has had time to develop a sufficient number of intestinal flora equipped to handle the new rations, your horse may experience diarrhea. Similarly, a new diet can alter the pH level in the gut, which can cause irritation and the resulting diarrhea.

Other causes of diarrhea related to diet may include too many concentrates (grains, commercial preparations, soybean meal, oil, salt, and so on), too much legume hay, or an allergic reaction to a particular protein found in the diet.

And of course, many disease processes, including poisons, include diarrhea as a symptom.

Horses with diarrhea should be placed on a bland diet. Many practitioners like to give the horse some flavored yogurt (make sure it's the live culture variety) to make up for important microflora than can be lost during an episode. Administer about 7 tablespoons for four or five days. Add some vitamins and electrolytes to make up for those lost. You can also purchase supplements of gut bacteria. Sounds weird, but you can do it.

Equine Motor Neuron Disease (EMD)

This condition results from damaged nerve fibers; in fact it has eerie similarities with Lou Gehrig's disease. The primary cause seems to be a severe depletion of vitamin E. Therefore, all horses that have little opportunity to eat fresh forage should be supplemented with vitamin E.

Equine Degenerative Encephalomyelopathy

Equine degenerative encephalomyelopathy is a progressive neurological disorder occurring in horses (and zebras, too, in case you happen to have one). The condition appears similar to EMD in that the spinal cord and brain stem are most affected leading to leg weakness and loss of coordination. Genetic factors and insufficient vitamin E seem to be the primary causes.

Equine Protozoal Myelitis (EPM)

This disease is called by a parasite—*Sarcocystis neurona*. This nasty beast lives in the feces of possums, of all things. Possums do occasionally get into horse feed—in fact, I had to chase one off my back porch last night. However, it is hypothesized that a lot of this contamination occurs before the feed gets to your barn. The organism is destroyed by heat treatment, so if you fear the disease, buy heat-treated concentrates—it doesn't have to be extruded, although that kills everything. Pelleted feeds and steam-crimped grains are heat-treated sufficiently to destroy the protozoa. If your horse has actually comes down with this disease, consult your vet for advice about supplements. Some vets, but not all, recommend folic acid.

Fluorosis

Foals are most affected by this condition, which is caused by an excess of fluoride, either from certain kinds of phosphorus supplements or pasture contaminated by industrial waste or effluent. This disease involves the bones and teeth. Unfortunately, it's a difficult condition to diagnose, so you'll need do some detective work. Characteristic signs include mottled teeth in foals and young horses, difficulty in drinking cold water, and, in more advanced cases, standing in a humped position. The effects are not reversible, although further deterioration can be avoided.

Goiter

Goiter is caused by iodine deficiency and the subsequent decrease in thyroid hormone production. The anterior pituitary gland, wondering what can be the matter, then produces excesses of a thyroid stimulating hormone. This makes the poor thyroid practically work itself to death in a futile attempt to produce thyroxine, which causes the gland to swell. The treatment is to supply the necessary iodine in the horse's food.

Hyperlipemia

This is a general term referring to animals with high levels of lipids (fats) in the plasma. It can be brought on by sudden fasting or starving. Pregnant or lactating ponies, donkeys and Thoroughbreds may be particularly susceptible. This disease can be fatal, and in its severe form is irreversible. It seems obvious that the prevention is to make sure your equine is supplied with enough food.

HYPP (Hyperkalemic Periodic Paralysis)

This genetic condition (also called **Potassium-Induced Periodic Paralysis**—PIPP) originated with a single American Quarter Horse stud named Impressive. Horses with this disease cannot regulate potassium and sodium properly in the body. Affected horses periodically develop severe twitching and even, in worst cases, paralysis. Death can result. Horses with this condition must have their potassium intake kept at a normal and steady level, no more than 1 percent of the diet. Legume hays should be avoided, and grass hays like timothy fed instead. Cereal grains like corn and oats are low in

potassium and thus safe, although molasses and oilseed meals can substantially increase the potassium levels. Feeds with fibers like beet pulp may also be helpful. For severe cases, your vet can offer additional treatment including alkalinizing salts and diuretics.

Infections and Wounds

Although infections and wounds are not a product of poor feeding, affected horses can be helped with increased amount of protein, calories, and zinc. Vitamins A, B complex and C are also useful.

Kidney Disease

Decrease calcium and phosphorus intake and give the renally-impaired horse plenty of water. Alfalfa and other legumes are high in calcium, so they should be avoided. The amount of protein that should be given is controversial. Conventional wisdom says that kidney damaged horses should be on a low-protein diet, but other experts believe that since the kidneys don't work as well in processing it, the horse needs more protein in the diet in order to get enough. The jury is still out on this one.

Laminitis (Founder)

Laminitis is a mysterious and dangerous disease, often caused by a nutritional error on the part of the horse owner. Many a horse has gotten into the feed bin overnight—and thence to his doom. Overfeeding of wheat or corn is another danger. Lush green grass has also been blamed for a type of founder to which older ponies, usually geldings, are particularly susceptible.

One of the most common and dangerous feeding problems can occur when you feed your horse a meal rich in grain and low in fiber. The small intestine finds itself overwhelmed with work, and may not get a chance to finish processing the meal before it is moved along to the hindgut. The cecum is thus presented with large amounts of soluble carbohydrates, which should have been taken care of in the small intestines. As the cecum tries to process the grain, it makes not only its usual complement of volatile fatty acids, but also lactic acid. EEK! The lactic acid lowers the natural acidity of the cecum to a point where those acid-loving bacteria that were doing so much of the work are killed off. In a way, I suppose we could consider them suicidal bacteria, but it's really more of an accident. No matter what their motivation, as the bacteria begin to die, they in turn release deadly endotoxins, and your horse gets really sick with grain laminitis or colic. Keep grain meals small. Remember, at least half your horse's food should consist of forage.

In founder, the tissues inside the hoofs swell and press against the hoof wall, resulting in excruciating pain. The laminae, thin tissues that attach the hoof wall to the coffin bone, can separate. If rapid action is not taken, it can cause irreversible damage. Although all horses can be affected, "easy keepers" seem to be at the greatest risk.

Juicy spring plants are low in fiber, but can contain up to 25 percent protein and the same amount of highly digestible carbohydrates. If an animal has been used to a lower quality, less digestible feed, an abrupt change in diet can kill off the bacteria that were dining on the former food. The dead bacteria release endotoxins that result in so-called "grass founder."

To prevent founder:

- Store all feeds well away from thieving horses
- Do not overfeed your horse on high-energy grain or allow unlimited access to spring grass
- Increase feed or spring grazing times gradually
- Don't over-exert your horse
- Don't give your horse water until he is properly cooled

Liver Disease

Increase simple carbohydrates, and add B complex vitamins, and vitamins E and C. Horses with liver disease often do better on a lower protein diet, so as a rule forgo the alfalfa and feed grass hays instead. Legume hays, however, contain an amino acid balance that is excellent for liver disease. Ask your vet. Corn and sugar beet pulp also contain amino acid mixtures that tend to correct imbalances caused by liver disease, so corn should be the grain of choice, while sugar beet pulp can be added a filler. The horse should be allowed all the forage he wants.

Orthopedic Injuries

Bone injuries often respond well to supplements of protein, vitamin A and vitamin D (balanced with increased calcium and phosphorus).

Respiratory Disease

Horses with respiratory problem need a dust-free diet insofar as possible. Use top-quality hay—moistened if necessary. Hay pellets or cubes are also a good choice.

Selenium Toxicosis

This condition occurs when horses get excess selenium, either from selenium accumulating plants or from excess supplementation. Most of plant-induced cases are derived from plants growing on alkaline soil, especially in areas of low rainfall. See Chapters 5 (Minerals) and 14 (Poisonous Pastures) for more details.

PONIES, WHO don't require much in the way of high-energy foods, are particularly subject to some types of laminitis.

Tendon Injuries

Increase vitamin A, and supplement with copper and zinc.

Tying-Up Syndrome (Azoturia, Monday Morning Sickness, Exertional Myopathy, Transient Exertional Rhabdomyolysis)

This disease appears when a performance horse takes a rest, then goes back to work. The signs are cramps, and an inability to move. The urine turns dark. Underlying causes are unknown, but culprits may include carbohydrate overloading, faulty fat metabolism, vitamin and mineral deficiencies, endocrine abnormalities, electrolyte imbalances, and viral infections. Because the cause is uncertain (and is probably variable), the recommendations are equally diverse. Certain horses seem regularly affected.

Many experts say to reduce the high-energy food while the horse is at rest. Some experts believe that tying-up syndrome can be avoided by reducing to one-third or eliminating grains from the diet on rest days. Instead, these horses should be given high-quality hay and extra fat (1 cup) in the diet. However, large amounts of alfalfa hay or cubes should probably be avoided by horses in training.

It has also been shown that many horses that experience azoturia have low levels of the electrolytes potassium, sodium, or calcium in their bodies. The addition of these minerals can sometimes prevent a recurrence. Some horses benefit from vitamin E, selenium, thiamin and chromium supplementation. Another variety of azoturia is equine polysaccharide storage myopathy, a condition found in Quarter Horses. It is treated in much the same way as transient exertional rhabdomyolysis.

With any kind of tying up, it's important to feed grain only in proportion to exercise, and fed grain should never be increased suddenly. Always reduce the amount of grain fed when the horse is not working.

Worms

Grazing near the dirt as they do, horses frequently fall prey to a distressingly large variety of worms. Worm infestations can cause your horse to drop weight, lose energy, and get sick. The most common sorts of worms affecting your horse include large strongyles (bloodworms), small strongyles (redworms or cyanthostomes), ascarids (roundworm), oxyuris (pinworms), gastrophilus (botworms), and anoplocephala (tapeworms). These creature compete for nutrients with your horse and cause physical symptoms as varied as irritation to the mouth or digestive tract, coughing and nasal discharge, fever, appetite loss, colic, diarrhea, and damage to the gut walls. Worm cycles last from days to months, and in the case of roundworms, can remain encysted for years. Bot worm infestations work a little differently in that they come from eggs laid by the bot flies on the horse's hair and are licked off by the horse. Regular worming is absolutely essential to keep down the population of all species.

Worms can be controlled, but never completely eliminated by the judicious use of anthelmintics (wormers), good feeding practices, careful pasture maintenance (including manure removal), and frequent cleaning of the horse's stall. Compost manure for a year before spreading on a pasture.

Simply raising the feed bin can help control worms by keeping the horse's mouth away from places where worms congregate, so to speak.

Feeding Vices

Cribbing

Cribbing, or chewing on stall wood, is a vice that is mostly caused by sheer and utter boredom. Horses have evolved naturally to walk around all day long, nibbling as they go. They are not clams; they need work to do, and things to experience. When deprived of these things, they start chewing. Some items seem preferable to others—most horses like soft wood, for instance. Although some people think that cribbing results from missing phosphorus in the diet (and recommend a bran mash), the most obvious solution is to get the horse outside more. Cribbing is considered an unsoundness in horses, and if continued over a long period can result in a horse's wearing down his front incisors. Cribbing horses are also typically underweight.

Feed Scattering

Some horses seem addicted to throwing their food all around the stall. Of course, they not only waste food this way, but also risk not getting enough nutrition. To make things even worse, after the food-flinging episode, the horse apparently thinks better of his rash actions, and then goes picking about in his bedding for it, devouring nasty worms and other unwholesome things in the process.

If the horse is indulging in this habit because he is objecting to his food, you might try changing it to something more palatable. Do so gradually. Otherwise, your only solution is to use a very narrow feeding tub—or even a nosebag.

Gobblers

Gobbling food is an unhealthy habit, one that can lead to colic, choke, and diarrhea. It's especially severe if the horse is being fed whole grain. Gobblers can be forced to slow down by placing a heavy chain or rocks in the bottom of the feed tub. It also helps to use a very large tub and spread the food around as much as possible.

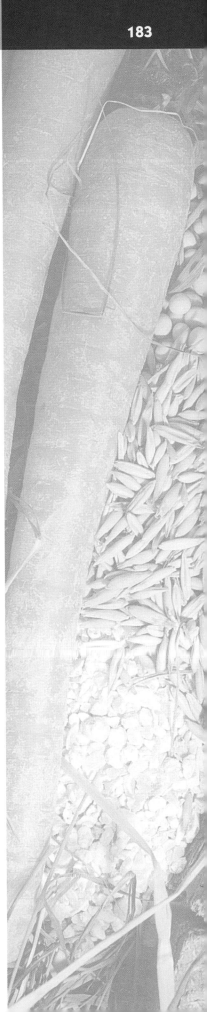

Mealtime Madness

This interesting malady comes in two forms. Some horses attack their fellows at feeding time. This is instinctive behavior, and there's not much you can do to change their disposition. Such animals obviously need to be fed separately.

Other horses become desperate for dinner when they hear the grain rattling, see you approach, or even know that it's dinnertime. They stamp, kick, neigh, and carry on in their stalls. Some can seriously damage themselves in their excitement over dinner. I don't know any way to stop this kind of behavior, except to feed the horse on schedule. If there are a bunch of horses, feed the noisy ones first.

Manure Eating

This "vice" is normal and possibly even healthy in foals, which need to pick up the correct bacteria from their mother's manure. In older horses, the problem may be caused by a diet too high in grain and too low in fiber. If you suspect this is the case, up the hay intake. Some people think the addition of B complex vitamins is helpful in treating this problem. And of course, it always helps if you keep the stall, pasture, and paddock well picked up.

Pica

Pica is deranged appetite. It is seen in people, dogs, and horses—and in most other mammals as well. Typically a horse with pica begins eating non-food items like rocks, manes, tails, dirt, or even bones. It is theorized that many animals with pica have a phosphorus, iron, copper, calcium, or roughage deficiency.

Wind Sucking (*Aerophagia*)

Some horse grab the top rail or a fence post with their teeth, arch their necks, and start gulping air. This wears down the teeth and leads to digestive problems. Horses seem to do this for fun, although boredom increases the activity. Many people spray a repellent material on the fence top whose noxious odor keeps horses away. Others use a strap around the throat which prevents the horse from gulping air. A commercial product called Nalmefene may also help. (They use it in humans to treat alcoholism, if that's any comfort to you.) The use of this drug is forbidden in competition horses by the AHSA. ▬

Poisonous Pastures

PARACELSUS SAID, "IT BETTER BENEFITS a man to know one herb in the meadow, but to know it thoroughly, than to see the whole meadow without knowing what grows on it." This is especially true if said herb is a poisonous one.

Poisons wear many masks; alkalis, glycosides, acids, resins and amines are just a few of their disguises, and horses are extremely predisposed to all kinds of adverse reactions from toxins in their food. Cows, who may share the pasture and feed have bacteria in the rumen to detoxify many deadly substances before they reach the small intestine. Horses don't have that luxury. The poisonous stuff enters the intestine and moves quickly into the bloodstream before detoxification can take place.

FOR MOST PLANT poisonings, there is no treatment a lay person can give. Call your veterinarian, and do not attempt to make things worse by dosing your horse with tranquilizers or pain medication. Since horses cannot vomit, one of the best antidotes to poison is not available. The only things you can do is get your horse to a quiet place, blanket him if necessary, and wait for the vet to arrive. Prevention is the best cure. Remove all poisonous plants from your pasture—or else keep your horse out of the pasture.

SOME CATTLE feeds have urea added as a supplement. The rumen of the cattle can turn urea into protein. The horse does not have this ability; the small intestine absorbs the urea before it gets to the cecum. Urea is poisonous to horses, although they can usually tolerate it at the level at which it is added to cattle feed.

Luckily, many species of toxic plants are not appetizing to your horse, so he won't eat them. Unfortunately this is not universally true. Very young growing poisonous plants often seem to be more tasty than older ones, a fact that is true of most plant foods. And while horses need to gobble down large amounts of some poisonous greenery before it affects them, in other cases, a tiny amount will do the fatal trick.

If your horse gets into trouble with any of the poisons below, call your veterinarian immediately! This list is not inclusive; many other poisonous plant species exist. Further, many plants go by several different common names, and two decidedly different plants can share a name. If dealing with a case of poisoning, identify the plant and give its Latin name, as well as any common ones you know, to your vet or animal poison control center.

Awful Aquatics

Algae

Certain species of blue-green algae (cyanobacteria) release toxins into the water after the death of the organisms. Horses may become seriously ill if they drink from a pond following a heavy algae bloom. Algae species likely to cause poisoning include *Oscillatoria agardhii*, *Nodularia spumingena*, *Aphanizomenom flos-aquae*, *Coelospaerium kutzingianum*, *Gloeotrichia echinulata*, *Anabaena spiroides*, *Anabana flos-aquae*, and *Anabaena circinalis*. Possibly the most dangerous is *Microcystis aeruginosa*, which causes many serious outbreaks every year. Symptoms include tremors, weakness, bloody diarrhea, and convulsions. In a worst case scenario, sudden death from hemorrhage or liver failure can result.

Beastly Bushes and Vicious Vines

Boxwood (*Buxus sempervirens*)

This wildly popular landscaping plant is found all over the country. I can't stand the smell of the thing myself, but that's perhaps a personal prejudice. It is full of alkaloids and is extremely poisonous to horses; in fact a mere pound of leaves can kill one. It causes respiratory failure.

Burning Bush (*Euonymous atropurpureus*)

The burning bush is a glorious autumn sight in our neck of the woods—the mid-Atlantic and mid Midwest regions of the country. It turns a brilliant flaming red and holds its color well after other plants have dropped their leaves. It can, however, cause colic and diarrhea in horses, although such poisoning is not common. Still, it should not be planted in horse pastures. No one is sure what poison is involved.

Castor Bean (*Ricinus communis*)

This southern bush contains ricin, one of the most dangerous poisons known. Horses won't eat castor beans by choice, but since the stuff grows wild it can accidentally get mixed into hay or feed. A mere mouthful can kill a horse. To make things worse, the symptoms of poisoning, including sweating, trembling, and loss of coordination, may not show up for hours—or even days. By that time, it's often too late anyway. Nearly all affected horses die. These plants are common denizen of tropical areas.

Hydrangea (*Hydrangea spp.*)

This ornamental grows throughout the United States (except the Southwest). It contains a poisonous principle related to cyanide, and horses that consume a large amount of it can develop gastroenteritis and bloody diarrhea. Horses can die from this plant.

Kochia (*Kochia scoparia*)

Most of the time this Midwest plant is harmless, even nutritious, to horses, although it does contain a substance that interferes with thiamin absorption. It seems that the plant becomes toxic during periods of extended drought; the thiamin loss can cause blindness (which can be corrected by the administration of thiamin).

Labrador Tea (*Ledum columbianum* and *Ledum glandulosum*)

This small bush grows wild in the moist, mountainous west. It causes nasal discharge, repeated gulping, collapse, coma, and death. Liver and gastrointestinal toxicity can result from ingesting small quantities of these plants.

Mesquite (*Prosopis glandulosa*)

Mesquite grows wild through the Southwest and into the Plains. It is most dangerous in the dry summer and fall, when its toxic principal, arabinose, becomes most concentrated. Its seeds and pods can produce colic-like symptoms. And, although not poisonous, its hideous thorns can tear up a horse's intestines.

Mock Azalea (*Menziesia ferruginea*)

This landscaping bush of the Northwest contains grayanotoxins which produce nasal discharge, gulping, and gastrointestinal distress. Other plants with grayanotoxin are the mountain laurel, rhododendron and pieris japonica. Horses have died from ingesting this plant.

Oleander (*Nerium oleander*)

This lovely southern ornamental is sometimes called dogbane (there are other dogbanes, too), but it isn't any better for horses. The entire plant contains cardiac glycosides, and a mere OUNCE of leaves can kill a big horse. Don't plant it around a horse pasture, and if it is there, remove it carefully and far, but don't burn it. The smoke is toxic too. The plant causes cardiac arrest.

ANY PLANT known to be poisonous to other animals is probably poisonous for horses too.

OCCASIONALLY you will note the abbreviation spp. after the scientific name of the plant. This means that the plant comes in a variety of related species.

FOR AN excellent guide to most horse-poisonous plants, I strongly recommend The Horse Owner's Guide to Toxic Plants, by Sandra M. Burger. This inexpensive book contains clear photographs of common poisonous pasture plants in flower, bud, and leaf, as well as good line drawings of the whole plant.

Pieris Japonica (*Pieris floribunda*)

This ornamental shrub is common on the East coast. The classic symptoms of grayanotoxin poisoning are repeated gulping, nasal discharge, and bloating. Affected horses may grind their teeth.

Rosary Pea (*Abrus precatorius*)

This Florida vine has highly toxic seeds. The toxic agent is abrin, which is released if the seeds are thoroughly chewed. Just one seed can kill a horse, although it is said that a resistance to the toxin can be built up over a number of months, if anyone cares to try it.

Saltbush (*Atriplex patula*)

This western plant grows in salty soils with a high selenium content. Eating too much of this plant can induce selenium poisoning, whose characteristic signs include loss of hair and ridges and cracks in the hoofs. In severe cases, the hoofs can actually separate.

Sweetpea (*Lathyrus spp.*)

This lovely ornamental vine is found throughout the United States. The entire plant is poisonous, but the seeds are the worst. A horse has to consume a fair quantity of them over a few days, but if poisoned, the active principle, beta aminoproprionitrile, causes severe lameness, which may be irreversible.

Wild Jasmine or Day-Blooming Jessamine (*Cestrum diurnum*)

This ornamental plant, found in Florida, Texas, and California, contains a substance that causes hyper-absorption of calcium, thus causing hyper-calcium toxicity in horses. Night-blooming jessamines are poisonous, too, but from a different toxic principle.

Yellow Jessamine (*Gelsemium sempervirens*)

This southern evergreen vine has toxic flowers and roots, especially dangerous in the winter and spring. The poison, a form of strychnine, can cause weakness, respiratory problems, and convulsions.

Yew (*Taxus* family)

All members of the yew family are extremely toxic. The evil substance is the alkaloid taxine and only a very little of it can kill a horse or other livestock by causing cardiac arrest. Near where I live, a man cut down his Japanese yew hedge, and thinking the cows in the field next door might enjoy the stuff, he kindly tossed it over the fence to them. The cows did indeed enjoy the treat, and the next day 25 of them were lying dead in the field with their legs sticking straight up into the air. That's the problem with yew. Animals

like the stuff to the point of seeking it out. This makes it different and more dangerous than many other poisonous varieties. Don't plant yew anywhere near your pasture.

Felonious Flowers

Bindweed or Morning Glory (*Convolvulus arvensis*)

This invasive plant is often found twining along fence wire. It contains tropane alkaloids in all parts of the plant resulting in colicky symptoms in horses that ingest them.

Some of the most common poisonous plants. Pam Tanzey.

Poison Hemlock

Deadly Nightshade

Oleander

Horsetail

Buttercup

St. John's Wort

Yew

Bracken Fern

Buttercup (*Ranunculus aris* and others)

That sweet childhood favorite? That delightful little wildflower that graces our marshy meadows? You bet. The active ingredient is ranunculin, which turns into the irritant protoanemonin as it is chewed. It flowers mostly from April through June. This plant is not even native to the United States, by the way—it was introduced from Europe. Now the nasty little weed has worldwide distribution.

Its toxicity varies with its state of growth and is most poisonous while in flower. Not all species of buttercup contain the toxic principle ranunculin. It is not deadly, in any case, but causes colic and diarrhea. Most animals hate its bitter taste, and so avoid poisoning; however, the very fact that the plant is seldom eaten encourages its spread. And in a few cases, some horses seem rather to develop a taste for the stuff—much like tobacco or scotch in humans. (Cows who eat buttercups produce reddish, nasty tasting milk.) Interestingly, dried buttercup is no longer poisonous, and so is safe if found in hay. However, that seems to be when some horses acquire their taste for it.

Buckwheat (*Fagopyrum esculentum*)

Although usually grown as a cover crop only to enrich the soil, buckwheat is sometimes ground as used as a grain; however, it should be not fed to horses since it can cause intense light photosensitivity in some animals, especially those with white skin.

Alsike Clover (*Trifolium hybridum*)

This perennial legume is similar to the common red clover, but the flower head is a white/pink, and the leaves lack the characteristic chevron pattern of red clover. It is commonly grown for pasture or hay! All green parts of the plant are dangerous when wet; the plant is safe when dry. It is found throughout the country. Horses eating it can develop a special type of photosensitivity (trifoliosis), and lesions on the skin, especially when the pasture is wet. This condition is sometimes called "dew poisoning." Some animals also develop a mild colic or diarrhea. Continued exposure to the plant can bring worse symptoms, including possible liver disease. Horses should be removed from a pasture containing it, although this is not a commonly reported toxicity.

Crimson Clover (*Trifolium incarnatum*)

Crimson clover grows throughout the Northeast and Midwest. Although it's not poisonous, it can be dangerous to horses when they ingest it. The plant has little barbed hairs beneath the flower heads, and when dried at an over-ripe stage, can cause both colic and impaction.

Red Clover (*Trifolium pratense*)

The delicious red clover is healthful, as long as it's not moldy. Red clover mold in hay produces a fungal toxin called slaframine, which induces salivation, bloating, stiffness, and even blindness. Horses grazing on lush green clover have been known to founder.

Sweet Clover (*Melilotus spp.*)

Sweet clover is a good feed, so long as it doesn't contain dicoumarol, which can happen when it gets moldy. Dicoumarol, a malevolent mold found in moldy sweet clover pastures, can cause a vitamin K deficiency and subsequent. It contains a mycotoxin related to the rat poison warfarin that destroys vitamin K in the body, thus reducing clotting ability. It would take a few weeks to actually develop, but when it does it can cause death; in pregnant mares it can also cause abortions.

Autmun Crocus (*Colchicum autumnale*)

This beautiful cultivar can be fatal to horses that eat the plant or bulbs. The toxic principle is the alkaloid colchicine. The only symptom is gastrointestinal distress, although on rare occasions, death may result from consumption.

Death Camas (*Zigadenus spp.*)

This plant, which comes in several varieties, mostly poisonous, grows throughout the country. It contains steroid alkaloids and produces a variety of poisonous symptoms. Horses will generally consume it only if other food is not available. Both fresh and dried versions are poisonous.

Dogbane (*Apocynum cannabinum*)

Dogbane, sometimes called Indian hemp, grows all over the United States. It is full of alkaloids and cardiac glycosides. It's pretty toxic, but horses seldom eat it.

European Hemlock (*Conium maculatum*)

Despite it name, European hemlock grows pretty much everywhere; it is most famous for having killed Socrates. This of course is not the stately hemlock tree, but a nasty weed. Its poisonous elements (several alkaloids) are most concentrated in the seeds, but the entire plant is toxic. This plant is a biennial—it is more poisonous in the second year than in the first. Horses sort of like hemlock, which is really too bad. The plant is a killer, and horses can die in hours or days after ingestion. Find this plant and get it out of your pasture.

Fitweed (*Corydalis spp.*)

Fitweed grows all over the country, except for the West Coast and deepest South and Southwest. It contains alkaloid poisons that can kill a horse

within hours. Symptoms include panting, staggering, and seizures (hence the name "fitweed.")

False Hellebore or Indian Poke (*Veratrum viride*)

This perennial grows throughout the country; it is mostly found in swamps, wet woods and meadows. It contains several kinds of steroidal alkaloids. Although horses won't eat the stuff unless nothing else is around, its effects are daunting; they include digestive disorders, respiratory paralysis, and death. Pregnant mares will abort or give birth to deformed foals.

Groundsel (*Sencio spp.*)

This weed is common is the dry areas of the Southwest and Great Plains. The toxic principle is pyrrolizidine, a toxin that destroys the liver. All parts of the plant are poisonous. Fortunately, horses will only eat the stuff if nothing else is available. The greatest danger is when groundsel gets incorporated into hay. Groundsel poisoning is hard to track down, since the symptoms (weight loss, depression, and abdominal pain) may not appear until several months after the plant is eaten.

Water Hemlock (*Cicuta maculata*)

If anything is worse than the European hemlock, it is the water hemlock, which, as its name suggests prefers a boggy acre. It is found through the United States and Canada. The active principle is cicutoxin, which causes severe convulsions. This stuff is so deadly that one mouthful can kill a horse in 15 minutes. The juicy spring shoots are tasty to horses.

Horsetail (*Equisetum arvense*)

Horsetails grow in swamps throughout the country. They contain aconitic acid, thiaminase and palustrine. Green plants are more toxic than dried, but horsetails in hay, fed over a period of a few weeks, can produce a severe enough poisoning to cause death. Symptoms include weakness and staggering.

Hound's Tongue (*Cynoglossum officinale*)

This western weed is a European import. The toxic principles are pyrrolizidine alkaloids, which affect the liver. Symptoms of poisoning often don't show up for months. The entire plant is poisonous, even when dried, but horses find it tasty.

Indian Paintbrush (*Castilleja spp.*)

Although the brilliant orange Indian paintbrush, which grows throughout much of the country, is not poisonous, it does accumulate selenium. So if the soil is selenium rich, this plant can be dangerous. Affected animals exhibit all the signs of selenium poisoning.

Jimmyweed (*Haplopappus heterophyllus*)

This woody weed of the Plains and Southwest is very poisonous to horses; the toxic principle is tremetol. It is even dangerous to foals whose dam eats the weed, since the contaminated milk can kill the foal. The poison can take a couple of weeks to take effect, but only a few pounds can destroy liver and kidney function. Symptoms include tremors, frequent urination, stiffness, and knuckling of the fetlocks.

Jimsonweed (*Datura spp.*)

Jimsonweed, a member of the very toxic nightshade family, grows throughout the country. (Its unfortunate discoverers were members of the Jamestown colony. They made a salad out of the stuff.) It is common in over-grazed pastures, and is easily recognized by this showy blue trumpet-shaped flowers. Even small amounts can cause death; fortunately, horses do not usually eat the plant. Symptoms include thirst, colic, convulsions, and sudden death. The most poisonous parts include all green parts and the unripe fruits.

Easter Lily (*Zephyranthes atamasco*)

This southern lily, a member of the amaryllis family, is toxic, although the precise poison is not currently known. Symptoms include diarrhea and staggering. Horses won't eat the things unless nothing else is available.

Locoweed (*Astragalus and Oxytropis spp.*)

This infamous plant of the West is not only poisonous (both fresh and dry), but also very palatable to horses. The poisonous principal is swainsonine, an alkaloid first identified in an Australian plant named darling pea—an instance of false advertising if I ever heard one. Locoweed has several methods to attack your horse. First of all, many varieties are selenium soakers, and can give your horse an overdose of this vital but toxic metal. Other species go after the nervous system, whence comes the name "locoweed." Indeed horses eating the stuff may act as if they are crazy, even though these symptoms may not appear until several months after the horse has been eating the plant. Typical symptoms include head bobbing, excitement, and over reaction to stimuli. If horses are not removed from the area where locoweed thrives, they can die.

Lupine (*Lupinus ssp*)

Not every species of this glorious blue plant (which grows everywhere in the country) is toxic, but enough of them are to make you suspicious of all. The seeds are the most toxic part of the plant; the poisonous principles include quinolizidine and piperidine alkaloids. Affected horses have problems breathing; they may go into convulsions and die.

Milkweed (*Asclepias spp.*)

Milkweed is found all over the country except the Pacific Northwest. There are both broad and narrow leafed species, with the latter more poisonous than the former. The toxic principle is a cardiac glycoside similar to that in oleander. Milkweed poisoning often results when the plant is baled in hay.

Mistletoe (*Phoradendron villosum*)

The white-berried mistletoe is a parasite of oak trees. It grows throughout the country, and horses that like to browse may ingest the stuff. It contains a variety of poisons. Death comes suddenly, with few symptoms; gastrointestinal upset may result from sublethal poisoning. So hang mistletoe all over your house if you like—but don't throw it in the pasture.

Monkshood (*Acinitum napellus*)

Monkshood is a member of the buttercup family. It grows in damp places throughout the United States and is toxic through and through. It contains aconitine and similar alkaloids. Symptoms include weakness, restlessness, and bloating. Affected animals may die within hours.

Common Nightshade (*Solanum americanum*)

Nightshade grows throughout the country, and horses may be drawn to it. Its unripe berries are the most poisonous, being full of the glycoalkaloid solanine. Some people say that the ripe fruits aren't poisonous, but I wouldn't eat them anyway. Nightshade causes severe neurological and gastrointestinal disorders.

Silver Nightshade (*Solanum elaeagnifolium*)

This plant grows in the Southwest. As a member of the nightshade family, its poison is similar to that of the common nightshade. Unlike common nightshade, however, it is the ripe fruit of the silver nightshade that is most toxic.

Rape (*Brassica napus*)

This unpleasantly named plant is a member of the mustard family; it is found throughout the country, but is most likely to infest pastures in the North. It contains several toxic compounds of the glucosinolate group, and can cause severe digestive upset, including colic, as well as thyroid, kidney and liver problems.

Other plants in this family, including kale, white clover, rutabaga and turnips, interfere with iodine intake. Horses dining upon these delicacies could use extra iodine supplement.

Rattlebox or Rattlepod (*Crotalaria spp.*)

This handsome plant with its bright yellow flowers grows throughout the northeastern part of the country. (It's called rattlebox because you can "rattle" the seeds in their dry pods.) It's a common wildflower that has poisoned many a horse; the toxic principle is a pyrrolizidine alkaloid that causes liver failure. The toxin is present in greatest quantities in the seeds, with lesser amounts in the leaves and stems. Symptoms include circular walking, weakness, and diarrhea.

Sacahuista or Beargrass (*Nolina texana*)

This plant is confined to the Southwest. No one is sure what the toxic principle is, but it seems to be concentrated in the flowers. Horses don't prefer beargrass, but will eat it if other forage is not present. The plant affects the liver and kidneys, but produces few overt symptoms. Beargrass can kill a horse.

Senna or Coffeeweed (*Cassia spp*)

Sennas, especially the seeds, contain a variety of poisons, not all of which are known. Some have deleterious effects on skeletal and heart muscle, and on the liver. Senna grows throughout the eastern and southern parts of the country west through Texas. It takes a while (several days to weeks) for the toxins to build up in the horse's system. When it does, the horse may stagger and his urine turns red or brown. Horses can die because of damage to the heart muscle. However, senna poisoning is more common in cattle than in horses.

St. John's Wort (*Hypericum perforatum*)

Alas, this medically valuable plant has its darker side. The villain is hypericin, a plant pigment that does bad things to horses. (Unfortunately, horses like to eat the plant.) This pigment causes a photosensitivity that is especially marked in white horses. It creates a skin reaction that is quite painful. Increased heart rate and diarrhea are also observed. St. John's wort grows throughout the United States and Canada.

Snakeroot (*Eupatorium rugosum*)

Snakeroot is found through the Plains areas, from Canada down into Texas and the Southeast. Its toxic ingredient is tremetol, which severely damages the liver and kidney. It is most deadly in the summer and autumn, and is frequently mixed into hay. Tremetol can pass from the dam into her foal through milk, which is why the resulting event is sometimes called "milk sickness." Symptoms include tremors and sluggishness.

Sneezeweed (*Helenium spp.*)

The weed grows on overgrazed pastures all over the United States and Canada. One of its common names, Staggerwort, gives you an idea of what its primary toxin, helanin, does to your horse—makes him stagger around. He can also foam at the mouth, which at least suggests the "sneeze" part of sneezeweed. The whole plant, but especially the seeds, is toxic.

Tarweed (*Amsinckia intermedia*)

Tarweed is yet another western plant containing pyrrolizidine alkaloids. The seeds are the most toxic, and as is the case with so many of these plants, symptoms may not show up for months after the horse begins ingesting the plants. The main signs are yellowed eyes and mucus membranes, wandering, and abdominal pain. Animals who have deteriorated enough to show jaundice will die.

Yellow Star Thistle (*Centaurea solstitialis*)

This unwelcome member of the sunflower family is found throughout the country except around the Great Lakes region. It didn't come from here originally, however—it's an import from the Mediterranean. A similar plant, Russian knapweed, comes from Russia, of course. No one knows what the toxic principle is, but horses seem to like the stuff, especially as the season wears on. Whether the plants get tastier, or whether horses just get used to it is not known, either. Whatever it is, it causes a condition called "chewing disease." This horrible, horrible disease, technically known as nigropallidal encephalomalacia, causes a vicious kind of brain damage that makes it impossible for the horse to chew. Affected horses invariably starve to death. The poor things stand with their mouths open to receive food, but cannot chew it. Once these symptoms appear, the horse must be euthanized. Horses must eat the stuff for some weeks to be affected, so if you see any of this thistle in your pasture, get rid of it.

Ferocious Ferns

Bracken Fern (*Pteridium aquilinium*)

While not exactly poisonous, bracken fern, which grows world-wide, contains compounds (thiaminases) that inhibit the absorption of thiamin, and thus can cause a deficiency in that vitamin. Luckily, horses won't eat the stuff unless other forages are hard to find, so poisonings are uncommon. Symptoms apparent after eating the plant for a month or more include loss of coordination and blindness.

Gruesome Grasses

Arrowgrass (*Triglochin maritima*)

This grass grows in swamps throughout the United States and Canada. Its leaves contain prussic acid—that's cyanide. Symptoms include rapid breathing, hyperactivity, bright red mucous membranes, convulsions, and death. A few pounds of the plant are a potentially lethal dose.

Sagebrush (*Artemisia spp.*)

Sagebrush, which lives throughout the Western U.S., contains volatile monoterpenoid oils, which are most potent during the fall and winter. These are neurotoxins. Although horses don't care for sagebrush, they will eat it if nothing else is available. Abnormal behavior and unexplained falling may occur after eating sagebrush for several days. If affected horses are removed from the source and fed properly, they will recover. This is in contrast to poisoning from locoweed, which is permanent.

Sudangrass (*Sorghum sudanense*)

Sudangrass and its hybrids contain compounds, including prussic acid, that cause muscle weakness, urinary problems, abortions, and, in severe cases, even death! Johnson grass (S. halepense) has much the same effect. Do not allow your horse to eat these grasses.

Tall Fescue (*Festuca spp.*)

Although there is nothing toxic per se about tall fescue, which makes an appropriate pasture grass for horses, older varieties can be infected with an endophyte fungus and associated toxins that can spell disaster for brood mares. The toxins can cause lower reproductive rates, abortion, lower milk production, prolonged gestation, and problems for the foal. (It doesn't help matters when we consider that fescue is probably the most common pasture grass.) Never allow pregnant broodmares on this grass. Get rid of it and plant the fungus-free variety.

Toxic Trees

Apple Trees (*Malus sylvestris*)

Oh, no. Not the apple tree. Yes, I'm afraid so. It's the seeds. They are chock full of cyanide. Now, if a horse threw away the core, there would be no problem. But horses gobble up the core and its seeds along with the rest of the apple. It takes about a cup of apple seeds to poison a horse, though, so a little treat won't hurt, but horses have indeed been poisoned by gobbling up (or down) large numbers of windfall apples from the ground.

Avocado

Avocados grown in southern California, and their bark, leaves and fruit are poisonous to horses. Swelling can develop around the mouth and head; they can resemble a snakebite, and have been so misidentified.

Black Locust (*Robinia pseudoacacia*)

The black locust is sometimes known as simply the locust tree—or to make

things even more confusing—as the yellow locust. Whatever you want to call it, though, this Eastern native can be dangerous. The youngsters have wickedly sharp spines (our property was full of the things when we bought the place). This is good, since the spines encourage horses to stay well away from them. The entire plant is poisonous; it contains glycoside robitin and two nasty phytotoxins: robin and phasin. (It seems a shame to name a poison after a lovely bird, but there you are. I didn't name it.) The real danger of this tree is that is makes such excellent fence posts. Locust is very hard, almost impervious to everything, and so is very popular for this purpose. Unfortunately, more than one bored horse has been poisoned from stripping the bark of the post and chowing down. Although seldom fatal, the effects can include weakness, chilled limbs, irregular pulse, diarrhea, and rear end paralysis. Call you vet if your horse has been eating your locust fence.

Black Walnut (*Juglans nigra*)

Although the husk of the black walnut is poisonous to dogs, and the whole tree contains a growth inhibitor that destroys neighboring trees, the black walnut has another way of getting at horses. This happens when people unthinkingly use black walnut shavings for horse bedding. The horse doesn't have to eat the stuff to get sick. Even a few black walnut shavings can sicken or even kill a horse by inducing laminitis and respiratory difficulties.

The tree is not generally a problem (for horses) in the pasture, and some people like the walnuts, although they are pain in the neck to shell.

Wild Cherry (*Prunus spp.*)

Cyanide again. Both the fruit and leaves of the wild cherry contain cyanogenetic glycosides. The leaves, especially when wilted, are the worst. Fresh or thoroughly dried leaves are relatively harmless. If a horse drinks water after devouring the leaves, the cyanide is quickly released into the bloodstream and the horse can go into convulsions. Brain, heart and lungs are all rapidly damaged. Death follows soon thereafter. (Apricot and peach trees have the same properties, but cherry is the worst of the lot.) Fortunately most animals will not seek out cherry leaves if more palatable forage is available.

Chinaberry (*Melia azedarach*)

The 17th-century Italian physician wrote of the chinaberry: "It bringeth death even unto beasts." The American poet Conrad Aiken wrote a very nice poem about a chinaberry tree, but then he probably didn't know that its berries are poisonous to horses. In fact the whole tree is full of alkaloids and saponins, but the berries are undoubtedly the worst—and horses will eat the things. Then they get colic followed by convulsions. The tree grows throughout the southern United States, although its native home is in Asia.

Eve's Necklace or Texas Sophora (*Sophora affinis*)

This ornamental tree, a member of the pea family, grows mostly in Texas, although its range extends to Oklahoma, Louisiana, and Arkansas. It produces elegant yellow flowers, but the dangerous parts of the plants are its black pods and the seeds they contain. Affected horses lose coordination and tremble. Some even fall down, and severe cases can result in respiratory paralysis or even death. Keep the animal quiet and call your vet for supportive treatment if you believe your horse has been poisoned by this tree. A smaller tree with similar range and properties is the Necklace Pod (Sophora tomentosa).

Golden Chain or Bean Tree (*Laburnum anagyroides*)

This southern ornamental tree is full of alkaloid poisons through and through, although the seeds are the worst. Symptoms include agitation, un-coordination, convulsion and coma; many horses die from asphyxiation. There is no treatment for this kind of poison, just keep your horse away from the tree.

Horse Chestnut (*Aesculus hippocastanum*)

Along with the poisonous black locusts I have on my property, I also enjoy the company of the toxic horse chestnut. I would dislike this loathsome tree even if it weren't poisonous, since its blossoms stink to high heaven and practically choke me every spring. By the way, these toxic chestnuts are not related to the TRUE chestnut, the kind you like to roast by an open fire.

It's not for nothing that this tree is also called the stinking or fetid buckeye. It grows from New England down through a large portion of the East and southern Midwest. This tree, I may add, is not native to this country. It was, for some unknown reason, brought here from southeastern Europe. It is poisonous throughout, including its shiny brown seeds, which come encased in hideous spiny capsules. Unfortunately, horses like to eat horse chestnuts, which may be why they call them that, for all I know. Horses especially enjoy the tender young plants, which along with the seeds, are the most toxic parts. The poison appears to be a combination of alkaloids, saponins and the glycoside aesculin. Although most horses will not die from eating horse chestnuts, it can make them pretty sick; the toxin affects both the nervous system and the gastrointestinal tract.

The buckeye is very similar to the horse chestnut, and belongs to the same genus—aesculus.

Oaks (*Quercus spp.*)

Oaks are everywhere, aren't they? And while the oak is one of the noblest of trees, it has its downside. All oak trees produce acorns, and all acorns are poisonous if eaten in large enough quantities. The offending elements are

tannin and gallotannin. Oak trees may have the same chemicals in their bark, new leaves, and buds. Tannin destroys the epithelial cells of the digestive tract and causes a multitude of symptoms, including abdominal pain, thirst, and loss of appetite. Horses will eat oak products if other forage is scarce. The symptoms may go on for a week or more, and unless treated, 85 percent of horses can die from kidney failure. Call your vet—calcium hydroxide introduced through a nasogastric tube may save your horse's life.

Peach (*Prunus persica*)

Like its relatives, all parts of peach trees contain cyanide. Especially the leaves. This doesn't bode well for horses, and horses ought not be grazed in peach orchards, where they can come down with convulsions and die.

Red Maple (*Acer rubrum*)

One of the most beloved shade trees of the eastern United States, the red maple, is toxic to horses. Both leaves and bark are poisonous, although no one knows why. It doesn't matter if the leaves are fresh or wilted, either, although some people say that wilted leaves are by far the worst. This doesn't mean that your horse will collapse and die after eating a maple leaf or two—but a sufficient number of them (about five pounds) will cause death. About 18 hours after ingestion, the horse will develop a severe anemia and methemoglobinemia, a condition in which the red blood cells that do remain will be unable to transport oxygen. This is what usually kills the horse, and suddenly too. Of course, you can't see anemia, so you need to watch out for the signs: lethargy, weakness, appetite loss, pale gums, dark brown or red-tinged urine. Pregnant mares will abort. If you even suspect your horse has been dining on maple, call your vet immediately. He will administer intravenous fluids and oxygen. Blood transfusions or replacement may also be necessary. This is an extremely serious condition, which unless caught very early is usually lethal. Never tie your horse out close to a red maple, and don't plant them in your pasture. Horses don't favor the taste, but as we all know, a bored horse might eat anything.

And So On

The list I have given here is a mere sample. Other plants which have been identified as poisoning horses include azaleas and rhododendrons (leaves), delphiniums (all parts), parsley (leaves), poinsettia (leaves and sap), poppy (roots and leaves) and rhubarb (leaves).

In addition, many feed additives designed for cattle or other farm species are poisonous to horses. Chief among them are rumensin (monensis sodium), an antibiotic used in the cattle industry, which can produce blindness and death in horses. Never allow your horse to eat out of an uncleaned trough previously filled with cattle feed! A growth-promoting compound called salinomycin commonly fed to cattle is also deadly to horses, as is lincomysin, often fed to pigs. Horses should eat horse food. That's a pretty simple rule!

Ouch Plants

In addition to plants that can poison a horse, many plants contain bristles, prickles, thorns, and other protective devices that are dangerous to horses. Such plants include burdock thistles, *(artium spp.)*, awn grasses *(Aristida spp.)*, oat, barley, rye, or wheat awns, sand burrs *(Cenchrus spp.)*, bristle grasses and foxtails *(Setaria spp.)*, horse nettle *(Solanum carolinense)*, stinging nettle *(Urtica spp)* and cockle burrs *(Xantium spp.)*.

Selenium Accumulator Plants

These plants absorb so much selenium that eating them can poison your horse. They include two-grooved milkvetch *(Astragalus bisulcatus)*, golden weed *(Haplpopappus engelmannii)*, woody aster *(Xylorrhiza glabriuscula)*, prince's plume *(Stanleya pinnata)*, white prairie aster *(Aster falcatus)*, broom *(Guterrezia sarothrae)*, gumweed *(Grindelia spp)*, saltbrush *(Atriplex spp.)*, Indian paintbrush *(Castilleja spp.)* and beard tongue *(Penstemon spp.)*.

CHAPTER

15

Supplements and Concentrates: The Extra Edge

A SUPPLEMENT IS JUST THAT
a supplement. It can add to, but not truly replace,
a good basic diet. And the average horse, on a
good diet, does not need supplements. No supplement can turn a worn-out nag into a gleaming
top-of-the-line champion. The annoying but oh-
so-simple truth is that most horses that are in bad
condition simply need more food. In some cases
they need better food.

That being said, we should note that certain
supplements, for certain horses, can make an
important difference. One important factor that
horse people need to consider is the availability
of feed and hay in their area. Dog owners all over
the country have pretty much the same choices,

but horse people are often limited to what is available locally. Drought, soil conditions, and farming practices and preferences all affect what the horse owner can choose. This is one reason why supplements, which are available nationwide, may be important for the average horse owner.

It is critical to remember, however, that a supplement is meant to correct a deficiency. If your horse is getting the proper nutrients in his diet, supplements are unnecessary, and may actually be harmful.

Ideally horses should receive all their required nutrients in their food. Unfortunately, every year this becomes more difficult. Why is this? Well, we can blame acid rain for one thing.

Acid rain is a product of power plant emissions and some mining operations. As its name suggests, it acidifies whatever it falls on. It's invisible and dangerous. For example, pristine mountain streams in New Hampshire are looking clearer than ever; that's because acid rain has lowered their pH level to about that of beer. These streams are crystalline because nothing grows in them.

Acid rain has equally deleterious effects on the soil, especially in the Northeast, where the problem is most serious because the prevailing winds bring pollution from the midwestern power plants and industries to the New England skies. The resulting rain lowers the pH of the soil, and depletes it of calcium and other good minerals, while allowing aluminum, which may be a poison and in any event has no known biological function, to be absorbed into the plants. Horses then eat the plants, getting not enough of the good stuff and possibly too much of the bad.

As I said, some horses can benefit from the use of certain supplements; for others supplementation could be useless or dangerous. The three important factors to remember when considering any supplement for your horse are:

- Is it safe?
- Is it effective?
- Is it necessary?

Safe and effective supplements should meet the following criteria, some of which are on the label. In other cases, you'll need to do your research. Select supplements with labels that provide a guaranteed analysis. You need to know exactly the potency of any supplement you feed your horse. Guessing could be dangerous, or at least, ineffective.

- The label should provide complete information, listing all ingredients—including fillers. The correct Latin names of the plant components, potency, dose information, lot number, and expiration date should be on the label as well.

- The supplement should carry the Good Manufacturing Practices Seal (GMP) issued by the National Nutritional Foods Association or ConsumerLab.com (CL) Seal of Approval. The GMP assures product quality and safety, while ConsumerLab.com is an independent supplement testing service. It publishes reports on ingredients, potency, and bioavailability of ingredients.

- The supplement should be produced according to U.S. Pharmacopeia guidelines. If the product passes, the label should state so.

- Ingredients should be organic, and of human-grade quality (even if the specific product is designed for animals). This information, unfortunately, may not be on the label.

Getting Realistic about Supplements

If a supplement is going to do your horses any good, it needs to be supplied in the proper amounts—and that's more than you might think. In fact, most supplements only provide a little extra of what a normal horse needs, just a few percentage points. So if you've had to supplement a seriously deficient horse, you'd be giving him about a pound of vitamins and minerals a day. That's not cheap either—I've seen people gulp when they check the price of supplements. And I don't blame them.

Protein

Most horses get plenty of protein and their constituent amino acids in their diets. Horses that don't get enough protein may also be lacking in carbohydrates and fats, and reveal their lack by a thin and undernourished appearance. Usually a horse that needs more protein also needs more food. Still in some cases, particularly in growing horses, and lactating mares, extra protein can be beneficial. As a matter of nomenclature, any feed containing 20 percent or more crude protein is considered to be protein supplement.

Common protein supplements include:

- Alfalfa meal: Grind the alfalfa, and heat dry it, and you have alfalfa meal. This is a good source of many nutrients.

- Cottonseed meal: This is a popular protein supplement, but should not be used with young foals; it has an unbalanced amino acid profile, being very low in lysine.

- Brewer's dried grains: This is a mixture of used hops and the extracted residue of barley malt. It's high in both fiber and protein.

NOT ALL supplements designed for human beings are appropriate for horses. Don't use ANY supplement unless you know it is safe for your horse.

SOME PEOPLE give their horses dried chicken manure as a protein supplement. Once heated, it's supposed to be safe. I just cannot recommend feeding a horse chicken manure. Sorry. I don't have a good reason. I just don't like the idea.

- Canola meal: This is a popular supplement in Canada, which is a prime grower of its source, the unsavory sounding rapeseed. Actually rape (*Brassic napus*) is a member of the mustard family. The stuff originally comes from Europe, and it makes a nice birdseed, as well.

- Extruded soybeans: Soybeans add both fat and protein to the diet.

- Linseed meal: Although linseed meal is a protein source, the fat residue (left from the oil) has the additional benefit of making your horse's coat shine, although the effect is not so marked as with unsaturated oils. Do not use linseed meal as a supplement for young foals; its amino acid profile is unbalanced.

- Soybean meal: Soybean meal is easily the most popular protein supplement. It is heat-treated, inexpensive, convenient, and loaded with protein. It is also palatable for horses, and a good choice when available pasture or hay is low in protein, or when you are feeding a growing, aged, or lactating horse. In other words, if you are feeding alfalfa, soybean meal is not needed. The best soybean meal is clean and light-colored. Mix it well into the feed.

- Animal sources. Some people use animal-based protein supplements, which are sometimes cheaper—but sometimes not. Animal-based protein supplements contain a lot of fat, however, which makes them hard to store. Horses also find them less palatable that vegetable protein. This should not be surprising. However, animal proteins are usually rich in lysine, and fishmeal (mostly menhaden) contains both lysine and methionine. Milk products like dried milk, casein (a milk

Beet pulp. Helen Peppe photo.

protein), or dried whey are also commonly used. Whey is probably the most common, since dried whole milk and casein can be quite expensive. These products have plenty of lysine and are high in protein and minerals. But they are low in the fat-soluble vitamins.

When purchasing a protein supplement, make sure that it provides a complete source of protein containing all the essential amino acids: lysine, methionine, tryptophan, histidine, valine, leucine, isoleucine, phenylalanine, threonine, and arginine.

Fiber and Other Carbohydrate Supplements

Beet Pulp

Beet pulp is a byproduct of the sugar-making process, at least it is when sugar comes from sugar beets rather than from sugar cane. After the sugar has been extracted, the beet chips are shredded for pulp. It is almost always soaked first, which reduces dust and makes it easy to chew. This is a definite plus for horses who may be suffering dental problems or who have respiratory difficulties. Some people think that unsoaked beet pulp can swell up in the gut and injure the horse, but no evidence supports this theory.

Beet pulp has an ADF (acid detergent fiber) rating of 28 percent, which makes it digestible. Its TDN is 68.7 percent. It is low in protein, phosphorus, carotene and vitamin D, but high in calcium and energy. Shredded or pelleted beet pulp is sometimes added as a fiber source and supplement for

Beet pulp pellets. Helen Peppe photo.

hay or pasture. Beet pulp can be used alone or combined with molasses to increase its energy.

Wheat Bran

Bran is the outer layer of the grain kernel—it is removed during the flour-milling process. Bran provides highly digestible fiber, as well as some protein. However, it has a major drawback; it contains 12 times as much phosphorus as calcium. If a horse received nothing but bran, he could eventually develop the condition known as "big head," giving the horse a ghastly appearance.

Its use as a purported laxative or colic-preventative is probably folklore. (Some of the recipes I have seen include mineral oil and Metamucil in the mash. The mineral oil is a laxative.) I am personally convinced that this folklore got started with Black Beauty, in which the equine characters were frequently fed bran mashes to help them recover from some particularly gruesome experiences. However, in moderate amounts it does no harm, despite the objection of some that it forms enteroliths (intestinal stones). It doesn't.

Some people find that bran mash improves a peckish horse's appetite, and some others use it hide medicine in. However, don't add calcium supplements to a bran mash, since the can bind to the phytic acid in the wet bran. Horses needing calcium shouldn't be eating bran anyway. My personal opinion is that bran mashes are more trouble than they are worth.

Rice Bran

This is a relatively new supplement to equine diets. Like wheat bran, rice bran is left over from the milling process, and contains a good amount of calories, protein (13 percent), and crude fiber (11.7 percent). But it is significantly different from wheat bran in that it contains about 20 percent fat. (Be careful—this makes it more likely to go rancid.) A pound of rice bran equals a half-cup of vegetable oil. So rice bran is a great addition to your horse's feed if you would like to add fat to his diet. You can buy it as an extruded powder, or in pelleted form. Rice bran, as a fat source, is much more stable than oils, and is sometimes a good deal more palatable to horses, especially in warm, humid climates when oil can get really nasty.

Rice bran does, however, contain the same calcium:phosphorus imbalance as wheat bran—a ratio heavily loaded in favor of phosphorus. Thus rice bran should never be a major proportion of the diet (no more than 5 percent); if it is, the calcium:phosphorus ratio must be corrected.

Chaff

Chaff is chopped up oat or barley straw or very low-quality hay. It has almost no usable nutrients (it's mostly lignin), but can be useful to keep a bored

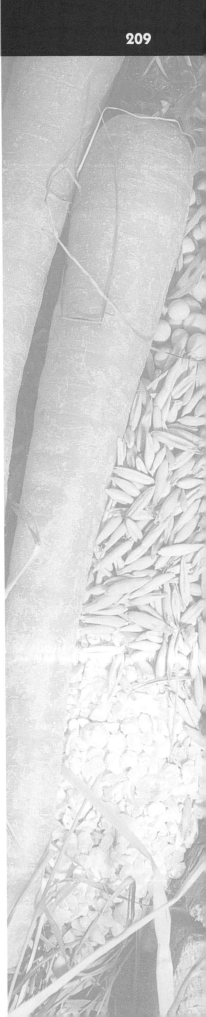

horse happy. It is also used to keep a dieting horse feeling full without adding calories, or to provide a fiber filler for a colic-prone horse.

Grain Hulls

Grain hulls, especially oat hulls, which are very high fiber (50 percent more than hay) are sometimes used to "bulk up" a horse's diet without adding calories.

Molasses

There are lots of different kinds of this interesting syrup, believe it or not: cane (blackstrap), beet, refiner's, citrus, wood and starch. Blackstrap and beet molasses are the kinds most often found in horse feeds. It is added to horse feed to keep down dust and improve the taste of the food.

Molasses contains about 54 percent TDN and lots of energy. It may help pick up the appetite of a reluctant eater. Blackstrap molasses is also high in calcium (not because of anything actually in the molasses, but because of the processing used in its manufacture). Molasses is low in protein and most vitamins, but does have a fair amount of niacin and pantothenate. Its energy content is similar to that of oats, although this energy comes from sugar rather than starch. The main danger of molasses is that the carbohydrates and moisture it contains can increase mold growth during the hot summer months. Mix about four ounces per day into the food.

Potatoes

Yep, you can feed your horse potaotes—and you don't even have to cook them. Their nutrition level is similar to corn, although horses aren't crazy about them, and large amounts can cause loose manure. They may also cause choke, although the risk is reduced if they are fed at ground level. At any rate, if you are low on other feed, you can try giving your horse up to 20 pounds of potatoes a day. Of course, you won't use any that are rotten, sprouting, or green. I actually don't expect anyone reading this book to start feeding her horse potatoes. But it's nice to know you can. French fries may be appreciated but perhaps not appropriate.

Lipid (Fat) Supplements

Vegetable oils are sometimes provided as a source of energy and fat in the horse's diet. They are also used as a binder for pelleted foods. They have no carbohydrates and no protein—just fat and energy. Yet this is not always a bad thing, since today's performance horses require plenty of both.

Most horse feeds contain only about 5 percent (or less) fat, but horses can benefit from fat supplements. In fact horses seem to be able to handle a diet of 20 percent fat in the total diet, so long as the change to a higher fat diet is made gradually. It's especially nice for their skin and coat, and high levels improve performance substantially. Fat is also good for elderly horses, or for horses who are not "easy keepers." Vegetable oils provide three times more digestible energy than an equal weight of cereal grain, and between 3.5 to six times as much if you calculate by volume. So when you add fat, you can reduce the total amount of feed as long as your horse is getting enough protein and other nutrients.

One of the amazing properties of fat is that it increases the amount of dietary energy available for growth, lactation and work even without an increase in calories. It does this because it decreases the amount of energy used for heat; this in turn decreases the body's heat load and leaves more energy available for other things. It does seem to be true that working horses in hot weather suffer much less stress if extra fat is added to the diet.

If your horse's diet lacks essential fatty acids, he may have a dry, coarse coat. He is also prone to skin lesions and infections. You can supplement your horse's diet with as much as three ounces of polyunsaturated corn or cooking oil per day. This will help keep his coat in peak condition. However, if you are using fats as an energy source, perhaps to replace grain, you'll need to add about eight ounces of polyunsaturated oil to the feed per day. The increase should be made gradually over a period of two or three weeks. Horses can use supplemented fat surprisingly well, considering that it is not part of their natural diet.

To complicate things, the more polyunsaturated fats that a diet contains, the higher the requirement for selenium and vitamin E. This is because left completely unopposed, polyunsaturated fats oxidize to peroxides in the muscle cell walls and blood. This reduces muscle efficiency. Polyunsaturated fats can also degrade into superoxide radicals, which cause inflammation, and more serious damage to cell walls.

Vitamin E helps prevent this problem, as does the selenium-containing glutathione peroxidase. That's why horses on high-fat diets should be getting supplements of vitamin E and perhaps selenium. Some parts of the country produce foods with more selenium than other parts. If you live in a selenium-deficient area, you might consider getting supplements; however, too much selenium is toxic. (Check with your veterinarian to find out what is the case in your area and whether or not he recommends a selenium supplement.) Generally, you can supplement vitamin E at 10,000 IU per 100 ml (about 3 1/2 fluid ounces) of added vegetable fat or oil.

Horses on a fat supplement may also require extra protein, which can be supplied in a protein supplement like soybean meal. This is especially necessary if the diet is based on grass hay, which tends to be low in protein anyway. For every additional four ounces of fat in the diet, add an equal amount of high-quality protein supplement like soybean meal.

Perhaps surprisingly, horses can use both plant and animal fats. Studies have shown that horses seem to greatly prefer corn oil, which is 90 percent digestible, to all others. However, they will readily consume sunflower, soybean, or blended oils, especially if they are introduced gradually into the diet.

Horses can even be taught to eat animal fats (which are cheaper), although they don't like them as well, which is not, after all, surprising. Horses are pretty strict vegetarians. The commonly fed animal-source fat, beef tallow, will not be eaten by most horses unless it is served warm enough to be in liquid form. I don't think many people want to be heating beef tallow in their kitchens to feed to their horses. Spend the extra money and use corn oil. It will easier on you and the horse.

In short, you can feed your horse almost any kind of fat that he will tolerate, with one exception. Don't use the so-called "ruminant-protectant " fat that is sold in some feed stores. Horses are not ruminants.

Once easy way to add fat to your horse's diet is to simply add a fat-supplemented commercial feed. A feed is considered fat-supplemented if it contains more than 3.5 percent fat (which is pretty low, actually.) The advantage of this method is that appropriate levels of other nutrients are already calculated for you and supplied in the feed.

For more information about the role fat plays for endurance horses, see the chapter on Feeding for Performance.

Mineral Supplements

Minerals can be added in either organic or inorganic form. Some minerals are more easily absorbed in one form than the other. Trace minerals are sometimes added in a chelate or proteinate form, which are extremely well absorbed—so well, in fact, that most supplements of trace minerals don't include more than 30 percent in a chelated or proteinated form. One hundred percent chelated minerals might be too much of a good thing. Chelation is beneficial if it increases a mineral's absorption to a proper (not excessive) rate, which can be affected by other minerals in the diet. Again, if the animal doesn't need the mineral in the first place, it is unwise to add it in any form.

Phosphorus

Horses subsisting entirely on legume hays may need a phosphorus boost. But the correct balance between calcium and phosphorus must always be maintained as seen below.

SOME PEOPLE give their horse an entire sunflower plant to eat. This all-purpose plant not only contains fat, but also protein and fiber. Sort of like a miracle food.

OLDER HORSES especially can benefit from some additional calcium. Add about two ounces of dicalcium sulfate for very old horses. If your horse needs more phosphorus than calcium, try monocalcium-dicalcium phosphate.

SOME nutritionists recommend the use of chelated minerals. A chelated mineral is a metallic element (like zinc, iron, or magnesium) which is "bound" to another substance, usually an amino acid. Chelated minerals do seem to be better absorbed—at least by cattle—but the jury is still out on their benefits for horses.

Calcium and Phosphorus Supplements

Calcium added to high-grain, high-wheat bran, or high-oxalate diets helps increase absorption from the small intestine. Calcium is also important for hard working, reproducing, and growing horses. Maintenance horses usually get plenty of it in their feed.

Since calcium must be kept in proportion to phosphorus, it is best to supplement them together. Common sources include dicalcium phosphate, limestone (calcium carbonate), oyster shell, or bone meal. High grade (38 percent) limestone may be added when only calcium needs to be added to the diet. When both calcium and phosphorus are needed, choose dicalcium phosphate. Do not use steamed bone meal, which is sometimes sold as a calcium/phosphorus supplement. It can carry anthrax, and that is something we have all had quite enough of, I think. Besides, horses hate the stuff.

The label on all calcium and phosphorus supplements should supply the maximum and minimum percent of each ingredient.

Potassium Supplements

Although the average horse gets plenty of potassium from his pasture or grass hay, a horse in heavy training on a high grain, alfalfa diet may require potassium supplements, especially if he is sweating a lot. Potassium chloride is cheap and can be added to feed.

Trace Mineral Supplementation

Some equine diets may be low in important trace minerals like copper, iron, zinc, magnesium, or selenium. To be sure your horse is getting enough of these, you can simply buy mineralized salt blocks. It costs only a little more than regular salt, but contains all the trace minerals that may be lacking in your horse's diet. Although excessive amount of certain trace minerals are poisonous, minerals added at this level are quite safe.

Magnesium

Performance horses can often do with additional magnesium in the diet, especially if they are not getting alfalfa. It can be supplied in the feed in the form of magnesium oxide (about 53 percent magnesium). Other frequently used magnesium supplements are magnesium carbonate (28.8 percent magnesium), magnesium chloride (12 percent magnesium), and magnesium sulfate (9 to 16 percent).

Selenium

Performance horses may benefit from increased selenium in the diet. And it may be necessary for all horses in selenium-deficient areas. Typical selenium supplements include sodium selenite and sodium selenate.

Manganese

Since grains are low in manganese, performance horses may need a supplement. It is also believed that a supplement is beneficial to horses with tissue damage due to inflammation, Manganese supplements include manganese sulfate, manganese carbonate and manganous chloride.

Iron

If iron must be supplemented, which is rare since the body maintains it well for periods of time, it should be supplemented in the form of ferrous sulfate, not ferric oxide or ferrous carbonate. (Some horses have been injected with iron dextran, a form of iron which causes allergic reactions in animals.). The best supplements include correct amounts of other trace minerals as well. However, iron should never be supplemented unless a confirmed anemia or iron deficiency exists. This includes foals. Even when iron supplements do not produce a toxicosis they can lead to increased bacterial infections. It's important to remember that too much iron can actually cause anemia.

Salt (Sodium Chloride)

All horses should have salt supplements, since neither grass nor hay contains enough. Simply throw down a slat block, preferably mineralized. (A mineralized salt block is only slightly more expensive and provides most of the needed trace minerals.) Your horse will eat salt free choice, and there's no danger of his over-dosing on the stuff. The more your horse sweats, the more salt he needs in his diet.

Copper

Both forage and grains can be too low in copper for horses, especially foals. Research shows that foals not getting enough copper in their diets are at risk of osteochondrosis and other developmental orthopedic diseases. You can provide the correct amount directly to the foal, or better, to the pregnant dam before the foal is born. Copper sulfate can be used as a supplement.

Iodine

In iodine deficient soils, like around the Great Lakes, supplementation is beneficial. This is so easy to provide—just give your horse iodized salt, which contains 70 ppm of iodine.

Zinc

Zinc deficiencies are rare, but certain horses on poor pastures can do with a zinc supplement. Zinc methionine complex is said to be excellent for hoofs. Common zinc supplements include zinc sulfate, zinc chloride, zinc oxide and zinc carbonate. Zinc sulfate is the easiest for your horse to absorb.

MANY SORTS OF nasty bacteria need iron to grow. Therefore, horses with infections should not be given iron supplements— you'd only be giving aid and comfort to the enemy.

Electrolytes

If you have nothing horse-specific at the moment, you can give your horse human electrolytes. One ounce of electrolytes per four gallons of water is plenty.

Vitamin Supplements

Supplementation of most vitamins is unnecessary for maintenance horses, since they can make most of their own in house. However, certain horses, on certain kinds of diet, or who are suffering certain specific conditions, can benefit from the supplementation of certain vitamins.

In general, horses can benefit from vitamin supplementation (vitamins A and E) if they are denied pasture or fresh high-quality hay, as might horses on a high-grain diet, especially if the grains are ground up and processed. Horses undergoing a course of antibiotics benefit from supplements of B complex vitamins and vitamin K. That's because antibiotics inhibit cecal and intestinal bacteria, and consequently their production of these vitamins. Sick or stressed horses may also benefit from an all-around supplement. However, most horses on good diets need no extra vitamins.

One caveat—vitamins and minerals must be in balance; some of them can act as antagonists to others. Copper and iron can oxidize some vitamins, unless the latter are "protected" by special coatings, usually in the form of gelatin or sugar.

Vitamin A

Vitamin A is a common and inexpensive supplement. It is one of the two vitamins horses cannot make in house (the other is vitamin E); this vitamin degrades very quickly in hay; in fact, its loses about 9.5 percent of its vitamin A activity every month. Many commercial feeds already are already fortified with it, but if you don't store the food correctly, the vitamin A content can diminish.

Your horse doesn't need vitamin A if he is on green pasture most of the year; in fact, since vitamin A is fat-soluble, it is stored in the liver for up to three to six months. Only if your horse is doomed to live in a stall most of the year without access to green pasture would vitamin A be a needed supplement. If you do supplement with vitamin A during the winter, you can omit it when the horse is turned out to pasture.

You should not need to supplement more that 2,000-3,000 IU/kg of diet. Total amounts over 20,000 IU/kg are toxic, producing stunted growth, bone problems and reduced clotting time—which can in turn produce internal hemorrhaging. The only way your horse can get vitamin A toxicity is through over-supplementation.

B Vitamins

B vitamins are found pretty abundantly in fresh forage; horses can also synthesize them in their gut (with the help of those friendly and charming microbes). So most horses do not need a B complex supplement. However, horses doing strenuous work may benefit from a supplementation of B-complex vitamins: thiamin, riboflavin (B_2), niacin (B_3), pyridoxine (B_6), pantothenic acid, folicin, cyanocobalamine (B_{12}), biotin, cholin, inositol, and paraaminobenzoic acid. Weanlings and horses with chronic illness may also benefit from supplementation of B vitamins, which are not stored in the system.

THIAMIN (VITAMIN B_1) is of special importance. This vitamin, which is normally synthesized in the cecum and colon, may be deficient if your horse is living on poor-quality hay or grain. You can supplement with 3 mg/kg (1.4 mg/lb). Very high performance horses may need 5 mg/kg (2.3 mg/kg). Thiamin is also useful for elderly horses that have trouble maintaining weight. For such animals, brewer's yeast, a rich source of thiamin, makes a good supplement. Thiamin supplements are safe and may be useful for performance horses; various brands contain between 100 and 1,000 milligrams per ounce.

Some people believe that large does of thiamin has a tranquilizing effect, but the opposite may in fact be the case. (Very high doses of injected thiamin have been shown to cause over-excitability.) Besides, giving a horse a shot of *anything* to tranquilize him, medical reasons aside, indicates a problem with the trainer—not the horse.

PANTOTHENIC ACID, although it is not usually needed since it is made in the horse's hindgut, can be easily added as the calcium salt (*calcium pantothenate*). It is readily available as a supplement.

Under normal conditions, *pyridoxine* is not required as supplement. However, performance horses or horses who living on poor-quality pasture may benefit from such a supplement. The normal dosage is about 25 milligrams per day.

Although it is unlikely that your horse needs *choline*, it can be supplemented in a dose of 500 milligrams per day in the form of choline chloride.

FOLIC ACID is sometimes used as a supplement for horses with equine protozoal myelitis. This is controversial and under further investigation.

There has been a fair amount of fuss about the values of *biotin* for hoof health, with a good deal of evidence showing that it really does work. At least, it works well in pigs, in case your pig needs a touch up in that area. Of course, so many factors come into play here—including genetics, far-

rier care, and stress that a little extra biotin in the diet is no guarantee to improve the hoof of any particular horse. In any case, you'll need to be patient. Remember, that the hoof grows form the coronary band down, and any improvement will take six to nine months. The suggested supplement is usually 15 to 30 milligrams per day.

Vitamin B$_{12}$, or cobalamin, is manufactured by the bacteria in your horse's gut; however animals in poor condition, especially those with parasites, may benefit from a supplement. Some people also think it helps performance horses, or for those horses consuming a diet low in cobalt.

Vitamin C (Ascorbic Acid)

Although horses can make plenty of vitamin C for normal maintenance, horses under stress do benefit from a little extra. It is also a useful supplement for aged horse (over 20 years). Some people believe horses benefit from a vitamin C supplement in hot weather or during periods of growth.

You can buy oral supplements of 5 to 20 grams per day, although it must be said that horses have problems absorbing oral doses of the stuff. In fact, it's been estimated your horse would need to eat about 20 grams to raise the ascorbic acid level in the blood appreciably. Ascorbyl palmitate is more easily absorbed by horses than ascorbic acid or ascorbyl stearate. (This makes horses unusual. Most species can't absorb ascorbyl palmitate well at all.) Efforts to supplement horses with vitamin C injections, either IV or IM, have not proved workable. Either the vitamin doesn't stay in the system, or it causes irritation.

Vitamin D

Horses regularly spending time outdoors in the sunlight, or who eat sun-cured hay get plenty of vitamin D. However, horses unlucky enough to spend day after day in a dark stall, without sun-cured hay, may suffer a deficiency. Regular working or pleasure horses can do well with supplements of 300 to 600 IU/kg (150 to 300 IU per pound) of diet while pregnant or lactating mares need 600 IU/kg. Foals will need 800 to 1,000 IU/kg (400 to 800 IU per pound), because growing horses require large amounts of this vitamin for good bone and tooth development.

Do not over-supplement this vitamin. Amounts only 10 times the recommended doses can result in toxicity, perhaps even less if the horse is getting too much calcium as well. Get your horse out in the sunshine to avoid the problem. Vitamin D toxicity is very dangerous and usually means death due to liver destruction.

Vitamin E

Although most horse feeds contain enough vitamin E to maintain your horse, studies show that supplement of 50 to 100 IU/kg (25 to 50 IU per pound) in the diet will increase his resistance to infections. Supplements normally use synthetic, rather than naturally occurring forms of vitamin E. The synthetic forms, which have been esterified, are more stable than naturally occurring or synthetic alcohol forms. The widely used one is DL-alpha tocopherol acetate. This being said, I should note that many horse professionals prefer the natural form of the vitamin—D-alpha tocopherol. It is very important to keep your stabled horse well supplemented with this vitamin, which is lost in hay during storage.

Heavily exercised horses, especially those that live in low-selenium areas, can also suffer muscle disease (myopathy) associated with exercise. (Recall that vitamin E and selenium work together.) A supplement of 100 IU/kg vitamin E can prevent this.

Vitamin E has long been used to boost the performance of working horses; performance horses that are not supplemented with vitamin E quickly deplete their supplies of the stuff. It is wise to add a daily supplement of 2,000 to 3,000 IU per day for such horses. However, vitamin E can also be helpful to ordinary horses that depend upon pelleted feeds. Sick and elderly horses, which may have weakened immune systems, can also benefit from the addition of vitamin E.

Pelleted feeds are produced through the use of tremendous heat, which destroys vitamin E. Fortunately, these feeds are nearly always re-supplied with vitamin E before they are sold. Grass hay also tends to be low in vitamin E.

Since hay loses most of its vitamin E during storage, you should supplement your horse's winter feed with it, especially if your hay is old or of poor-quality. Grain is also low in vitamin E. Even supplements, however, can lose vitamin E if they are improperly stored. Air and moisture are especially damaging to vitamin E. Horses that have plenty of fresh food are less likely to need a vitamin E supplement.

Vitamin E acts as a therapy for several conditions. Vitamin E supplementation (6 to 20 times that recommended in the diet for a healthy horse) will enhance the immune system and lessens clinical signs of disease. Remember that this vitamin is not toxic; extra supplementation will not hurt your horse. In addition, adding vitamin E to a vaccine appears to increase its efficacy.

Some evidence now exists to indicate that equine degenerative myeloencephalopathy (EDM), a disease of the spinal cord, which manifests itself during the first year of life as un-coordination, may be reversed with supplementation of 6,000 IU vitamin E per day. A lower amount (1,500 to 2,000 IU)

ALCOHOLS, like tocopherol (identified by the ol on the end of the name) are esterified by adding part of an acid (such as acetic acid). The ending of the name then changes to ate (tocopherol acetate) to show that the compound is now an ester and has been esterified.

MANY experienced horse people swear vitamin E acts as a natural calming agent for hot horses.

may also act as a prophylactic to prevent a horse from acquiring the disease, which appears to have a genetic predisposition component.

Another nervous condition, equine motor neuron disease (EMND), a rare but lethal disease of certain nerve cells, can be treated with 6,000 to 9,000 IU vitamin E, and prevented with 2,000 IU vitamin E, per day. Young horses (under two years) are most at risk from this disease.

Yet a third neurological disease that can be treated with vitamin E is equine protozoal myeloencephalitis (EPM). This disease, which is caused by a protozoal parasite, can sometimes attack very quickly, but in other cases its onset is gradual. Like many neurological problems, signs include un-coordination, weakness, and rear end paralysis. The parasite must be killed with medications, but research indicates that adding 700 to 900 IU vitamin E will speed and strengthen recovery.

Herbs

Americans currently spend about three and a quarter billion dollars on herbs every year. They can be used alone, or in combination with other forms of therapy—as long as you know exactly what you're doing, which isn't always easy. The study of herbs is a lifelong endeavor, and Western medicine is just coming to understand it. Almost no one, including holistic veterinarians, is an expert on all herbs; most deal with just a few they know well.

> **NOTE:** *Many common Chinese herbal preparations include ginseng, almond, tree peony, garlic, and even kudzu. Many of them also have strange and wonderful names like sky-full-of-stars, hare's ear decoction, and secret wine of harmonious marital relations.*

The FDA has classified herbs as supplements, and they may only be marketed as such—not as cures for diseases. Companies that sell herbs are not permitted to make claims about their healing properties, even though in many cases these are well established.

For one thing, no real formularies exist to establish dosage guidelines. For another, the quality of herbs varies considerably, and consequently many practitioners prefer to use the more easily standardized herbal extracts rather than whole herbs. Other practitioners, however, insist that extracts may exclude some of the very substances that help the herb work better. This is currently an unresolved issue. Whatever the case, it's important for consumers to know precisely what they are getting. Since there is no real quality control for herbs, they can be misidentified—or even contaminated. You can buy commercially prepared herbs specifically designed for horses, but you must take sensible precautions.

- Never buy an herbal product that doesn't list the Latin botanical name of the substance. This name should include genus and species.

- Buy only products that have an expiration date. Many have short shelf-lives.

- Know what part of the plant you are buying. Different parts have different uses.

- Choose only organically grown commercial (not wild-harvested) herbs.

- The age of plant at harvest is important for some herbs, like ginseng.

- Whole herbs are often preferable to extracts.

- Know how to store the herbal preparation properly.

- Choose the right form for your needs: tea, extract, compress, ointment, bulk herb, or capsules.

- Most of the time both dried and fresh herbs are equally suitable.

- Apply the correct dosage. Most labels give the dosage appropriate for a 150 pound human male, not an 1,100 pound horse. See a qualified animal herbal nutritionist.

- Herbs in large pieces last longer than the powered form.

- Since herbs work best for chronic conditions, rather than for emergencies, the best plan is to start slowly and dose until you get the desired effect. It usually takes at least a month before you'll notice any results. Use the "delivery method" best suited to the herb and your horse. In some cases, you can just sprinkle it over his food. In most cases, it's best to give supplements with your horse's meals—they are better absorbed that way.

Nutraceuticals

Nutraceutical is a new term. The word is a combination of "nutrition" and "pharmaceutical" and is defined as a food (or food ingredient) that has health benefits, including the prevention and treatment of disease. Nutraceuticals are neither food nor drug; this "neither/nor" designation allows them to escape most of the regulatory restrictions of both foods and drugs. For people, they are governed by their own (somewhat lax) guidelines. For animals, however, it's a different story. The FDA still has control over animal feeds, so we're left with the bizarre situation that nutraceuticals for animals are more strictly regulated than those for humans—even though we are almost always talking about the same substance. It's a weird world we live in.

Although nutraceuticals have been popular in Europe for decades, the term was first coined in 1976, here in the United States, by Dr. Stephen

NUTRACEUTICALS often work even better when they are combined for a synergistic effect.

MANY nutraceuticals, including those of dubious value, are derived from environmentally endangered plants or animals. Thousands of hapless sharks are killed every day for their cartilage alone. Many native plants, like Goldenseal, have been ripped from the ground in huge numbers. As a result, this once common wildflower has almost become extinct. Before using any nutraceutical, make sure that, in the case of plants, the substance is grown commercially, not poached from the wild, and for animals, that the species has not been driven to the brink of extinction. Bears were once hunted almost out of existence because some people thought that bile from bear gall bladder is an aphrodisiac. It isn't.

L. DeFelice, and is defined in the U.S. Dietary Supplementary Health and Education Act (D.S.H.E.A.) of 1994 as "any non-toxic food component that has scientifically proven health benefits, including disease treatment or prevention."

The D.S.H.E.A. stipulates that the functional component of the substance must be standardized in the nutraceutical product and it must be produced under good manufacturing practices. The product may then be labeled, describing its role and how it works. Nutraceuticals are intended as supplements only—not as a replacement for real food.

Nutraceuticals may be sold on their own, or may appear as additions within regular foods, like "high fiber" bread. Some nutraceuticals are genetically altered substances. One example is a specially modified oil that is high in Omega-3 fatty acid.

Closely related to nutraceuticals are the phytochemicals. These naturally occurring substances are found in fruits, vegetables, and grains. Nutritional research has determined their health benefits, especially their role in fighting disease. Important phytochemicals include flavonoids like anthocyanins, genistein, daidzein, as well as tannins, lignins and phenols.

Many nutraceuticals are also antioxidants. Antioxidants are unsaturated molecules, usually found as pigments in foods. They stimulate cell growth and provide other proven benefits, perhaps even preventing cancer. They appear to neutralize oxidation products (free radicals) produced metabolically from proteins and fats or from overexposure to sunlight or toxins in the environment. Free radicals are highly reactive molecules that cause damage to cells and genetic material; they are blamed for the initiation of many diseases.

Miscellaneous Supplements

Bacteria

Some owners like to give newborn foals or horses with digestive upset an oral dose of friendly bacteria like Lactobacillus to help out the microbes already present in the gut. No formal studies exist to show these are effective, but they certainly do no harm. Believers say they increase the number of cellulose-digesting microorganisms that live in the digestive tract.

Brewer's Yeast

Brewer's yeast is a veritable feast of vitamins, including thiamin. It makes an excellent supplement for older horses. Yeast doesn't normally live in the horse's hindgut, which is too acid for it, but adding yeast to the diet increases fiber digestion by about 8 percent, and improves digestion of phosphorus by nearly 25 percent.

Live Yeast Cultures

Yeast cultures are often called probioitcs and are used as a source of digestive enzymes. They tend to be about 50 percent protein, 40 percent carbohydrate, 8 percent minerals, and 2 percent fat. Lactating mares given yeast cultures produce milk with greater total protein. Some studies show that adding live yeast cultures may be useful for weanlings, lactating mares, and performance horses.

Chondroitin Sulfate

Chondroitin sulfate, although not naturally present in the horse's diet, has been shown to help strengthen connective tissue, a feature particularly attractive to owners of performance horses. This supplement is usually derived from the trachea of cows. Dogs chew these things up as treats ("moo tubes"), but horses are unlikely to consume cow trachea in the "raw state" without serious objection. This is a useful supplement, especially for arthritic horses.

Dimethylglycine (DMG)

This natural product has been used for many years by both human and equine athletes to enhance performance and speed recovery from exercise. It is fairly safe, but its effectiveness depends upon whom you ask. Some horses given the substance showed increased appetite—and increased aggression. By law, this product cannot be added to commercial feeds; people who want it must purchase it separately.

Dimethyl Sulfone (MSM)

Dimethyl sulfone, also called methylsulfonylmethane, is found in fresh forage. (It's also found in beer, which is of course why people drink beer. If horses didn't have grass to eat, they'd need beer, too.) Its most important role as a supplement is to provide sulfur in an easily available form. In addition to this laudable goal, may people swear that DSM cures or at least helps navicular disease, muscle soreness, arthritis and epiphysitis. But if it does, no one knows how. This supplement is not currently approved for adding to feed, so it must be bought and administered separately.

Feramo-H

This commercial product contains vitamin A and trace minerals. It may be a useful addition to feed lacking in these nutrients. Some people believe it improves the coat, darkening or giving it a dappled look. This product is also helpful in shedding an unwanted winter coat.

Kelp and Seaweed

These popular supplements can be dangerous if incorrectly used. Their high iodine level can cause goiter.

Mucopolysaccharides

These substances help repair cartilage around the joints; they also help prevent inflammation.

Octacosanol

This natural component of wheat germ and cottonseed oil has been widely used by human athletes to improve cardiovascular function. Whether or not it helps horses is debatable.

Sunflower Seeds

For an interesting change, try adding about eight ounces of black sunflower seeds to your horse's diet. They contain both protein and essential fatty acids for the coat. These are especially nice for horses on a grass hay diet.

Medicated Feeds

Every once in a while you may come upon a feed that is laced with antibiotics or other drugs. This stuff is not horse feed. It is meant for cattle, poultry, or swine and can be dangerous or even deadly to your horse. You will know a medicated feed when you see it, because the federal government requires the label to state that the feed bears the label MEDICATED directly under the name of the feed. Dangerous ingredients include antibiotics like bacitracin, chlortetracycline, erythromycin, neomycin, oxytetracycline, tylosin and sulfamethazine: growth promoters like melengestrol acetate, monensin, and lasalocid (these last two are extremely dangerous to horses); ethylenediamine dihydroiodide (EDDI)—an expectorant and iodine supplement: and wormers like levamisole. This stuff does not belong in horse feed. (Most of it doesn't belong in cattle, chicken, or pig feed, either, but that's another issue.)

Drugs

Drugs are not supplements; they are substances used to treat a specific disease, and should be available from your veterinarian by prescription only. Drugs are under the auspices of the United States Food, Drug, and Cosmetic Act. They have been subjected to a great amount of rigorous research, and their potencies and effects have been carefully documented.

Supplements, while generally quite safe, are not subject to the same standards as traditional drugs. The FDA forbids manufacturers to claim health benefits of many supplements, especially herbs, or indeed any substance that has not been clinically proven to actually promote health or fight disease. However, the newly formed North American Veterinary Nutraceutical Council works to establish scientifically valid guidelines for the development and administration of these substances. ▪

Appendix A

Conversion Tables

Painful though it is, it is sometimes necessary to convert one measurement into another. I've used U.S. Standard volumes, so if you're using British units, a British gallon is larger than a US gallon, being nearly five US quarts. Of course, the United Kingdom has gone metric, so this probably won't matter much to most people.

Few measurements in nutrition are so critical that you will need to follow these conversions to the last drop. A pint, for example, is close enough to half a liter (500 milliliters) so that I wouldn't worry about the difference.

To convert mg/k to mg/lb, divide by 2.2

To convert mg/lb to mg/kg, multiply by 2.2

United States Standard to Metric:

Weight

    1 pound = 454 grams
    1 pound = 454,000 milligrams
    1 pound = 0.45 kilograms
    1 ounce = 28.3 gram
    1 ounce = 28,300 milligrams

Volume

    1 pint = 472 milliliters
    1 quart = 946 milliliters
    1 quart = 0.946 liters
    1 gallon = 3.78 liters
    1 fluid ounce = 29.6 milliliters

Metric to United States Standard:

Weight:

    One kilogram = 2.2 pounds

Volume:

    1 liter = 1.06 quarts
    1 liter = 33.8 fluid ounces

Metric to Metric:

    1 gram = 1,000 milligrams
    1 gram = 1,000,000 micrograms
    1 liter = 1,000 milliliters
    1 milligram = 1,000 micrograms

Units of heat or energy:

The energy content of food is measured in calories. The actual definition of a calorie is the amount of heat needed to raise the temperature of one gram (the same as one milliliter) of water one degree Celsius (1.8 degrees F). This amount (called a small calorie) is too small to be useful in measuring the energy value of feed. Consequently, when we talk about food, we use the large calorie, which is equal to 1,000 small calories. This is also called a kilocalorie, or just plain calorie with the kilo being understood. The energy requirement of large animals, such as horses, is sometimes given in even larger units called megacalories (or Mcal), which are equal to 1,000 kilocalories (that's 1,000,000 small calories!). A human living on a 2,000-calorie-per-day diet would be consuming 2 Mcal per day.

Appendix B

Resources

Briggs, Karen. *Understanding Equine Nutrition*. The Blood-Horse, Inc. 1998.

Burger, Sandra and Anthony P. Knight. *Horse Owner's Guide to Toxic Plants*. Breakthrough, 1996.

Equine Research, Inc. *Feeding to Win*. Equine Research, 1992.

Ewing, Rex A. *Beyond the Hay Days*. PixyJack Press, 1997.

Kohnke, John. *Feeding and Nutrition: The Making of a Champion*. Birubi Pacific, 1992.

Lewis, Lon. D. *Equine Clinical Nutrition: Feeding Care*. Williams and Wilkins, 1995.

Ramey, David W. *Medications and Supplements for the Horse*. Howell Book House, 1996.

Ramey, David W. and Stephen E. Duren. *Nutrition in the Horse*. Howell Book House, 1998.

Schoen, Allen M. and Susan Wynn. *Complementary and Alternative Veterinary Medicine: Principles and Practice*. Mosby, 1998.

Sparks, Dave M. *Veterinary Notes for Horsemen: Feeding Horses*. Heartland Publications, 1998.

Way, Robert F. and Donald G. Lee. *The Anatomy of the Horse: A Pictorial Approach*. Breakthrough, 1983.

Wulff Tilford, Mary L. and Gregory L. Tilford. *All You Ever Wanted to Know About Herbs for Pets*. Bow Tie Press, 1999.

Index